MICHAEL PEARSON'S
TRADITIONAL
KNITTING

Aran, Fair Isle & Fisher Ganseys

New & Expanded Edition

DOVER PUBLICATIONS, INC.

Mineola, New York

Bibliographical Note
This Dover edition, first published in 2015, is a new and expanded edition
of the work originally published by William Collins Sons & Co Ltd, London,
and Van Nostrand Reinhold Company, New York, 1984.

International Standard Book Number
ISBN-13: 978-0-486-46053-6
ISBN-10: 0-486-46053-3

Manufactured in the United States by Courier Corporation
46053301   2015
www.doverpublications.com

Contents

List of Patterns

Patterns Notated

Patterns Written in Full

MICHAEL PEARSON'S
TRADITIONAL
KNITTING

Aran, Fair Isle & Fisher Ganseys

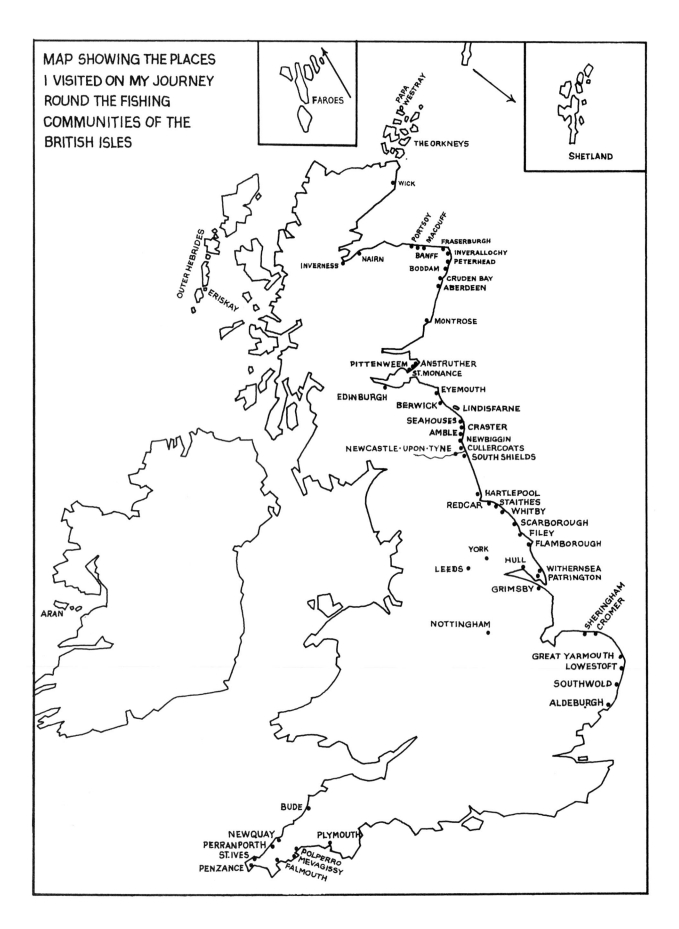

MAP SHOWING THE PLACES
I VISITED ON MY JOURNEY
ROUND THE FISHING
COMMUNITIES OF THE
BRITISH ISLES

FAROES

PAPA WESTRAY

THE ORKNEYS

SHETLAND

WICK

PORTSOY
MACDUFF
FRASERBURGH
INVERALLOCHY
BANFF
PETERHEAD
BODDAM
CRUDEN BAY
ABERDEEN

INVERNESS
NAIRN

OUTER HEBRIDES

ERISKAY

MONTROSE

PITTENWEEM ANSTRUTHER
ST.MONANCE
EYEMOUTH
EDINBURGH
BERWICK
LINDISFARNE
SEAHOUSES
AMBLE CRASTER
NEWBIGGIN
NEWCASTLE·UPON·TYNE CULLERCOATS
SOUTH SHIELDS

HARTLEPOOL
STAITHES
REDCAR WHITBY
SCARBOROUGH
FILEY
FLAMBOROUGH
YORK
HULL
LEEDS WITHERNSEA
PATRINGTON
GRIMSBY

ARAN

NOTTINGHAM

SHERINGHAM
CROMER

GREAT YARMOUTH
LOWESTOFT
SOUTHWOLD
ALDEBURGH

BUDE

NEWQUAY PLYMOUTH
PERRANPORTH
ST.IVES POLPERRO
MEVAGISSY
PENZANCE FALMOUTH

2

Preface

This is a book of celebration—a celebration of knitting within the way of life of inshore fishing communities that dot the coastline of the British Isles; a celebration of the people who practised this craft when knitting was essential rather than recreational—an act of survival rather than of fashion. It is a book about extraordinary knitters who, despite great hardship, developed these patterns whose origins are tucked away within centuries of oral tradition. Not surprisingly, it is the most remote areas of Britain that have continued longest with such age-old customs, those least touched by one of the greatest social changes the world has seen—the Industrial Revolution. It is also a book about my journey around Britain documenting the traditions before their way of life as inshore fishing communities disappears forever. From 1972 to 1984 I visited many places from Shetland to the Scilly Isles, from Aran to the Hebrides, researching within these communities their traditional craft, the place, their circumstances and lifestyle. Through my description of the places I visited; by talking to those in the community who still practise the craft of traditional knitting; by documenting their creations; by recounting their thoughts and feelings; by generating a sense of place through the reproduction of their history through photographs, I hope that I convey a sense of my experience at a deeper level than mere description. You will not find within these pages a comprehensive account of the traditions because this was not my intention. I was witness, I believe, to a special kind of creativity—a creativity much deeper than 'comprehensive'—a creative process that developed in circumstances that I was taught would be an anathema for self-expression. In this journey, I discovered that the vital creative element of this knitting was to remain within the constraints of tradition, and, by the simple virtue of its practise, it brings with it a natural tendency to encourage its use as a means of personal expression. I was to learn and was witness to the product and the process of their craft acquiring meaning; the abstract designs they chose to decorate their craftwork carried social messages: an expression of their identity as a community and as individuals.

I was to learn that the strength of traditional knitting lies in its ability to make each creation become a unique contribution to the development of the tradition where the past is evident by the rules and conventions that are followed; the present is manifest in the making; the future assured through its direct and intimate link with all that had gone before. I was witness to displays of knitting craftsmanship, the likes of which, I thought at the time, I would never ever see again.

As I began my journey, it was almost immediately apparent that the traditional lifestyle of the coastal fishing communities I was to visit had begun to change. There would be many places where the idea of research would be futile, as the local style of inshore fishing had been superseded by a series of circumstances; the most prevalent being 'weekenders' buying up local housing for holidays. My parents were among those 'gentrifying' these villages and I admit to being particularly disappointed to find no contemporary knitting activity in the community where I was conceived and born. My dream of my own identity pattern sequence and of every fishing village having a living, contemporary knitting pattern sequence was an impossibility. In consequence, fired up by this disappointment and as the last surveyor of this social phenomenon, it became all the more important that I should write my record in such a way that my act of witness and the story I tell should serve to fire your enthusiasm, so that you can participate in the continuation of traditional knitting in the knowledge that the knitting you generate is directly linked to the heritage you aspire to recreate.

I have, therefore, clearly defined the conventions and illustrated them step by step in those communities that still continue the tradition and where, within the context of primary experience, I have been witness to the creation of the patterns and the techniques that generated them. Here you will find fully written pattern instructions.

Where communities had documentary evidence of traditional knitting in the past, this secondary evidence has been acknowledged by detailing examples from the very rich source of knowledge held by library archives, museum collections, old publications and the family albums of those

I met on my journey. Here you will find graphic illustrations of pattern repetitions which you may like to choose for your own knitting.

In addition I have detailed the knowledge I gained from my travels about the processes necessary for you to develop your own pattern sequences. This information comes with the blessing and encouragement of those families I met who still continue the time-honoured techniques I have described.

My search began by building on the work of Gladys Thompson and Mary Wright with the intention of connecting with their research 'in the field'. I thought that if I had regular connections to those knitting families who had contributed to Gladys's and Mary's books, I would be able to state with certainty that the tradition continued. Despite the paucity of a living tradition, my travels around the British Isles was a rich experience; the following description will indicate to you, I believe, a little of the flavour of this research.

On my travels around the countryside there were many times when I had no contact to call on when visiting a new fishing village. It was my practise in the early days to visit the 'local' tavern. A stranger walking into a 'local' is, for the patrons, much like someone you don't know coming into your front room. It is considered an intrusion into your private domain—especially if you sit in someone's seat! So, having got the sudden silence and the turning of heads over with, I bravely battled to the bar and ordered a pint and surveyed the scene. (My quest, remember, was the search for intricate and interesting patterns decorating the ganseys worn by the fishermen.) On spotting a likely candidate, past experience even in those early days had taught me not to blast my way in, tap my chosen target on the shoulder and, by way of introducing myself, explain that I found the pattern on his gansey most intriguing. I also learned never to interrupt that most serious of games—dominoes. Apart from causing the poor fellow to splutter his pint over those dominoes, looking desperately for a way out, this approach somehow reduced the possibility of meeting the knitter who, of course, was usually his wife. By then, having politely answered my questions (we were, after all, talking about a subject of common interest) it was usually too much for him to continue.

Experience developed a more sophisticated approach. The answer lay in creating the situation where I was expected. I arrived early and visited the landlord, the local shopkeeper, and the coxswain of the lifeboat and outlined to them my 'mission', explaining that I intended to be in the pub that evening. Bush telegraph did the rest! So, wearing my own gansey, my visit to their local turned into an evening of knitting talk—comparing my pattern with local variations, because of course there would not be a man in the pub that wasn't wearing his gansey. And, although a stranger, for one evening I shared in the tradition which they have practised for generations. The men I have talked to, who were wearing the ganseys their wives have knitted, explained to me that they wore the ganseys as though they were made of gold.

By evening's end I left with invitations for afternoon tea the next day, and some serious knitting conversations in the home of one of the knitters. On arrival I would meet all the knitters from the village and be deluged with a lifetime's worth of knitting. I recorded their patterns and listened to details of their lives, and as the afternoon closed in, my arms laden with carrier bags full of home baking and their good wishes, I said goodbye, with a promise to send their patterns back in published form. Shame on me to think, when I first began, that my reception would be hostile and that these marvellous knitters would not reveal their patterns to me so that I could record them and make them available to everyone!

There has been only one occasion when I was refused patterns; you will find this story as you follow my journey into the world of traditional knitting. As you read about the tradition in these pages, I hope I make it clear that to understand what it means to be a traditional knitter you must participate, creating personal pattern sequences using traditional designs as creative inspiration. One day someone may come knocking at your door!

—MICHAEL PEARSON

Introduction
Traditional Knitting in Historical Context

Today, knitting is a gentle and satisfying pastime; yet not long ago it was an essential element in the incomes of a vast number of Britain's population. In this age of consumerism and mass production, it is easy to forget that most things had to be made by hand. Within the period that most concerns us (the last 100 years or so), family life in rural areas was extremely hard. There were many poor but willing hands ready to knit socks, gloves and stockings for English and Continental markets for very little pay. Indeed, the rewards were minimal in comparison to the efforts, but the extra income from knitting brought in by the wives of the fishermen and farmers was often crucial to their survival. The usual time needed to knit a gansey, for example, was about three weeks, working four hours a day. A very experienced knitter could perhaps complete one in a week. The reward for these labours at the turn of the century was the princely sum of two shillings and sixpence. In the unlikely event that a woman was able to knit up to fifty-two ganseys in a year, her income would amount to only £6 10s. At its best, such payment was only three-quarters that of a domestic servant, who could at least command the addition of roof, bed and board.

The heyday of this contract knitting, away from the clamour of industrialisation, was the middle of the eighteenth century, and Britain had been a major centre of commercial hand knitting for hundreds of years before this. Originally the knitters, exclusively male, operated within the guild system, similar to those of goldsmiths and silversmiths. The guild supplied the church and the court, using fine silk and gold thread to make hosiery and gloves of exquisite fineness. Apprentices served seven years before the production of their 'masterpieces' that enrolled them within their order. The influence of the guilds was powerful and their monopoly of the craft complete. For example, in 1571, the Cappers Act introduced a fine for any man seen in public not wearing 'a cap of wool, thicked and dressed in England, made within this realm, and only dressed and finished by some of the trade of Cappers'.

But changes, inevitably, were on the way. The Rev. Lee had invented a knitting 'frame' which was destined to revolutionise the whole craft some thirty years before the Cappers Act. The guilds,

Knitting on the quayside, Great Yarmouth.

Delivering wool on the Shetland Islands, 1882.

'In a cottage industry the entrepreneur supplies the materials required to produce sundry articles to the workers in their homes where the labour content of the manufacturing process is provided, having the advantages of keeping overheads at a minimum. Once made the entrepreneur collects the products and arranges for their sale. In a cottage industry where equipment in the form of special tools and simple machinery was required, these may have been owned by the workers, or sometimes the entrepreneur would supply them with the materials. The domestic form of organisation of a manufacturing process is particularly suited to the production of knitted goods.

'When Lee invented his knitting device, these frame knitting machines, although bulky, were initially used under the domestic system. Machines, however, did not entirely supercede hand knitting. Production in the knitter's home predominated until the factory system developed in the middle of the nineteenth century. Even then, hand knitting under the cottage system survived until the earliest twentieth century in the Yorkshire Dales and a number of fishing communities. Today, both hand and machine knitting based on the cottage system still flourish in the Shetland Isles'.

(Martin Harvey, *Knitting International*, December 1977.)

Bringing home peat on Stornoway, 1878.

exercising their power, had the inventor banished to France where he languished in poverty. But industrialisation of such an essential craft could not be staved off indefinitely. By the mid-seventeenth century merchants had brought in the new machines. Soon though, many of them were housed, together with their operatives, under one roof: the irreversible shift from a rural to an industrial economy had begun.

In the communities away from the fast rising industrial centres, the old cottage industry still managed to survive, though it was never again to be a major economic force. The old hand knitters of the Dales, Northumberland, Norfolk, Leicestershire, Cornwall and Scotland became a legend; they survived the mechanisation by making up garments with patterns that were impossible to knit on machines.

In this way, their manner of life was maintained and their traditions and folklore preserved. The industrial economy, meanwhile, gave rise to a further development in knitting: the new middle classes, responsible for the servicing and development of knitting 'factories', themselves continued hand knitting as a genteel and exclusively female pastime. By the nineteenth century, delicate knitted lace covered the innumerable objects that cluttered the typical middle-class Victorian household. By the 1890s, the introduction of regularly published pattern leaflets was ample evidence of the importance of knitting to a class of women with a vast amount of leisure time.

This pastime, in turn, became directed to commercial ends and thus began the modern wool supplier. The patterns and designs produced by the suppliers concentrated on developing hand knitting according to prevailing fashion trends. Traditional styles were, of course, in demand, but they were usually adapted to meet other requirements regarding shape, style, colour and, in particular, amateur knitting technique. The adapting of the rules of Fair Isle and Aran has given rise to misconceptions about their origins. One popular mistake was to think that the knitting of Fair Isle was identified by a specific two colour pattern, usually a Tree of Life and star, concentrated around the yoke. The image is, at best, a tasteful adaptation determined by commercial considerations and it bears little relation to the original tradition. Again, within the tradition of Aran knitting, the practise of using only two needles, instead of knitting in the round, has become universal, yet it is unlikely that the garments were made in this way 150 or even 100 years ago.

Wherever knitting was essential, the authentic patterns were jealously guarded. Not only did the men folk need the protective warmth as they went about their daily work, their families needed the extra income that a knitting wife brought in just to survive. Many of the pictures in this book—of women standing knitting as they wait at the port for their husbands and brothers—may look quite charming. The reality is that they are classic evidence of the exploitation of people desperate to increase inadequate and irregular incomes.

Observing first hand for myself, living within these communities, I have witnessed the decline in the industry and watched the older communities breaking up and so it was my desire to document their treasured traditions before they disappeared forever. As I have indicated already, the research shows that in some areas it is already too late, the only remaining information being in the form of

Knitting in the round with long, double-pointed needles, Scarborough, 1890.

Cornish fish wife, *c.* 1890.

'...not only are the units widely dispersed, but the number of individuals to whose income knitwear contributes, is extremely high. There are few homes in the rural areas which do not earn something from the industry, and this method of topping up wages from other sources is quite invaluable in preserving the rural life. Earnings from hosiery are as widespread as earnings from crofting and in many cases they are both more substantial and certain. Fishermen, crofters and housewives alike enjoy the advantages of this system, which in many cases can make a crucial difference to their standard of life'.

Planning for Progress: Shetland Woollen Industry, p. 24, Highlands and Inland Development Board, Special Report No. 4, April 1970.

A fishing family in their Sunday best, 1920s.

documents and old photographs in the archives of museums and the albums of the fishing families. These treasured artifacts, of course, bear their own lively witness to a vanished past, and their collection and examination for patterns will be a pleasurable frustration.

Knitters and fish gutting group.

Knitting Aids and Techniques

Before we begin the journey around the fishing communities, I've included this section on knitting techniques. This is a general discussion and I have been more specific, where necessary, at the beginning of each section. An introduction to some of the aids used by older knitters to help them in their craft will give you a better understanding of the atmosphere in which they lived and worked—an atmosphere evocatively illustrated by the pictures in this book. These old-fashioned knitting aids do not simply provide a historic flavour; the modern knitter can learn a lot from them. Contract knitters in the Shetlands still use techniques that have existed for many generations to help them achieve their quotas in the best possible time.

'…leather knitting belts are still sometimes used…personally, I prefer the safety pin stuck firmly in the bodice a little above the belt on the right side…I have seen a bunch of feathers used, stuck in the belt…'

(Mrs Leith 'Skennes', Orkney.)

'A "Wisker" was a bunch of straw stuffed inside an old sock and tied to the waist…'

(Mrs Keith, Lossiemouth, 1959.)

'The knitter always wore a belt around her waist into which was tucked her knitting sheath in a slant-wise position on her right hand side. Instead of knitting with straight needles they used curved "wires" or "pricks" which allowed a minimum of movement…The speed was gained by moving the arms in a beat-like movement rather like striking a drum'.

(Marie Hartley, *The Old Hand-Knitters of the Dales*, 1951.)

Mrs Curwen, Foula, Shetland Isles, 1902.

Below and opposite page: Knitting aids from the Marie Hartley and Joan Ingilby collection.

Historical Aids

The technique of knitting is slow and throughout its history many ideas have been devised to speed it up. The most significant technique in hand knitting is the anchoring of the working needle so that the knitter could use the fingers of the right hand to move the stitches from the left-hand needle, enabling the average knitter to speed up productivity to 'two cuts' or four ounces of wool in an evening.

The most popular forms of anchor were the sheath and the stick, strapped or pinned to the waist. In addition, tapes with a clasp at one end were often used; known as top crooks, they kept the worked fabric pulled out of the knitter's way, both for convenience and evenness of tension. Since contract knitters had to work at a phenomenal speed and did not need, except occasionally, to look at their work, they would often labour in the evenings with very little light; they therefore made rattles, which they inserted in the balls of wool to help find them if they got dropped in the dark. Examples of these knitting aids are shown in the photograph below and on page 11, which are all taken from the magnificent collection of Marie Hartley and Joan Ingilby at the Upper Dales Museum in Hawes, Wensleydale.

Sheaths, Sticks, Whisks, 'Thrattle' and Rattles

Sheaths were the simplest forms of anchor, easy and cheap for the knitter herself to make. The longest lasting were made of leather and stuffed with horsehair, but they could be created out of nothing but an old sock and some straw. Even a tightly packed bunch of feathers would serve the purpose. The sheath was usually attached to a belt worn around the waist, and the pointed end of the working needle stuck into it to hold it steady and leave the knitter's right hand free.

Sticks were a more elaborate kind of anchor; indeed, some of them were highly ornamented. The two on the right of the photograph on

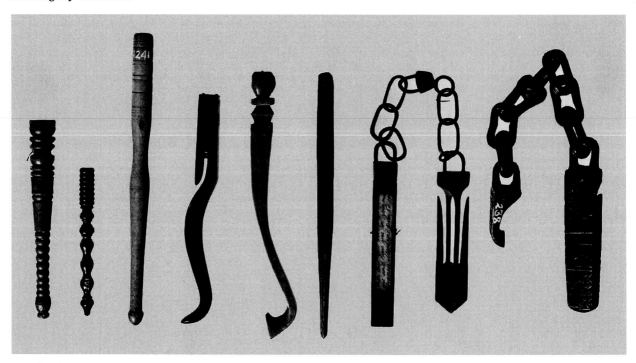

page 10 feature hooked blocks at one end to which balls of wool were attached. These two are also decorative, being carved from a single piece of wood in a linked-chain effect; one bears a sentimental motif, the other a carving with a knitter's initials.

The photograph below shows a variety of other aids. The two sets of curved needles on the left would have been used in fine and coarse knitting. The knitting stick in the centre is of the goose wing type common in the Wensleydale area; it would have been secured with the belt (*see figure 1*). Beneath the belt you can see a top crook. The spring clasp was inserted into the bottom of the garment being knitted and the tape went round the knitter's waist and was secured at the end around the knitting stick. The round object beneath the top crook is a rattle made from a length of the 'thrapple' (lower larynx) of a goose. It has dried peas put inside and then the narrower end is brought around and inserted into the other. Next to the rattle is a small needle holder, made of silver. As the knitting lengthened, the tape would be drawn around the knitter's body, pulling the work around her side and back out of the way. This technique possibly relieved the hands from some of the weight of a heavy garment; but it was mainly employed to keep the garment away from the legs when the knitter worked as she walked—a very common practice.

The knitters of the Dales extended the technology of hand knitting by the use of aids such as these; they were so fast that speeds of 200 stitches a minute were considered commonplace. Mrs Martha Dinsdale of Wensleydale, one of the last, was asked how long she took to knit a pullover: 'Ye'ed to be a terble good knitter to deu yan i' a day,' adding that when they got to the last stitches they used to think of the money. When she was told about knitting slowly, with straight needles, she was most amused and said, 'They ought to 'a' larned ye better!'*

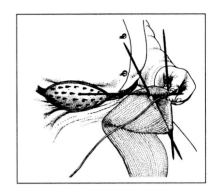

Figure 1 Knitting in the round with a 'whisk'.

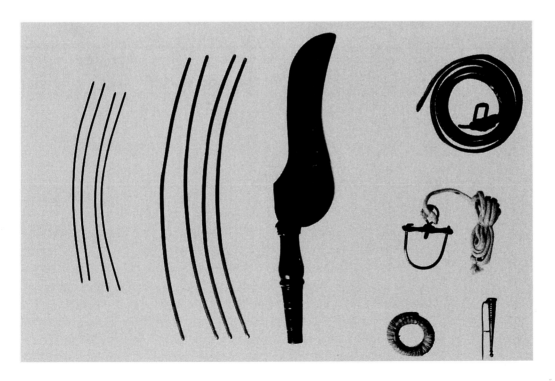

---

* Interview recounted by Marie Hartley in *The Old Hand-Knitters of the Dales,* 1951.

Knitting in the Round

The traditional, and most natural, way to knit is 'in the round'. For the ganseys and Fair Isles discussed in this book, it is the only method which will give you the authentic shape of the garment, a shape related to the bridal shirts and smocks of earlier centuries where the garments have drop shoulders and no shaping on the body. The sleeves, knit down from the shoulder, can be easily unravelled from the cuff and reknit to make the best possible repairs to frayed cuffs and worn elbows. The tube shape of the body is fairly close fitting for warmth, while gussets under the arms provide a freedom of movement.

If you already knit, the method you most likely are using, where you knit with two needles making shapes which then have to be sewn together, owes more to dressmaking and tailoring than knitwear. While this method may be justified to accommodate difficult shaping demanded by fashion trends, over and over again seasoned knitters of the 'in the round' method will give you an excellent piece of advice: 'Never, ever sew when you can knit'. After all, most people hate stitching the knitted pieces together—knitting in the round, together with the grafting of seams, does away with this tiresome chore. Perhaps more importantly, in my opinion, the major virtue of knitting in the round is that the work is always seen from the right side, so that when knitting ganseys the purl and plain stitches do not have to be 'reversed' when working from the wrong side. When knitting Fair Isle in the round it makes the working of two strands so much more manageable that you always knit exactly what you will eventually see on the pattern. Furthermore, once you have mastered the technique, you will find that it makes for a very even tension. It has always been my experience that turning the garments and working, say, alternate purl rows to make stocking stitch often causes unevenness.

With Aran patterns it is a little different. It is difficult to determine whether Arans have always been knit over two needles, as they invariably are today. It is not, on the whole, very likely, since the convention for knitting this type of garment comes from a solid tradition of knitting in the round. Most of the historical research into Arans dates from the 1930s—a period when fashion designers and wool manufacturers were adapting old patterns for the amateur knitter, when it was customary in these circles to work with two pins. I have therefore accepted the established convention of working Arans over two needles and sewing the pieces together. Their shape is, nonetheless, the same as traditional garments—straight on the body with drop neck sleeves—except that they have no underarm gussets.

Figure 2 illustrates knitting in the round. The normal method is to use four needles, the stitches are divided evenly over three of them and the fourth used to work the stitches. This number of needles is, however, restricting when knitting up the body of the garment, which for an average man would measure about 40 inches (102 cm) and it has been general practice to use five needles. With four needles on the stitches and one to work with, the load on the pins is reduced. In some parts of the country—northern Scotland, Norfolk,

Cornish girls knitting, 1850s.

Figure 2 Knitting in the round, using double-pointed needles.

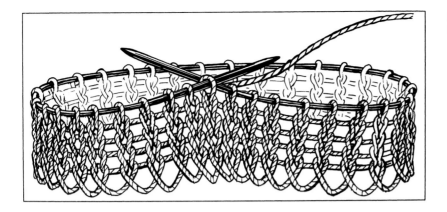

Figure 3 Knitting in the round, using modern circular twin pins.

and Cornwall, in particular—some knitters would use up to eight or ten small sock needles to hold the work!

For all its seeming complication it is a very easy technique. There is, however, one snag for the beginner. There is a tendency to alter the tension of the stitch when moving the work from one needle to the next. If the same crossover position is maintained it can lead to an unsightly column of stitches, especially apparent on plain knitting. The answer is simply to vary the crossover point by a few stitches every time and, with practice, the tension will even up.

Knitting in the round makes it essential for you to mark your half rounds to delineate where the side seams will fall, so that you know where to start the underarm gusset and to divide for the back and front yokes. You can do this in two ways. On ganseys and Fair Isles that are patterned all over, the pattern repeats will usually enable you to note the position of the seam lines, although it is a good idea to mark the stitch with a short length of contrasting thread or wool. On a plain gansey the best way to mark the half round is to purl the seam line stitches on every round so that they make a distinctive line all the way up the side of the garment. You will then have no trouble identifying the correct stitch when it comes to increasing for the gusset. A last point to note is to cast on equally over the number of needles you are using and make sure that the work does not become twisted when you begin. If you use circular twin pins as an alternative to double-pointed needles, this is especially important as you will have a great number of stitches on the needle when you cast on.

Not surprisingly, certain points are more important for some styles of knitting than for others. For the two-colour and multi-coloured work of Fair Isle, for example, you may think that knitting in the round matters less because there is no pattern dependent on the use of purl stitches, the entire design coming from the use of different coloured wools. In fact, the tension of the yarn (improved by knitting in the round) is especially important. When working with two colours, the yarn not in use has to be carried across the back of the knitting. Those of you familiar with Fair Isle work will be aware that there are two ways of doing this. One is the 'weaving in' method, by which the free yarn is woven into the back of every other stitch until it is needed again. The traditional method, however, is considered to be 'stranding,' whereby the yarn 'floats' across the back of the work *(see*

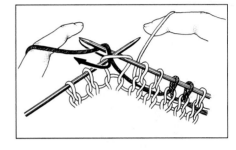

Figure 4 Holding the contrast yarn with the left hand while the background colour is being worked.

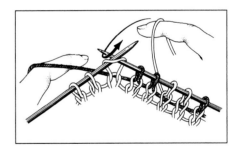

Figure 5 Working the contrast yarn while the background colour is held out of the way.

figures 4 and 5 on page 13). It is easy to see that with the latter method an even tension is critical to the success of the final garment. Altering the tension by turning and working a wrong-side purl row increases the danger of the yarn or the stitches being pulled too tight and the resulting work lying unevenly

Continental Knitting Method

In connection with two-colour work, it is worth mentioning a particular way of holding the needles, known as the Continental Method. In the English method of knitting, 'Western Uncrossed', the strand of wool is held in the right hand, and I suspect that most British people try to knit Fair Isles with both colours of wool controlled by the right hand. On the continent, and in particular for our purpose, on the island of Shetland, it is more usual for the wool to be controlled by the left hand: it is pulled behind the working loop on the left-hand needle and flicked through by the right needle, on which it stays. Once you get used to this technique, you will find that you can work much faster than with the more usual method. *Figures 6 to 9* explain how it is done. It is also possible to use a combination of both methods, controlling one colour with each hand.

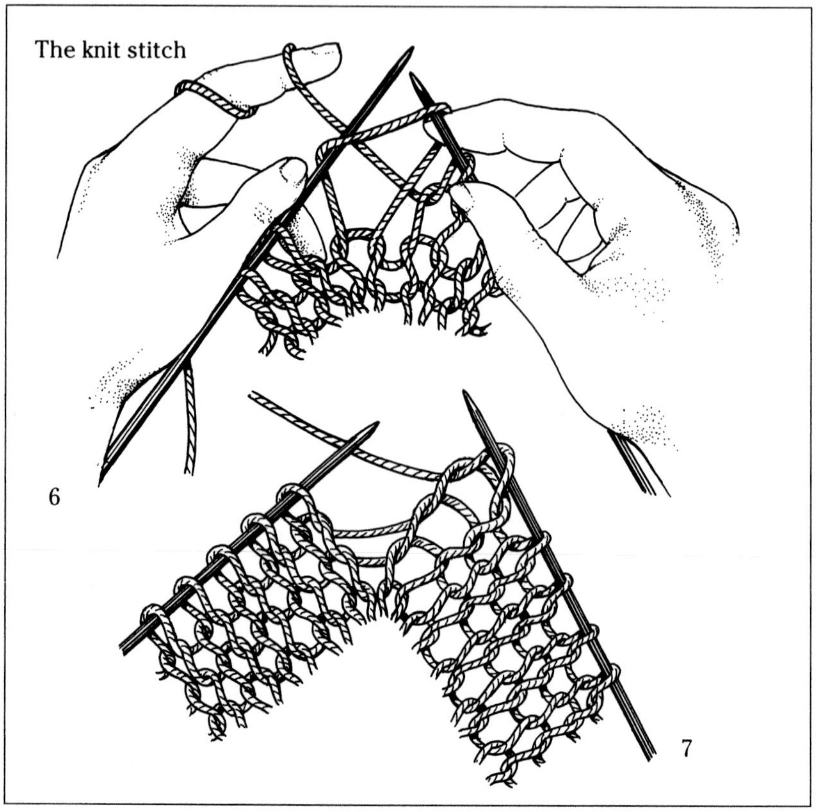

CONTINENTAL KNITTING METHOD
Hold the yarn in the left hand around the index finger and away from the needle, which is held between the thumb and second finger leaving the index finger free to work the yarn.

Figure 6 Place the right needle through the first stitch on the left needle. Pick up the yarn with the point of the right needle.

Figure 7 Pull a loop through to form a stitch on the right needle, slipping the loop off the left needle at the same time.

The knit stitch

6

7

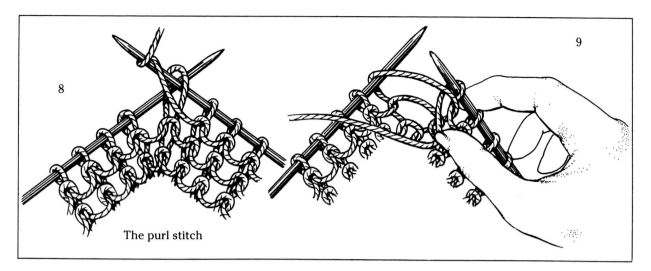

The purl stitch

Figure 8 Hold the needles in the same way, but keep the yarn to the front of the work. Insert the right needle into the next stitch to the front of the left needle and loop the yarn round it.

Figure 9 Take the yarn back through the stitch to form a new stitch on the right needle, slipping the loop off the left needle at the same time.

An Introduction to Pattern Structure, Pattern Sequence and Reading Pattern Instructions

One of the purposes of this book is to give you the opportunity to arrange your own patterns. This is the next logical step for an adventurous knitter. Avid knitters have always set great store by the ability to copy or adapt other people's patterns within the confines of the traditional shape, construction, and pattern conventions. Many a tale has been recounted to me of fisher lassies vying for a seat in church behind a particularly fine example of knitting, though always accompanied by a few chuckles—is the girl more interested in the handsome knitting or the handsome wearer?

The patterning traditions that make folk knitting so fascinating probably grew up for practical rather than aesthetic reasons, except in the case of multi-coloured work. The essential attribute of the fishermen's garment was warmth, and the most efficient method of creating warmth is to knit in a way that uses up more yarn than plain knitting and that creates air pockets. If you knit plain stitch back to front, as it were (*i.e.,* a purl), and place this next to a plain stitch, the loops will lie in different directions, increasing the thickness of the material. The most suitable places for this extra warmth are the yoke, upper sleeves, and the welt; though, of course, the patterning can be extended over the whole garment, as with Arans and the more elaborate ganseys.

This extra layer of insulation, then, is made up of the relationship between the plain and the purl stitch, which is crucial in the creation of patterns. The two stitches are, technically, the same; it is just a matter of which part of the stitch is allowed to lie forward on the face of the knitting. In the fisher gansey tradition, purl stitches usually provide the raised pattern on a plain background; with Arans, it is plain stitches, often 'travelling' diagonally across the work in cables, that provide the decorative element on a background of reversed stocking stitch. In Fair Isle it is the second yarn travelling behind the main body of work that provides the extra layer.

'In our day research now claims that the purl stitch was known in the year 1555.... I do not know who may have it now, but 20 years ago Sir Alex Seton, a direct descendant of Mary Seton, had in his possession an old Latin reader which confirms the purl stitch as French in origin.

The old reader was issued by the famous French printing firm, Estiennes, typographers to the King of France. It belonged to Mary Queen of Scots while she was a schoolgirl of thirteen at the ancient French monastery of St Germain. On the blank leaves of the book are notes written by the girl queen while she was engaged in mastering the art of knitting socks.

Her knitting notes are written in Old French and begin thus: 'Quand vous voudrez commence la chauffe, faite douge VI pinct, et en faite un doit sans estreicy, et puis fait cinq estrouy de dis en dis.... [When you wish to begin the sock make 12 stitches and knit a finger length without taking in, and then do five purl every tenth stitch....]'

(John London, *Scotland Magazine*, 1957.)

Norfolk fisher gansey, worn by
Mr Alex Kerr.

How Patterns Emerge

If you were to imagine yourself experimenting with this relationship between stitch and background it is quite easy to understand how patterns emerge. For example, the result of placing the raised surface of a purl stitch in a progressive increase relevant to the purl stitch of the previous round is a diagonal. The logical conclusions of this are patterns like the herringbone, the open and closed diamond, the flag, etc. Similarly, alternating knit and purl stitches over equal distances, and then repeating them over several rounds, results in the rib; variations of this are the basket stitch and the many combinations of moss or Bird's Eye stitches. Such experimentation by creative knitters is more than likely to be how patterns emerged, although a more lyrical explanation is that they were consciously trying to represent certain designs or symbols. It is perhaps more probable that the patterns were discovered first by accident, then by experimentation and finally assigned names by association.

Over centuries of knitting, many patterns have emerged and excellent research has revealed that most in common use have at some time decorated the various articles made under the contract knitting system, such as socks and gloves. The traditions were usually oral and passed down from mother to daughter, though the complex two-colour patterns were often also notated in graph form to aid the memory.

This gradual assimilation of technique is one possible explanation of why, in the case of fisher ganseys, particular patterns have been identified with certain villages. Great pride was taken in these patterns and it is said that at one time it was possible to identify a fisherman's origin by the pattern on his gansey. This notion is unfortunately somewhat of an urban myth. There is no historical record that I can find where someone identified a fisherman's origin from the pattern on his gansey. A more correct observation is the point I made that particular patterns have been associated with particular villages. In my research I spent enough time in the places I visited to be able to identify the significant knitter in the community. She was a knitter prepared to take risks with the ability to skilfully create her vision with enthusiasm and to happily pass on what she learnt to her community of knitters who naturally looked to her for leadership. The consequence of this process led to the fishermens' ganseys taking on a village 'signature'. In Fair Isle knitting, it was individual creativity that counted, especially since the number of original knitters on the island itself cannot have been very great. The tradition of personal experimentation with colours and patterns continued when mainland knitters took up the technique. The identification of Aran patterns goes much more by families: certain patterns would be passed down in a family through many generations and would never go outside it. So it can be seen that the oral origins of the patterns and techniques described in this book have a lot to do with the final appearance of the garments.

How to Read the Patterns

The pattern sequence is now your choice—you are not constrained by your local tradition or sense of obligation to your family. In the following section I reveal what I consider to be major pattern trends and I show you how to choose pattern sequences and place them in harmonious order. At this point I would draw your attention to the photographs illustrating this section. I think they portray reasonably clearly that the level of expertise required for knitting ganseys is within the grasp of children. I mean this with no disrespect, because I would be the first to agree that at first sight the structure and method appear impenetrable. If, however, you take up the challenge, you will have to agree the approach to gansey knitting is one of simplicity.

In my first edition nearly all the patterns in the book did not include instructions for making a whole garment. I followed the traditional way. It was simply a matter of choosing patterns that appealed, then knitting them up as small samples and then laying them side by side to create satisfying combinations. All that was then necessary was to work the chosen patterns symmetrically into the number of stitches required for the chest size.

At the time I expressed the notion that such a task was a little daunting. In fact, I need not have worried as the general level of knitters' expertise was quite high. Today I am advised that the level of knitting in terms of the self-generation of patterns is not so skilled. With this in mind I have made the following adjustments. For every village or community I have visited, where knitting in the traditional manner is practised, I have made up complete patterns that you may follow. In addition, I have introduced to this edition a method of reading stitch sequences which I previously published when knitters were at a similar creative nexus nigh on thirty years ago. When I first read knitting patterns it was a completely literal affair—there were no visuals apart from a photograph of the pattern and the instructions were written out to be read and knitted stitch by stitch.

Graphics played little part until we began to see Japanese yarns appear on the market with completely visual instructions. I remember the excitement even today. In consequence, I have gone halfway by noting that the very nature of making fisher ganseys and Fair Isle knitting has a visual metaphor which is easily translated to instruction. The gansey is made up for the most part with only one stitch presented to the front or the back of the fabric, either a knit stitch or a purl stitch, and Fair Isle knitting has one stitch that is either in the background or in contrast. These stitches occur in rounds to make up the fabric, so the following instruction translation is therefore:

Make a table headed with columns of Knit and Purl repeating: K P K P K etc. Item the rounds and insert number of knit and purl stitches, as per pattern *(see chart top of page 18)*.

Similarly, make a table headed with columns of Background and Contrast repeating: B C B C B C. Item the rounds and insert number of Background and Contrast, as per pattern *(see chart bottom of page 18)*.

Mary Jane and Elizabeth Joliffe, Polperro, Cornwall.

Little girl knitting, Polperro.

17

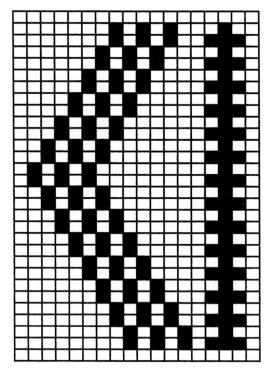

	K	P	K			K	P	K	P	K	P	K	
Round 1		3				1	1	1	1	1	1	8	Round 1
Round 2	1	1	1			1	1	1	1	1	1	8	Round 2
Round 3		3				2	1	1	1	1	1	7	Round 3
Round 4	1	1	1			2	1	1	1	1	1	7	Round 4
Round 5		3				3	1	1	1	1	1	6	Round 5
Round 6	1	1	1			3	1	1	1	1	1	6	Round 6
Round 7		3				4	1	1	1	1	1	5	Round 7
Round 8	1	1	1			4	1	1	1	1	1	5	Round 8
Round 9		3				5	1	1	1	1	1	4	Round 9
Round 10	1	1	1			5	1	1	1	1	1	4	Round 10
Round 11		3				6	1	1	1	1	1	3	Round 11
Round 12	1	1	1			6	1	1	1	1	1	3	Round 12
Round 13		3				7	1	1	1	1	1	2	Round 13
Round 14	1	1	1			7	1	1	1	1	1	2	Round 14
Round 15		3				8	1	1	1	1	1	1	Round 15
Round 16	1	1	1			8	1	1	1	1	1	1	Round 16

Continue round 17 as round 14. Round 18 as round 13 etc. to round 30.

Annie Jane Nelson's Craster pattern, 17 sts and 28 rds.

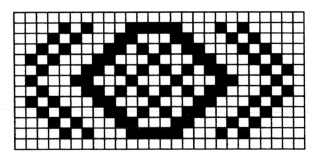

	B	C	B	C	B	C	B	C	B	C	B	C	B	C	B	C	B	C	B	C	B	C	
Round 1	24																						Round 1
Round 2	4	1	1	1	3	5	3	1	1	1	3												Round 2
Round 3	3	1	1	1	3	2	3	2	3	1	1	1	2										Round 3
Round 4	2	1	1	1	3	2	1	1	1	1	1	2	3	1	1	1	1						Round 4
Round 5	1	1	1	1	3	2	3	1	3	2	3	1	1	1									Round 5
Round 6		1	1	1	3	2	1	1	1	1	1	1	1	1	2	3	1	1					Round 6
Round 7	1	1	3	2	3	1	3	1	3	2	3	1											Round 7

24 sts and 13 rds. Round 8 to round 13
as round 6 to round 1.

Fair Isle Pattern

Knit rules:
Rules for reading visuals – read right to left
Rules for reading word instructions – read left to right
When knitting your instructions – knit right to left

The majority of graphics patterns displayed are bounded by a single
column and row. This boundary plays no part in the structure of the
pattern and its repetition

Traditional Knitting: The Fisher Gansey

What better way can there be to describe the unique knitting of England and Scotland, than to use the words of one of the fisher lassies. She is describing how to knit a 'Sunday Best' gansey, which is knit on fine needles—often twelve stitches and nineteen rows to the inch. With many interesting borrowings from the craft of weaving, Lily McKay's description (in the Buchan dialect of the Moray Firth) of how to knit a gansey went something like this:

'Nae . . . I couldna' follow a pattren. So I put them on my memory. We had different pattrens. We used to work a lot with the diamond sometimes single, sometimes double. There was the hairt, yes the hairt pattren and the anchor. Och, there were lots of different ganseys. My neighbour made some awfa bonnie ganseys, she wove some bonnie pattrens.

It was a a'four ply wool, an awfa lang weav. We knitted them on four needles, right round aboot. And then you lifted the sleeves and did them on four needles frae the top and then you took them in and shapet the gushet; and then you wove a bit withoot any intakes and then tak in to come doon and mak yer cuff. It was singles at the bottom. We warpet it frae the fit, you see, on four needles—a good lang tail, setting the rib and after let oot. You didna put on so much on the tail, but let oot a score to mak it mair full and to keep the tail tichter kind. Nae mony dis them by hand: that was a thin dress—the working anes swere wi'thicker wassit and wi'thicker needles for winter and done mostly plain. This is a Sunday Best ane'.

(Quote by Lily McKay [91 yrs], August 1983, Buchan, Moray Firth, Scotland. Noted by Alison McKay and reproduced by their kind permission.)

Origins

It should be evident by now that the traditions I am describing have their origins and their expression intimately connected with pre-industrial production and trade. The word 'gansey', it is claimed, is derived from 'Guernsey', because of this island's association with knitting. It is also generally considered to be a dialect corruption of the word as it appears time and again throughout the country, each area claiming it for its own. Almost without exception, however, 'gansey' is used to describe the seamen's seamless jersey or pullover; although, in Scotland it is an old word that describes any kind of pullover. Interestingly, if one digs a little deeper and sources the word 'jersey' we find that it is described as a 'garment made of stuff'. Stuff is described as a fabric made entirely of 'worsted'. Worsted is described as 'well twisted yarn of long stapled wool'.

Sunday Best ganseys, east coast of Scotland, c. 1890.

19

Mr Coppelman and his son, Filey, c. 1907.

I have noted that one may easily be brought to the conclusion through the broader derivation that the name of the garment itself owes its origins to the island of Guernsey, and this island's production of machine-made guernseys manufactured by Renouf. I am now drawn to the notion that its name is associated with the worsted 'wassit' yarn that has been produced in Guernsey for some considerable time. If we look at the history of spinning in the 16th century, the Channel Islands were renowned for producing a fine worsted, 'Jersey Stocking'. Lewis Paul's patent of 1738 refers to combed wool as 'jersey' and in 1882 Beck's *Draper's Dictionary* states, 'Jarsey is still the local name for worsted'. Similarly it would be incorrect to assume that the knitting industry of the Channel Islands preceded the knitting industry of the British Isles, which gave rise to the patterns and traditions of the Fisher Gansey.

The Conventions of Pattern Construction

This section explores the considerations and conventions that have evolved by determining where and in what combination we place patterns of our choice on the gansey that will be our creation. You will note that there is a similar discussion within the Fair Isle tradition.

The Purl Stitch on Plain Knitting

Before delving into these patterns it is first necessary to understand how the purl stitch works on a plain stocking stitch ground.

When a purl stitch is presented vertically in columns the stitch disappears and pulls the work in, and when used in combination with plain stitches becomes the basis for knitting the welt.

When a purl stitch is presented as stitches in rows, the stitches stand out from the plain knitted ground like a band. The combination of a plain knitted round, followed by a purl round, followed by another knit round is known as a garter stitch.

When plain and purl stitches are presented alternately so that in each round at no point are there more than three or four purl stitches next to, or on top of each other, we obtain a second textural grounding standing out from the plain stocking stitch ground. The simplest example of this is the moss stitch combination.

In Annie Jane Nelson's pattern on page 18, you will note that this convention is further exploited by placing purl stitches on top of each other, which makes the pattern stand out even more effectively from the ground. This combination is used where a large pattern is required as a method for shaping the pattern at a less acute angle than there would be using a single moss stitch combination. I strongly recommend that no more than four purl stitches are placed in such a

McGarry Kelly, Whitby. His gansey pattern is based on P3, K3 set within horizontal bands of garter.

McGarry Kelly gansey pattern: K3, P3 moss stitch, set in garter stitch panel

P	K	P		
	knit		Round 1
		purl	Round 2
	knit		Round 3
		purl	Round 4
	knit		Round 5
		purl	Round 6
	knit		Round 7
3	3		Round 8
	knit		Round 9
	3	3	Round 10
	knit		Round 11

Repeat rd 8 to 11 for required depth, ending with rd 7 to rd 1

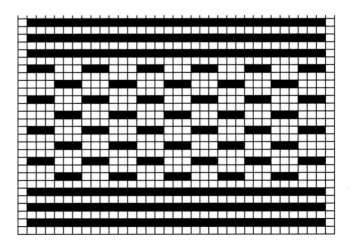

manner, as any additional stitch would make the work appear as a column, and therefore begin to disappear from the background (as we have already discovered in the knit two, purl two combinations). In addition, it is suggested that not more than four are placed together horizontally unless there is a definite intention to change the texture of the ground, such as in a basket stitch or a ladder stitch combination.

Before and after each pattern a plain knitted round has been inserted with each pattern set sequence. This is the framing you must do for the pattern to stand out clearly. The patterns worn by McGarry Kelly and Scraper Smith illustrate this concept beautifully.

Background moss stitch variations edged by garter stitches.

Please note: a moss stitch and a garter stitch are not single stitches.

Moss stitch: A single purl and knit stitch lay side by side in and round, and are then presented alternately after being separated by a knit round.

Garter stitch: A knit round folowed by a purl round. Repeat.

Moss stitch set in garter panel.
Repeat rd 6 to rd 8 for required depth, ending rd 5 to rd 1

P	K	P		
	knit		Round 1	
		purl	Round 2	
	knit		Round 3	
		purl	Round 4	
	knit		Round 5	
	1	1	Round 6	
	knit		Round 7	
1		1	Round 8	
	knit		Round 9	

Double moss stitch set in garter panel.
Repeat rd 6 to rd 8 for required depth, ending with rd 5 to rd 1.

P	K	P		
	knit		Round 1	
		purl	Round 2	
	knit		Round 3	
		purl	Round 4	
	knit		Round 5	
2		2	Round 6	
	knit		Round 7	
	2	2	Round 8	
	knit		Round 9	

Triple moss stitch set in garter panel.
Repeat rd 6 to rd 9 for required depth, ending with rd 4 to rd 1.

P	K	P	K	P		
			knit		Round 1	
				purl	Round 2	
			knit		Round 3	
				purl	Round 4	
			knit		Round 5	
2	1	3	1	1	Round 6	
			knit		Round 7	
	1	3	1	3	Round 8	
			knit		Round 9	

Basket stitch set in garter panel.
Repeat rd 6 to rd 9 for required depth, ending with rd 5 to rd 1.

P	K	P		
	knit		Round 1	
		purl	Round 2	
	knit		Round 3	
		purl	Round 4	
	knit		Round 5	
	3	3	Round 6	
	3	3	Round 7	
3		3	Round 8	
3		3	Round 9	

Betty Martin stitch set in garter panel.
Repeat rd 6 to rd 10 for required depth, ending with rd 5 to rd 1.

K	P		
knit		Round 1	
	purl	Round 2	
knit		Round 3	
	purl	Round 4	
knit		Round 5	
1	2	Round 6	
1	2	Round 7	
knit		Round 8	
1	2	Round 9	
1	2	Round 10	

Pattern Sequencing

Horizontal Panels

The conventional sequence with horizontal panels is to work plain stocking stitch for the body and moss or double moss variations set in horizontal panels at the yoke. The plain area is always separated from the pattern area by garter ridges. The number of ridges has been recorded as an indication of the number of children in the family. Each horizontal pattern is edged by a plain knit round and then separated from the next horizontal pattern by garter stitch rounds, usually the same number as the first garter ridge panel. It is usual when knitting horizontals from the yoke to let the gusset be the start and end point of the first horizontal repeat. Horizontal panels on the arm are normally a repetition of the body sequence— begun after a few rounds of plain knitting to settle the stitches picked up around the shoulder.

IMPORTANTLY, never pattern below the elbow, otherwise, after the elbow has worn through, unpicking stitches from the cuff and pulling back past the hole in order to renew the sleeve, will disturb the pattern and cause problems.

Vertical Panels

Annie Jane Nelson's pattern on page 18, the photograph illustrating the pattern from Craster in Northumberland *(page 106)* and the section that informs you on determining patterns repeats *(pages 26 to 27)* clearly reveal the need to separate major pattern elements from each other. Here we have a single element—the zigzag, 'local name' for the Road to Crovie. The device used to separate the pattern is known as a 'seeding column' and follows the same rule as horizontal panels. Each major vertical element always begins and ends with a plain knit stitch to set the pattern in the plain knit ground.

The seeding column diagrams illustrated indicate the minimum number of stitches to successfully divide major vertical elements. You may note that this device is flexible enough to add stitches to, which is often essential for ensuring the correct number of stitches for accurate sizing. The most common of these seeding columns in addition to those illustrated is the 'rope' or 'cable', and in some villages, knitters have increased the seeding column to match the number of stitches in the 'major' vertical element.

Where the convention is to repeat a vertical pattern element it is advised that the number of repeats be equal on the front of the garment and the back. When the choice of major vertical patterns is different, it is advised that each pattern repeat will have the same number of stitches.

Horizontal and Vertical Panel Combinations

When we are enabling a pattern sequence that has vertical and horizontal expression my major advice is to employ the use of graph paper and place your choice of pattern side-by-side in order to work out your ideal relationship. The more complex the verticals and horizontals the more is the requirement to knit up a swatch of at least half a round. This will ensure that you have picked up enough stitches for your pattern repeats to work together and fit the size you desire. If you choose patterns that are unequal to each other it will be necessary to ensure that your patterns are odd so that the centre of the pattern can coincide with the centre front and back. The largest of your unequal patterns should be at the centre and the remainder of your pattern choice repeated on the left and right edge of the centre pattern. You will find examples of swatches on pages 62 and 63 knitted by Phoebe Carr of Thorne, a highly acclaimed knitter within the canal and keelboat community of the Humber estuary.

The more complex the pattern combinations I was a witness to, the more the likelihood that they were a personal expression.

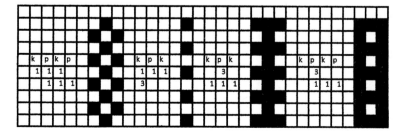

Seeding patterns made up as minimum columns dividing major pattern elements

Patricia Hanson's 'Crown and Anchor' pattern combination she knitted for her friend Squire was such an example (below). The number of stitch and row versions of these two patterns was considerable. Patricia explained that when she got past the initial lack of familiarity with the technique of graphing she quite enjoyed working with the many variations. She added that the extra work must have been worth it because Squire had many affirmative comments at the golf club bar.

Graphing is also useful when altering the basic template for knitting a gansey. Mrs Dorothy Pickering graphed up a design interpretation based on a Wick gansey pattern *(see page 144)* and knitted a bright blue gansey with pronounced neck shaping and personal pattern preferences.

Squire's Crown and Anchor golfing Gansey made by Patricia Hanson.

The Anchor, 19 sts & 32 rds

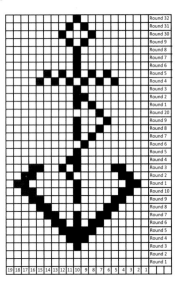

The Crown, 21 sts & 16 rds

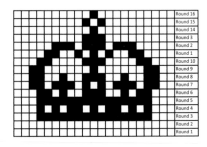
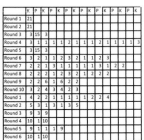

Moss diamond and Chevron Interlace, 18 sts & 24 rds

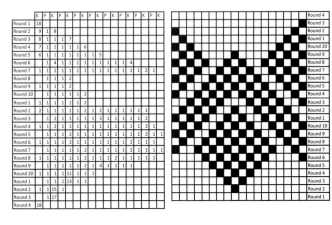

In the context of personal expression, Mrs Dorothy Pickering's source material for her splendid interpretation of Anchors, heapies and trellis diamond patterns on this child's sky blue gansey are displayed on pages 144 and 145.

Taking Measurements

Figure 10 Taking measurements.

A Chest size 40" (102 cm)

B Base to armpit (not too tight) 15" (38 cm)

C Overall height (nape of neck to base) 25" (64 cm)

D Arm length to shoulder including cuff 20" (51 cm)

E Chest height (armpit to nape of neck) 10" (26 cm)

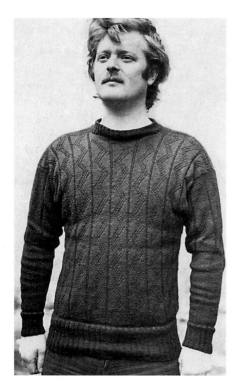

Craster pattern (Sunday Best). The pattern sequence is as follows: Seeding is 3 sts and 2 rds. Zigzag is 14 sts and 30 rds.

Constructing Ganseys

When you measure for a woollen garment *(see figure 10)*, it is usual to allow at least an extra 2 inches (5 cm) on the actual chest measurement so that the pullover is not too tight. Do not do this for the moment, though, since it may be necessary to increase the number of stitches in order to accommodate evenly the patterns you have chosen and this will provide the extra width for you.

Having got the measurements, you then work out the number of stitches you will need to achieve the chest width. Remember that you will need to cast on for the entire width when knitting in the round, but only for half the width for knitting the front and back separately. The number of stitches will depend on the tension: it is absolutely crucial to knit up a tension swatch before you go any further. As an example, let us take the 5-ply worsted wool used for ganseys, worked with No. 12 (2¾ mm) needles. In stocking stitch, knit up a square measuring at least 4 inches (10 cm), lay it out flat and count your stitches and rows over 1 inch (2.5 cm). It should be seven stitches and ten rows. If there are more or less, try bigger or smaller needles until you have achieved the correct tension. Do not be tempted to avoid this step: it isn't worth it.

Using the measurements in the example shown, to make the width of 40 inches (102 cm) for the chest, you will need 40 x 7 stitches, *i.e.* 280. Suppose that for a pattern you have picked zigzags which take up fourteen stitches, separated by seeding panels of three stitches. Each combination will be seventeen stitches wide, and this has to divide evenly into the overall number of stitches so that there are an equal number of repeats front and back. Dividing 280 by 17 gives you 16, with eight stitches over. If our maximum size was 280 stitches, we could use this number, and knit the extra eight stitches plain, four on each side, to mark the sides. But that would make the gansey too tight, since we need a few inches play (5 to 7 cm) on the actual size. Seventeen times the pattern configuration would be incorrect, since the uneven

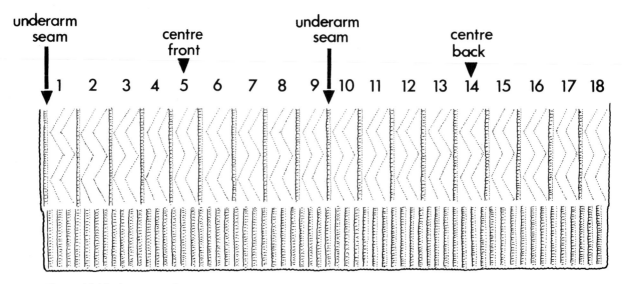

Figure 11 Marking seam lines.

number would mean that the patterns would not divide exactly between front and back. So the correct number of stitches needed is 18 x 17, *i.e.* 306 stitches. This will give nine full patterns each on the front and back, and will make a garment measuring 43 inches (110 cm), providing the extra width for comfort over the actual chest measurement. You can either cast on the 306 stitches or, to make a slightly tighter welt, cast on the original 280 stitches and increase evenly to make the extra 26 stitches over the first few rounds of plain knitting, above the welt.

To check where the seam lines will fall so that you will know where to divide the work for the sleeves or the underarm gusset, it is a good idea to sketch out your patterns over the whole width in a straight line and note the halfway mark, or half round. This will be the position of one seam and the other will fall where you cast on *(figure 11)*.

Every phase in the making of the gansey has practical applications, since it was designed primarily as a work garment for fishermen which, along with their oilskins and button-fronted moleskin trousers, had to stand the rigours and extremes of life at sea. The wool used is a 5-ply worsted of great strength and durability known as Seaman's Iron, and is tightly knitted and patterned to increase its insulating properties and turn water.

There you have it. A few sums are all that are needed. Using this example and the written-out patterns as a starting point, you will soon realise how simple it is to pick any pattern or combination of patterns in the book and work out your own sequence in the oral tradition from which these patterns originated. With practice, a knitter only had to look at a person to decide the number of repeats required to knit a gansey to size—one would be an 'eighteener', another a 'sixteener', etc. As far as the length count goes, it is not usually necessary to bother with counting rows; the best method is simply to note the actual length of the garment from the stitches on the needles.

The Underarm Gusset (Ganseys and Fair Isles Only)

The seam line *(see figure 11, "underarm seam", page 26)* on the half round of the body of the garment marks the point for the beginning of the gusset that allows freedom of movement under the arm, incidentally extending the length of the garment's life. The diamond-shaped gusset is always knit in plain knitting, and on Fair Isles with one colour only. Once it is worked out at the beginning of the sleeve, the same central stitch continues to mark the seam line which is carried all the way down the sleeve to the cuff *(figure 12)*.

The gusset is made as follows: when you are about 3 inches (7.5 cm) short of the length from welt to armpit, increase one knit stitch on either side of the seam line stitch that you have marked. Repeat this increase every fourth round, until the gusset is 19 stitches (3 inches or 7.5 cm) wide. At this point, divide for front and back by slipping the gusset stitches together with the

Beverly poses in a Rocket Gansey with Michael in his Craster Gansey, beneath Cullercotes Watchtower. 1978 editorial.

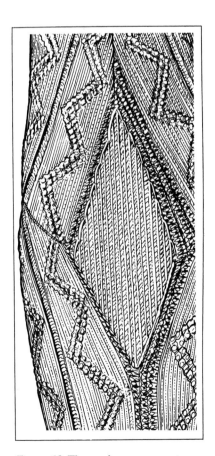

Figure 12 The underarm gusset.

stitches for the back onto a holder. Continue to work the front over two needles to the shoulder; then, still leaving the gusset stitches on the holder, finish off the back. When you come to work the sleeves, you pick up the gusset stitches, together with as many stitches as necessary evenly around the armhole. Keeping the gusset plain, decrease one stitch each side of it, and repeat the decrease to match the way you made the increase, until you are left with just the central stitch again. The rest of the sleeve is worked to the cuff in the normal way.

The Shoulder

When the front and back yokes are completed, the shoulders are the next to finish off. Of the various methods, the simplest is to take the shoulder stitches from front and back (you will have left the first lot on a stitch holder) and knit them together onto one needle, casting off at the same time. You can effect this 'grafting' either on the inside (by putting the right sides together) or on the outside, leaving a ridge.

There are a number of variations on this basic way of grafting the shoulder seams. The most popular method in Scotland is to knit an extra panel on one side only: either on the two fronts; or on, say, the left front and the right back. The seams are then grafted on the inside. This is an especially neat way to finish a Fair Isle, since it enables you to work a whole pattern panel whose centre line will fall exactly on the shoulder. Remember to subtract from the height of the yoke shoulders whatever extra you will create in the panels.

Another variation common on ganseys is to make a strap by knitting the last couple of inches on both front and back in a contrasting pattern to the rest of the yoke, and grafting the seams in a ridge that can be disguised as part of the pattern. *Figure 13* illustrates the 'rig and fur' pattern, which is a very popular shoulder strap in the North East. Looking a little like a ploughed field with ridges and furrows, it is constructed from three rows of garter stitch followed by two rows of plain knitting. The shoulder straps are cast off together to make a ridge on the outside that complements the pattern. Other shoulder strap designs are shown in *figures 14 and 15*.

The most spectacular method of all for a gansey shoulder strap is to knit it at right angles to the yoke so that it continues down the sleeve without a break. This shoulder 'saddle' is particularly effective on a fully patterned garment where the pattern will continue right down to the cuff: the configuration on the saddle forms the central element in the pattern on the sleeve. It is constructed as follows. First work out how wide your saddle will be, and leave off knitting the yoke to allow for this extra width. Then, on the needle holding the stitches of the left back shoulder, cast on extra stitches at the neck side, using a contrasting colour wool (the number of new stitches will determine the width of the saddle). Knit one row of the new stitches. Now, working exclusively in the main colour, place all the stitches next to those of the left front shoulder at the neck side, on the same needle. You will now have a strip of new stitches connecting the two shoulders across the neck. Using two needles, work a wrong-side (*i.e.*

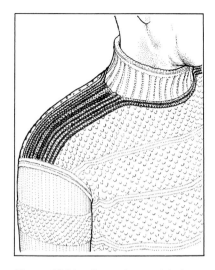

Figure 13 Northeast 'rig and fur' shoulder panel.

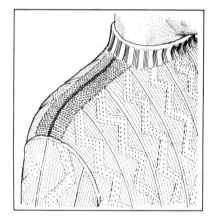

Figure 14 Shoulder grafted on the outside.

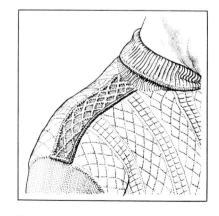

Figure 15 Scottish shoulder panel.

28

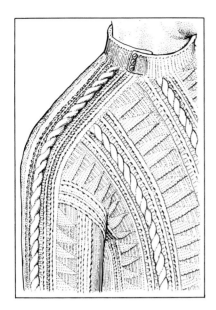

Figure 16 Decorative shoulder saddle knit at right angles.

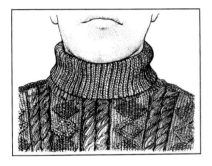

Figure 17 Polo neck.

purl) row in the pattern of your choice across the saddle stitches. When you get to the last stitch, work it together with the first of the shoulder stitches still on the needle. Turn, and repeat the procedure on the next row, knitting the last saddle stitch together with the first shoulder stitch. Continue in this way, taking one stitch from each alternate side at the ends of every row until all the shoulder stitches are used up. Leave the remaining stitches on a holder or safety pin to be picked up when you work the sleeve. When it comes to doing the neck, you simply pull out the contrasting wool in which you cast on the saddle, and pick up the stitches as part of the neck edge. *Figure 16* shows the beautiful effect of this type of 'saddle'.

The Neck or Collar

The most common collar on pullovers today is the roll, or polo neck *(figure 17)*. This modern method is not recommended for the pure traditionalist, though it does look well on a garment to be worn under a jacket. The method for the most traditional collar *(figure 18)* is to pick up evenly around the neck, and work 2 inches (5 cm) of knit two, purl two rib, then finish off with four rounds—two purl, two plain—casting off loosely. Most knitters do not include any shaping, so of course there is a tendency for the neck to drop with repeated wear. To get over this and preserve the life of the collar, you can work it with a slit edge at one side and make a couple of buttonholes. A buttoned collar is usually knit quite tight and high, but looser versions are sometimes made to wear over shirts *(figure 19)*.

This section concludes the instructions and conventions for knitting a gansey. Experienced knitters should have no problems in generating their own pattern sequences on a gansey to fit the size of their choice.

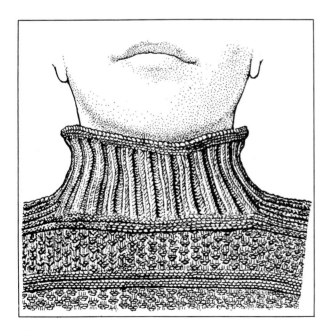

Figure 18 Traditional collar shape.

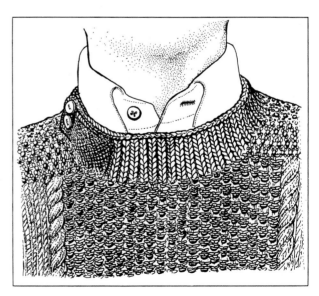

Figure 19 Buttoned collar.

The Fisher Gansey Patterns of Norfolk

My search for gansey patterns was at first concentrated around areas in North East England, where I learnt about my local knitting tradition. These introduced me to the influence of Scotland, and from there the next logical step was to see what could be found at the southernmost point of the fishermen's yearly travels.

The ports of Great Yarmouth and Lowestoft were the centre of the herring trade in southern England. On arrival I was immediately aware that the social mix of the communities was less well defined than up north, and that many people like myself had been there before me. On one hand, this made my job more difficult in that the communities had already broken up, and finding fishermen with anything other than an economic heritage would prove impossible. On the other, many people had documented the lifestyle and recorded the thoughts and aspirations of the fishing families before they broke up. After days of fruitless effort I turned to these sources—in the museums and archives—to get what I wanted. With a few notable exceptions this is where most of the information lay.

The demise of the fishing industry is well illustrated in Great Yarmouth. Fishing is no longer of importance and the town has turned to the countryside and to London and the South East for its economy. Fishing as it once was now lies in stacks of books and photographs in the archives of the Norfolk Museums service. Most of the material referred to the Scottish herring fleets and there were some rare photographs of the fleet, the fishermen and the women. But there was little documentation of local fishing and I had turn to villages further up the coast away from these two ports to get a sense of the local tradition.

The fishwharf at Great Yarmouth, 1910.

Mackerel fishing boats at Sheringham, Norfolk.

Group of fishermen on East Beach, Cromer, raise hats to wife of liberal MP, *c.* 1920s.

CROMER AND SHERINGHAM

I am indebted to Martin Warren, the Curator of Cromer Museum, who has taken a special interest in the ganseys of this particular area. He is responsible for a number of museums—one of which is a group of renovated fishermen's cottages devoted to displaying the lifestyle of the local inshore fishermen. It is well worth a visit. On seeing the exhibition one might be drawn to the conclusion that fishing was quite important to the township. This is not so: the fishing families were few and never ever solely survived on fishing. The tourist trade has always been important in recent history: the arrival of people from the cities 'pleasuring' during the summer months gave the fishing families an opportunity to hire their boats for pleasure trips, let out deckchairs and provide bed and breakfast accommodation to supplement their normal income.

The fishing was mainly for crab and lobster, but in the 19th century many men went on the 'Great' boats, dandy rigged luggers, locally built, that fished out of Grimsby and Hull; a few even used to spend the season with the Scottish fleets, and no doubt returned with a few Scottish patterns. Of course, there were relations with the Scots community when they visited: one of the gansey patterns in the museum was knitted by Mrs E. Kerr, who was a Scots lass herself. Her knitting reveals her heritage, as she used the Scots half flag as the major pattern. Despite the many examples of knitting in the Cromer Museum the town had never—as far as one can tell—had its own tradition or a pattern that was specially associated with it. The patterns in the museum come from Sheringham which had, and continues to have, a strong tradition.

But unfortunately I was not able to document them all. Of the remaining families that still knit, the West family is the most active and the museum has documented their knitting over three generations. The patterns are far and away the most beautiful in the collection and I was anxious to meet Mr 'Teapot' West and ask his permission to reproduce them. Mr West had, however, no intention of giving me, or anyone else, permission; he considered them exclusive to his family and said, understandably, that he did not like the idea of some stranger walking down the village streets wearing his pattern.

My entreaties about passing on his heritage for outsiders to appreciate, and warnings that maybe in the future his family would no longer knit, fell on deaf ears. His only concession has been to allow the museum to photograph them

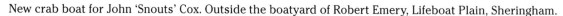

New crab boat for John 'Snouts' Cox. Outside the boatyard of Robert Emery, Lifeboat Plain, Sheringham.

for their archives. I was left with an increased understanding of the joy the fisher lassies of Scotland must have felt at pinching patterns and committing them to memory on sight! I was sorely tempted to do likewise, but out of respect for his wishes I acceded to his demand.

His ganseys are knitted in 3-ply wool using very fine needles (some on size 17) at a tension of twelve stitches and nineteen rows to the inch. I suspected that at some point in the past his family and others had supplemented their income by contract knitting, and that the fine needles they used had been passed down and used to knit the ganseys.

I asked him whether there was any special reason why they were knitted so finely but he could offer no explanation. I then asked whether his mother or grandmother had knitted for money—to which he replied that they had. He remembered his grandmother, in particular, knitting socks. Some entrepreneur had had a demand for finely knit socks and had set off the fisherwives of Sheringham to fulfil his orders. Why knitters should not have continued using fine needles elsewhere was more than likely due to the fact that most contract knitting was quite coarse at the turn of the century, since the fine knitting was usually done by machines.

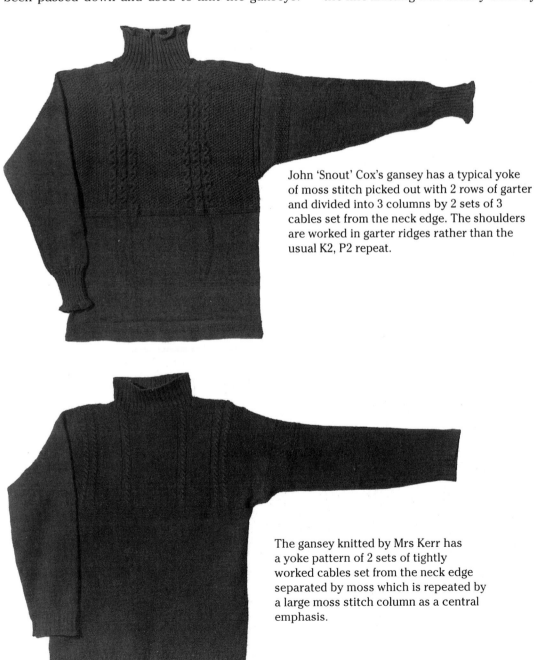

John 'Snout' Cox's gansey has a typical yoke of moss stitch picked out with 2 rows of garter and divided into 3 columns by 2 sets of 3 cables set from the neck edge. The shoulders are worked in garter ridges rather than the usual K2, P2 repeat.

The gansey knitted by Mrs Kerr has a yoke pattern of 2 sets of tightly worked cables set from the neck edge separated by moss which is repeated by a large moss stitch column as a central emphasis.

Most of the patterns shown here have been deciphered and notated from photographs I found in the museum at Cromer. Like Mr West's, they are all extremely finely knit. The ganseys worn by the Sheringham fishermen at the turn of the century *(below)* were classic work garments, concerned more with keeping warm than with elaborate patterning. The three visible ganseys display simple moss ladder variations: Potter Hardingham's pattern has a purl stitch surrounding 4 x 3 plain knit stitches, throwing them into relief. John's is a light 3 stitch moss pattern and Belsha's is a 4 stitch double moss pattern.

The children wore ganseys as well as their fathers, as can be seen from the school photograph of about the same date *(opposite page)*. One could no doubt surmise that it is the boys wearing the ganseys who come from fishing families. The gansey worn by one young lad *(back row, second right)* is of particular note. There is no seeding between the major configurations and the end result is a tessellated pattern over the whole of the yoke, which looks spectacular when worked over fine needles. It seems to have been a trait in this area at this time not to include any division between major patterns: the gansey knitted by Mrs Bishop for John 'Tar' Bishop beautifully illustrates this long-lived tradition echoed in the tessellated pattern of Mrs Esther Nurse of Lower Bodham dating around 1950 *(see page 38)*.

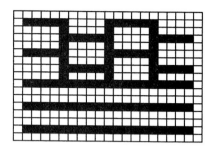

	K	P	K	P	K	P	K	P	K	P	K
Round 1			19								
Round 2	19										
Round 3	19										
Round 4			19								
Round 5	19										
Round 6	19										
Round 7			19								
Round 8	4	1		4	1	4	1	4			
Round 9			5		4	6	4				
Round 10	4	1		4	1	4	1	4			
Round 11	4		6	4	5						
Round 12	4	1		4	1	4	1	4			
Round 13			5		4	6	4				
Round 14	4	1		4	1	4	1	4			
Round 15	4	6		4	5						

Garter stitch panel.

Work basket stitch to desired dimensions and then work the first 7 rds in reverse to complete panel.

Potter Hardingham: 19 sts and 15 rds. Reverse basket stitch combination set in a double garter panel.

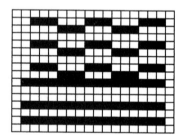

	K	P	K	P	K	P
Round 1				6		
Round 2		6				
Round 3				6		
Round 4	6					
Round 5	6					
Round 6				6		
Round 7	3	3				
Round 8			3	3		
Round 9	6					

Garter stitch panel.

Work moss stitch to desired dimensions and then work the first 6 rds in reverse to complete panel.

John 'Tar' Bishop: 6 sts and 3 rds. Triple moss combination set in a double and single garter panel.

Sheringham fishermen, 1890s. From the left: John 'Potter' Hardingham, John 'Tar' Bishop, Elijah Farrow and Belsha Johnson.

Belsha Johnson: 8 sts and 4 rds. 4-stitch moss combination set in a double knit garter panel.

	K		K	P	K	P
Round 1				8		
Round 2		8				
Round 3		8				
Round 4				8		
Round 5		8				
Round 6		8				
Round 7				8		
Round 8		4	4			
Round 9		4	4			
Round 10				4	4	
Round 11				4	4	

Work moss stitch to desired dimensions ending rd 1 to rd 8 in reverse.

Upper Sheringham School, *c.* 1890s.

Upprer Sheringham School; back row, second from right
16 sts and 9 rds

	K	P	K	P	K	P	K	P	K	P	K	P
Round 1		1	3	1	3	1	3	1	3			
Round 2	3	1	1	1	5	1	1	1	2			
Round 3	2	1	1	1	1	1	3	1	3	1	1	
Round 4	1	1	1	1	1	1	1	1	1	5	1	
Round 5		1	1	1	1	1	1	1	1	3	1	3
Round 6	1	1	1	1	1	1	1	1	3	1	1	2
Round 7	2	1	1	1	1	1	3	1	3	1	1	
Round 8	3	1	1	1	3	1	5	1				
Round 9		1	3	1	3	1	3	1	3			

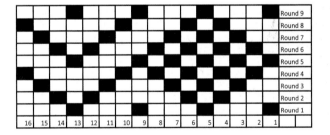

Upper Sheringham School; second row; third from left
15 sts and 20 rds

	K	P	K	P	K	P	K
Round 1	2	2	4	2	5		
Round 2	2	2	5	2	4		
Round 3		2	2	2	4	2	3
Round 4		2	2	2	5	2	2
Round 5	2	2	8	2	1		
Round 6	2	2	7	2	2		
Round 7		2	2	2	4	2	3
Round 8		2	2	2	3	2	4
Round 9	2	2	4	2	5		
Round 10	2	2	3	2	6		
Round 11		2	2	2	2	2	5
Round 12		2	2	2	3	2	4
Round 13	2	2	6	2	3		
Round 14	2	2	7	2	2		
Round 15		2	2	2	6	2	1
Round 16		2	2	2	5	2	2
Round 17	2	2	6	2	3		
Round 18	2	2	5	2	4		
Round 19		2	2	2	2	2	5
Round 20		2	2	2	1	2	6

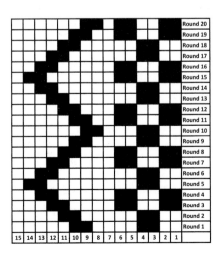

By the 1920s, seeded patterns were more common, as shown in the later fishermen's group *(above)*. Most of the ganseys in this photograph are machine-made, but two hand-knitted ones are clear enough to be deciphered—those worn by James Dumble *(standing, second right)* and 'Jimmy Coalie' *(standing, right)*. James Dumble's has a very interesting step configuration made up with garter and double moss stitch, while Jimmy Coalie's is decorated with a distinctive vertical herringbone and moss stitch sequence.

My last pattern from Norfolk is Henry Little's gansey, knitted by 'Pinnie' Little, who died in 1968 at the age of 76. It has 'had a bit of rough', as they say down here, but its fine knitting is still evident—it will have been worked with size 14 and size 16 needles. The gansey is knitted in tightly cabled columns separated by a simple purl diagonal repeat.

I hope that these provide a pointer for those of you who are enthusiastic enough to go to Cromer and see the remaining collection—notably the amazing patterns of 'Teapot' West.

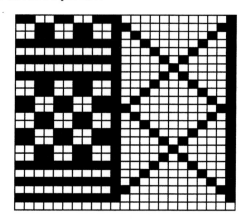

James Dumble: 16 sts and 11 rds. Double moss set within 3 garter rounds and edged with vertical column of open diamonds.

	K	P	K	P	K	P	K	P	K	P
Round 1	11	5								
Round 2		1	9	4						
Round 3	1	1	7	1	1	5				
Round 4	2	1	5	1	2	1	4			
Round 5	3	1	3	1	3	5				
Round 6	4	1	1	1	4	1	2	2		
Round 7	5	1	5	1	4					
Round 8	4	1	1	1	4	1	2	2		
Round 9	3	1	3	1	3	5				
Round 10	2	1	5	1	2	1	4			
Round 11	1	1	7	1	1	1	2			

Sheringham fishermen, 1920s, with beach inspector and friend.

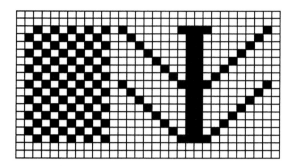

	K	P	K	P	K	P	K	P	K	P	K	P	K	P	K	P	K	P	K
Round 1	8	4	8	1	1	1	1	1	1	1	1	1	1						
Round 2	7	1	1	2	1	1	1	1	1	1	1	1							
Round 3	6	1	2	2	2	1	6	1	1	1	1	1	1	1	1				
Round 4	5	1`	3	2	3	1	5												
Round 5	4	1	4	2	4	2	1	4											
Round 6	3	1	5	2	5	1	3												
Round 7	2	1	6	2	6	1	1												
Round 8	1	1	6	4	6	1	1												

James Coalie 30 sts & 7 rds.
Vertical column of single moss edged by 2 opposing
purl diagonals seeded by 2 purl vertical columns.

Henry Little's pattern was knitted by 'Pinnie'
Little on size 14 and 16 needles. The gansey
is knitted in tightly cabled columns separated
by a simple purl diagonal repeat.

Henry Little: 16 sts and 7 rds cabling every 5th rd.
Tight cabled columns separated by a simple purl diagonal
repeat, set within a 3 garter panel at the beginning of the
gusset and finishing at the shoulders as a 'rig' (ridge) & 'fur'
(furrow) combination (looks like a ploughed field). This
relationship is echoed on the sleeves at shoulder edge.

	P	K	P	K	P	K	P	K	P
Round 1	3	4							
Round 2	2	1	1	3					
Round 3	2	2	1	2					
Round 4	2	3	1	1					
Round 5	2	4	1						

Mrs Bishop's pattern for John 'Tar' Bishop.
12 rds and 28 sts.

Mrs West, Mrs Bishop and Mrs Esther Nurse knitted very fine horizontal yoke patterns based on garter ridge and moss stitch variations, while Mrs Bishop knitted spectacular tessellated patterns over the yoke.

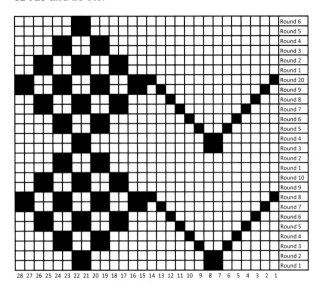

28 27 26 25 24 23 22 21 20 19 18 17 16 15 14 13 12 11 10 9 8 7 6 5 4 3 2 1

Mrs Bishop's pattern for John 'Tar' Bishop, 1900.

	K	P	K	P	K	P	K	P	K	P	K	P	
Round 1	6	2	12	2	6								Round 1
Round 2	6	2	12	2	6								Round 2
Round 3	5	1	2	1	9	2	2	2	4				Round 3
Round 4	4	1	4	1	9	2	2	2	4				Round 4
Round 5	3	1	6	1	5	2	2	2	2	2	2		Round 5
Round 6	2	1	8	1	4	2	2	2	2	2	2		Round 6
Round 7	1	1	10	1	1	2	2	2	2	2	2	2	Round 7
Round 8		1	12	3	2	2	2	2	2	2			Round 8
Round 9	16	2	2	2	2	2	2						Round 9
Round 10	16	2	2	2	2	2	2						Round 10
Round 11	18	2	2	2	4								Round 11
Round 12	18	2	2	2	4								Round 12

Mrs Esther Nurse: 23 sts and 10 rds.

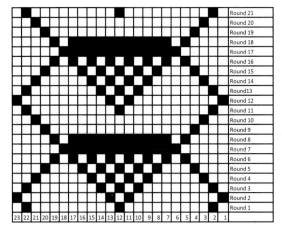

23 22 21 20 19 18 17 16 15 14 13 12 11 10 9 8 7 6 5 4 3 2 1

Mrs Esther Nurse's pattern, 1950.

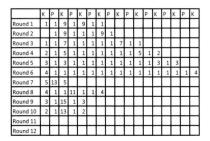

	K	P	K	P	K	P	K	P	K	P	K	P	K	P	K
Round 1	1	1	9	1	9	1	1								
Round 2		1	9	1	1	1	9	1							
Round 3	1	1	7	1	1	1	1	7	1	1					
Round 4	2	1	5	1	1	1	1	1	1	5	1	2			
Round 5	3	1	3	1	1	1	1	1	1	1	3	1	3		
Round 6	4	1	1	1	1	1	1	1	1	1	1	1	1	1	4
Round 7	5	13	5												
Round 8	4	1	1	11	1	1	4								
Round 9	3	1	15	1	3										
Round 10	2	1	13	1	2										
Round 11															
Round 12															

Scottish 'fisher lassies', walk arm in arm, along the wharf at Yarmouth, happy to have their photograph taken during a break in the activity of 'Skaning" (gutting) Herring.

The yearly migration of this fish from the Shetland Isles down the east coast of England would have many girls such as these follow the fish from port to port working in gutting crews usually 28th May to the 5th July as far as Yarmouth, and then on to Lowestoft till Armistice Day 28th November.

A gutting crew would exclusively consist of 3 women (their menfolk would be fishing, bringing their catches port to port as they moved down the coast). Two of the crew gutted, and the third would pack the fish into barrels. They would be paid, at the time of this photograph (1950), 1 shilling per barrel plus 15 shillings per week. It was not unusual, at the height of the season, to find the gutting crews working from 6am till 2am the following morning!

The Knit-Frocks of Cornwall

It was my intention, when visiting Cornwall, to approach it as I had the other areas of knitting, village by village, so that I could reveal a living tradition rather than resort to the archive departments for information. A glance at the map of Cornwall reveals a myriad of ports and havens; I assumed that my search for patterns would take a long time and that in those tiny villages would be a goldmine of information. I quite quickly realised that this was not to be. Many of the communities have little relationship with fishing, being historically trading ports for the industrial hinterland. Those places which had a fishing heritage now continue it in name only.

Cornwall has become the ultimate in tourism, an expression of the desire of the greater communities of our island to get away from their industrial atmospheres and seek somewhere completely different to spend their holidays. Thirty years ago everyone was content to go to their local seaside resort where the atmosphere was sufficiently different and the distance as far as they could imagine

themselves going. With the advent of foreign holidays due to the ease and excitement of air travel, these places have been relegated to day resorts. The exception is Cornwall. The beauty of its coastline, the picturesque character of its villages and its pleasant climate have been Cornwall's saviour. I write now as a northerner and my attitude is typical. For many in the north and in industrial Scotland, Cornwall seems the perfect holiday playground; in atmosphere it might as well be another planet—an ideal place to take 'two weeks off a year'.

At the turn of the century there were no major road or rail communications to Cornwall. The nature of the land lent itself to shipping; most of the major ports owe their existence to the movement of Cornish tin, china clay, stones, bricks and copper to the rest of Britain and to their usefulness as packet stations for the rest of the world. Today, most of the fishing has declined, yet at one time literally millions of tons of pilchards were caught and packaged for world markets. With the decline,

The St Ives fishing fleet, 1910.

Polperro, 1890s. Photo by Valentine.

the fishermen had to seek a new source of income. They achieved this by hiring out their boats for 'pleasuring' to the increasing numbers of city and industrial people who travel to Cornwall for their holidays. The income derived from this activity still plays a significant part in their economy today.

It was these major ports that I visited in my research. At first I was greatly encouraged: I found many knitters, although most of them made up plain Guernseys from the patterns of the nearby Channel Islands. I was spurred on by the knowledge that there were so many places to visit that in the end I would surely find some interesting patterns. But the result was negative.

The meeting I had with Mrs Jennie Thomas of Mevagissey was typical of many. When I asked her what patterns she did, she replied that they were always copies of the Guernsey, knit with a 'trail' (flap) instead of a welt in plain stitch and sometimes with a garter panel at the shoulder edge. I asked, 'Did you knit up any patterns at all?' and her reply was one I was to hear many times: 'All plain mostly. I have done cable or fisherman's rib as a pattern. Fisherman's rib was the only real one—if you could be bothered, as it took so long to knit. I knit mine with nine

needles—eight on the body and one to work with, forty-four stitches to the needle'.

Everyone I met I pressed for any memory they may have had of patterns, only to have confirmed again and again the fisherman's rib or the cable. I came to the conclusion that the knitters still practising in the old way no longer made up patterns.

This was a strange discovery because I was already aware that contract knitting had been a thriving industry which had been documented from the late 1700s to the 1930s. In other areas of research, a history of knitting usually meant that many patterns survived in practice. If one was to travel back in time to the villages one would be sure to find a group of knitters working away in the open air—up at the castle in St Ives, along the cliff path at the 'Peak' in Polperro, or around the wells in Newlyn. The knitters would group together and while away their precious spare moments gossiping and working. It was better to work out of doors since the dark navy yarn was difficult knitting at the best of times when working in pattern. Nowadays, the modern knitter tends to work at night indoors, with a powerful light over one shoulder to throw the pattern into relief.

Here in Cornwall contract knitting was concerned more with the production of ganseys than the

Fishermen from Flushing on the quayside, *c.*1900. They are wearing plain ganseys, one decorated with the name of the wearer's boat to attract custom from tourists.

knithose (socks and the like) we find in other areas of contract knitting. In Mary Wright's well-documented researches* she cites many examples of agents advertising for 100 to 500 knitters at a time. A Mr Broad of Liskeard and Messrs Tippet & Sons of Plymouth were typical of these agents working around 1830. This entrepreneurism was not only

---

* Mary Wright, *Cornish Guernseys and Knit-Frocks*, 1979.

Outside the Three Pilchards inn, Polperro 1856. Note the number of knitters taking advantage of the daylight while their menfolk ply their trade weighing the fish in preparation for market.

confined to the pursuit of profit; indeed, as early as 1790, the good works of the Fox and Tregilles families of Falmouth extended to the formation of a 'School of Industry' for the very poor. Maintained by public subscription, it accommodated up to sixty children, mostly girls, whose activities included 'to learn knitting'. In 1818 the Scilly Isles went the same way as Guernsey had two centuries earlier. Fishing declined and the economy had to be artificially stimulated by the formation of a School of Industry for the Scilly Isles. Local Cornish girls were sent over to teach the women and children how to knit and braid, and in August of that year the following advertisement appeared in the *West Briton*:

> 'The Committee of the society respectfully acquaint the public that they have constantly on sale, at their depot in Penzance, a variety of goods, manufactured by the poor of Scilly—*viz.*—
>
> Worsted and lambs wool stockings
> Men's Worsted and yarn FROCKS
> Cotton GLOVES, & men's BRACES
> Children's SOCKS, in wool & cotton
> Fine and coarse STRAW PLAIT
> Men's summer STRAW HATS
> Shoemakers THREAD
> Ladies small fancy articles in
> work-BAGS, NOTE-CASES, PINCUSHIONS etc.

Cornish girl knitting, 1850s.

Social responsibility apart, one can be sure that the good works of the merchant families did not impinge too greatly on their profits, since the fishing communities still experienced a poverty that in our times is hard to imagine.

The Bark House, St Ives, 1880. Photo by Edward Ashton. A group of children pose with the fishermen outside the Bark House where the fish were smoked. All the children are wearing their ganseys—the majority plain.

Old lady carding wool on the Isles of Scilly, *c.* 1890s. She will then spin it on the great wheel, sometimes called the 'muckle' or 'spindle' wheel.

Young 'Fish Jowsters' pose for the camera, St Ives, 1893. This photograph was part of the 'fisheries exhibition' in Truro. The young boy on the right is the only person wearing a gansey and this is a simple fisherman's rib.

A topsail Schooner in calm waters, St Ives.

Fisherwife working on a knit-frock on the headland at Polperro, 1904.

W. Nicholls, Captain Martin and J. Bath in Bude, 1906. The photograph
records the award for bravery given to Captain Martin for rescuing
two fishermen off Boscastle in 1906. Mr Nicholls's knit-frock is made of
horizontal bands of moss and garter. This was one of the archival photos of
fishermen that contributed to the conclusion that Cornish knitting had, by
the turn of the century, little to add to the tradition.

It was not until the appearance of trawlers and, more recently,
seine netters capable of catching whole shoals of fish in one
sweep, that the fishermen could command a decent standard of
living. Unfortunately, the very fact of fishing on such a large scale
contributed greatly to the eventual demise of the industry, by
fishing the seas dry. Conservation of fish stocks in the long term
was either not understood or went unheeded. It is easy to see why.
One has to have experienced regular nourishment and comfort
before one can turn one's attention to the plight of other species.

It seemed, therefore, that as far as present-day Cornwall was
concerned, gansey patterns were very thin on the ground. But
this was not the impression I had gained when I read previous
publications. One of these books was Mary Wright's. I went to see her
to discuss this problem and to get permission to draw upon her work.
She confirmed my assessment and concluded that in the past twenty
years the tradition had almost died out and her efforts had been to
catch what she could. Her research had therefore been very timely,
and I have included one or two patterns that derive from it.

So, yet again, I had to go back to the archives to discover what
the tradition was like at the height of the Cornish fishing industry.
I was fortunate enough to find many photographs of fishermen
wearing their ganseys, and my conclusion was that, with one or
two exceptions, the majority of patterns were fisherman's rib or a
horizontal seeded panel made up of various combinations of moss
stitch, separated by a row or two of garter stitch. It confirmed the
modern tendency to knit plain ganseys.

The most interesting patterns I have been able to find come from the work of Jonathan Quiller-Couch, who wrote about the life around his home of Polperro in the 1850s.* To illustrate his minute and studied descriptions of the lifestyle and atmosphere of his village, he worked in collaboration with his friend the photographer Lewis Harding. His portraits and studies of local life give us an opportunity to see the type of patterns the fisherwives knitted at that time.

It must be stressed, however, that the more illustrious patterns were the exception rather than the rule. In the group of three fishermen below, the most interesting pattern is that worn by J. Curtis, the man on the right with the little girl on his lap. It is made up of a horizontal double moss base band followed by vertical columns of open and closed diamonds, flanking a central column of closely worked chevrons. The attractive sleeve patterns of the central figure, Charles Jolliffe junior, have also been worked out *(see next page)*.

---

* Jonathan Quiller-Couch, *The History of Polperro*, 1856.

Fishermen, Polperro, 1850s.
Charles Joliffe snr *(seated left foreground),* Charles Joliffe *(centre),* John Curtis *(seated right with little girl on lap).*

POLPERRO PATTERNS

John Curtis: Chevron, closed moss diamond and split diamond, each element 19 sts and 17 rds separated by a 4-st moss seeding variation, sitting on 2 garter bands edging an 8 rd double moss horizontal panel.

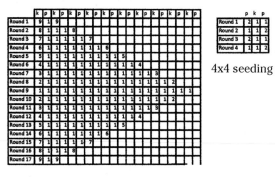

Chevron, 19 sts & 18 rds.

Closed moss diamond, 19 sts & 17 rds.

4x4 seeding

Open split diamond, 19 sts & 17 rds.

Charles Jolliffe Jnr
Single purl open diamond, 13 sts set in panel of 21 rds ending 2 rds of garter.

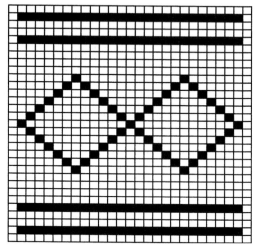

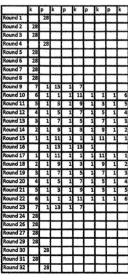

Most of the patterns worn by the boys in Lewis Harding's evocative photographs are typical fisherman's rib, with every other stitch knit into the row below for extra warmth. Fisherman's rib is ideal for children's ganseys as it is hardly worth spending all that effort on decorative patterns when they grow out of them so quickly. There is, however, one real advantage in knitting a gansey for a child: it will last much longer than a normal pullover because you can replace the arms when they are worn, by knitting down again from the shoulder to the cuff.

If you prefer making up a more adventurous pattern it is worth having a try at the pattern I have noted here, taken from this group of boys playing musical instruments *(below)*. The boy playing the triangle has a pattern very like that of J. Curtis of Polperro, except that the diamond is smaller and the closed diamond has been replaced with a 'heapy'.

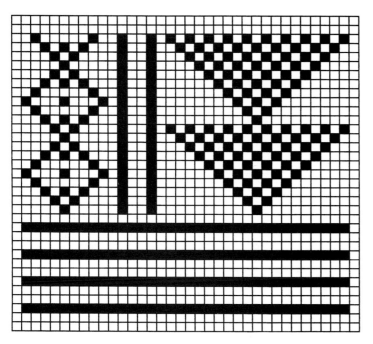

Triangle player: reverse heapy, 21 sts & 10 rds and split diamond, 11 sts & 10 rds with 3 sts seeding set in a band of 4 garter stitches

Boy musicians, Polperro, 1850s.

	K	P	K	P	K	P	K	P	K	P	K	P	K	P	K	P	K	P	K	P	K	P	K	P	K	P	K	P	K	P	K	P
Round 1	10	1	10	1	2	1	11																									
Round 2	9	1	1	1	9	1	2	1	5	1	5																					
Round 3	8	1	1	1	1	1	8	1	4	1	1	1	4																			
Round 4	7	1	1	1	1	1	1	1	7	1	2	1	3	1	1	1	1	1	3													
Round 5	6	1	1	1	1	1	1	1	1	1	6	1	2	1	5	1	2															
Round 6	5	1	1	1	1	1	1	1	1	1	1	1	5	2	1	2	1	3	1	3	1	1										
Round 7	4	1	1	1	1	1	1	1	1	1	1	1	1	1	4	1	2	1	2	1	5	1	2									
Round 8	3	1	1	1	1	1	1	1	1	1	1	1	1	1	1	1	3	1	2	1	3	1	1	1	1	1	3					
Round 9	2	1	1	1	1	1	1	1	1	1	1	1	1	1	1	1	1	1	2	1	2	1	4	1	1	1	4					
Round 10	1	1	1	1	1	1	1	1	1	1	1	1	1	1	1	1	1	1	1	1	1	1	1	2	1	5	1	5				

Fisher lads wearing typical Cornish plain ganseys, 1850s.

The Masters Holten and Curtis, Polperro. These ganseys are typical fisherman's rib, where the stitches are knit into the row below.

This photograph of Robert Stephen Hawker, vicar of Morwenstow, was commissioned by the reverend himself for sale within his parish, presumably to maximise on the novelty value of the relatively new technology of photography. According to his diary the sale was a success. He evidently always wore a gansey because he considered himself a 'fisher of men'.

The Revd Robert Stephen Hawker, Vicar of Morwenstow, 1858.

Revd Hawker: Solid basket combination set in single garter stitch band.

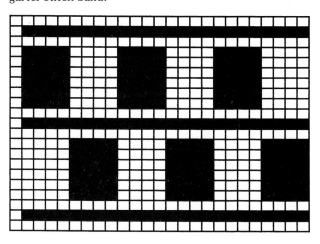

	K	P	K	P	K	P
Round 1	Knit continuous					
Round 2	Purl continuous					
Round 3	Knit continuous					
Round 4		4		4		4
Round 5		4		4		4
Round 6		4		4		4
Round 7		4		4		4
Round 8		4		4		4
Round 9		4		4		4
Round 10	Knit continuous					
Round 11	Purl continuous					
Round 12	Knit continuous					
Round 10	4		4		4	
	4		4		4	
	4		4		4	
	4		4		4	
	4		4		4	
	4		4		4	
	Knit continuous					
	Purl continuous					
	Knit continuous					

Porthgwarra fisherman mending
pots outside his home, 1903.

The Porthgwarra fisherman—seen mending his pots and drying
skate *(above)*—has bands of a simple pattern on his sleeves which fit
in well with the plain fisherman's rib that covers the yoke.

To finish my account of knitting in Cornwall, it only remains for
me to reflect on how much of a tragedy it is that the tradition should
be in such a poor state, especially considering the possibilities that
present themselves with the yearly pilgrimage from the industrial
Midlands and the art and craft atmosphere that pervades the area
today. With the early demise of the fishing industry many of the
indigenous population moved out—and the entrepreneurial activity
that revolved around the exploitation of tourism was practised by
many newcomers who had no previous connection with Cornwall's
heritage. The tourists' demand to identify with the history of fishing
was fulfilled by the import of machine-made knitwear from Guernsey
and all the other paraphernalia that goes with an 'alternative'
lifestyle. In Cornwall's case, commercial activity exploited the artists
and craftsmen who moved in when the fishermen moved out.

Porthgwarra fisherman hanging up skate to dry in a cliff cave, 1903.

The Keelmen of the Humber Estuary

While I was preparing to visit Norfolk and Cornwall I was invited to send some of my collection of ganseys to a knitting exhibition run by the Humber Keel and Sloop Preservation Society. Why, I thought, should people interested in boats which plied the inland waterways of England be interested in knitting? It turned out that various people in the society had noted the fishermen's patterns and wondered whether there was a similar tradition among the keelmen. There was, of course, and I rushed to catch what I could. I have included the patterns I found to illustrate that it was not just the fishermen who had a tradition of knitting.

Before notating these patterns, kindly given to me by the society, it would be appropriate to outline the history of the keel and sloop sailing men. The fact that there is a society to preserve their heritage is an indication that there are no longer any sloops or keels in active service carrying out the tasks for which they were originally designed.

The society has preserved two of these craft, the keel *Comrade* and the sloop *Amy Housan*; they sail out on special occasions and are chartered by enthusiasts. The last time they sailed was when they headed the flotilla of craft at the opening of the spectaculr Humber Bridge by Her Majesty

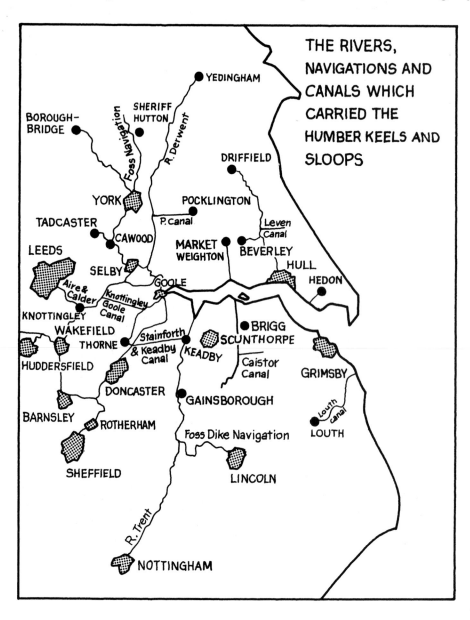

the Queen in 1982. It was an emotional sight; one could not fail to be moved by the juxtaposition of ages as these majestic boats—whose technology dates back to the Vikings—sailed in full rig under the vast bridge spanning the Humber estuary, the epitome of 20th-century structural engineering.

The keel and sloop are similar in design, the exception being in the rigging. They were built strong enough to withstand the cross-currents of the Humber estuary and the east coast where they plied their trade to Bridlington, Scarborough and Lowestoft, yet were shallow enough in draft to negotiate the waterways inland. They were the 'lorries' of their time—hauliers, rather than hunters. They carried enormous amounts up and down the canals and waterways opened in the 1790s, a vast and complex network of communication built to speed up the movement of materials from industrial West Yorkshire to the agricultural counties of Lincolnshire, Norfolk and Nottinghamshire. Their cargoes were grain, steel, coal, gravel, sand, bricks, flour, tiles, barley, maize, clay, phosphate—in fact anything and everything that required bulk carriage.

The tradition and the lifestyle of these keelmen have long since died away and, like their boats, their few remaining artifacts are preserved with dedication by the members of the society. Now that the boats have been overhauled and are in working order, the members of the society have turned to the other traditions of keelmen—one of which is the knitting.

Today, keelboat jersey knitting is a memory, yet in the past two years it has been stirring back to life with revived interest among enthusiasts. The distinctive feature of their patterns is the Central Star pattern, exclusive to this tradition. I have never seen it anywhere else in all my travels.

All the patterns are based on working extra wool into the yoke. The bottom half remains plain, with a little decoration over the welt. They have evolved beautiful horizontal bars at the crossover point between the plain knitting and the patterned yoke, much like the Hebridean ganseys. These horizontal patterns range from the simple garter stitch to sophisticated waves. The patterns I have documented come from ganseys knit in the 1930s and 1950s in 4-ply Guernsey wool. Such fine work tends to be too tedious for modern knitters, so the patterns have been translated for working in the thicker 5-ply worsted yarn, using size 12 and size 13 needles.

Mr and Mrs George Humphries on board their keel on the Calder at Heath, near Wakefield.

The market sloop *Bee (left)* and a keel boat on the Trent.

Mr and Mrs Alf Mullett on board their keel, *Gertrude*. A 'West Country' keel small
enough to go through the locks on the Calder and Hebble Navigation in the West
Riding of Yorkshire, she has been towed up to York and is waiting to discharge
her cargo at Leatham's Flour Mill.

The Committee of the Stainforth Aquatic Sports, *c.* 1914. All the members were keelmen, many of whom lived in Stainforth, a village between Thorne and Doncaster on the Sheffield and South Yorkshire Navigation. They and their families participated in traditional events such as sailing races, tug-of-war, greasy pole and seahorse race.

The market sloop, *Three Sisters*, in Barrow Haven, a creek on the south bank of the Humber, 1890. A regular service operated across the river between Barrow and Hull.

Mrs Jackson

The moss stitch and chevron patterns are worked above the welt at each side of the seam stitches. The body is knit plain for 10 ins and then the triangular patterns are worked, followed by the horizontal garter stitch ridges. The yoke follows with the star placed in the centre, flanked by two 6 st cables on every 5th round at the arrows.

Centre Star   ↓   ↓   Centre diamond   ↓   ↓   Chevron

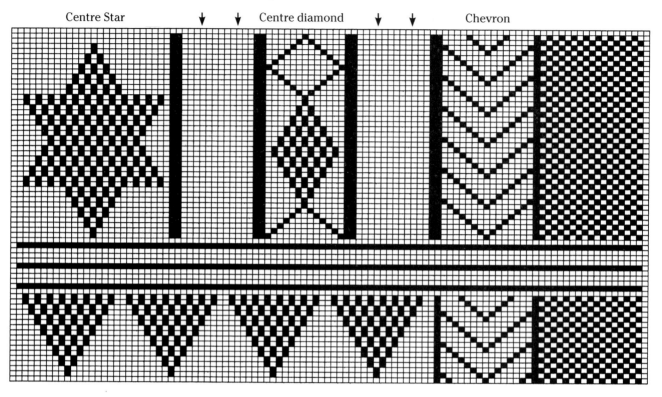

Reverse double moss triangle

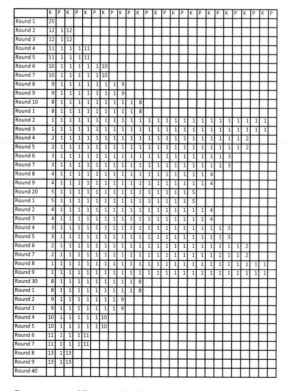

	K	P	K	P	K	P	K	P	K	P	K	P	K	P	K	P	K	P	K	P	K	P	K	P	K	P	K	P
Round 1	25																											
Round 2	12	1	12																									
Round 3	12	1	12																									
Round 4	11	1	1	1	11																							
Round 5	11	1	1	1	11																							
Round 6	10	1	1	1	1	1	10																					
Round 7	10	1	1	1	1	1	10																					
Round 8	9	1	1	1	1	1	1	1	9																			
Round 9	9	1	1	1	1	1	1	1	9																			
Round 10	8	1	1	1	1	1	1	1	1	1	8																	
Round 1	8	1	1	1	1	1	1	1	1	1	8																	
Round 2	1	1	1	1	1	1	1	1	1	1	1	1	1	1	1	1	1	1	1	1	1	1	1	1	1	1	1	
Round 3	1	1	1	1	1	1	1	1	1	1	1	1	1	1	1	1	1	1	1	1	1	1	1	1	1	1	1	
Round 4	2	1	1	1	1	1	1	1	1	1	1	1	1	1	1	1	1	1	1	1	1	1	1	1	2			
Round 5	2	1	1	1	1	1	1	1	1	1	1	1	1	1	1	1	1	1	1	1	1	1	1	1	2			
Round 6	3	1	1	1	1	1	1	1	1	1	1	1	1	1	1	1	1	1	1	1	1	1	1	3				
Round 7	3	1	1	1	1	1	1	1	1	1	1	1	1	1	1	1	1	1	1	1	1	1	1	3				
Round 8	4	1	1	1	1	1	1	1	1	1	1	1	1	1	1	1	1	1	1	1	1	4						
Round 9	4	1	1	1	1	1	1	1	1	1	1	1	1	1	1	1	1	1	1	1	1	4						
Round 20	5	1	1	1	1	1	1	1	1	1	1	1	1	1	1	1	1	1	1	5								
Round 1	5	1	1	1	1	1	1	1	1	1	1	1	1	1	1	1	1	1	1	5								
Round 2	4	1	1	1	1	1	1	1	1	1	1	1	1	1	1	1	1	1	1	1	1	4						
Round 3	4	1	1	1	1	1	1	1	1	1	1	1	1	1	1	1	1	1	1	1	1	4						
Round 4	3	1	1	1	1	1	1	1	1	1	1	1	1	1	1	1	1	1	1	1	1	1	1	3				
Round 5	3	1	1	1	1	1	1	1	1	1	1	1	1	1	1	1	1	1	1	1	1	1	1	3				
Round 6	2	1	1	1	1	1	1	1	1	1	1	1	1	1	1	1	1	1	1	1	1	1	1	1	2			
Round 7	2	1	1	1	1	1	1	1	1	1	1	1	1	1	1	1	1	1	1	1	1	1	1	1	2			
Round 8	1	1	1	1	1	1	1	1	1	1	1	1	1	1	1	1	1	1	1	1	1	1	1	1	1	1	1	
Round 9	1	1	1	1	1	1	1	1	1	1	1	1	1	1	1	1	1	1	1	1	1	1	1	1	1	1	1	
Round 30	8	1	1	1	1	1	1	1	1	8																		
Round 1	8	1	1	1	1	1	1	1	1	8																		
Round 2	9	1	1	1	1	1	1	9																				
Round 3	9	1	1	1	1	1	1	9																				
Round 4	10	1	1	1	1	1	10																					
Round 5	10	1	1	1	1	1	10																					
Round 6	11	1	1	1	11																							
Round 7	11	1	1	1	11																							
Round 8	13	1	13																									
Round 9	13	1	13																									
Round 40																												

Centre star, 27 sts and 40 rds.

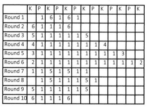

	K	P	K	P	K	P	K	P	K	P	K	P	K
Round 1	1	6	1	6	1								
Round 2	6	1	1	6									
Round 3	5	1	1	1	1	5							
Round 4	4	1	1	1	1	1	1	4					
Round 5	3	1	1	1	1	1	1	1	1	3			
Round 6	2	1	1	1	1	1	1	1	1	1	1	2	
Round 7	1	1	5	1	5	1	1						
Round 8	1	5	1	1	5	1							
Round 9	5	1	1	1	1	1	5						
Round 10	6	1	1	1	6								

Chevron, 15 sts and 10 rds.

Left chart table:

	K	P	K	P	K	P	K	P	K	P	K	P	K	P	K	P	K	P	K	P	K	P	K	P
Round 1	3	11	3																					
Round 2	3	1	1	9	1	1	3																	
Round 3	3	2	1	7	1	1	2																	
Round 4	2	3	1	5	1	3	2																	
Round 5	2	4	1	3	1	4	2																	
Round 6	2	5	1	1	1	5	2																	
Round 7	2	6	1	6	2																			
Round 8	2	6	1	6	2																			
Round 9	2	5	1	1	1	5	2																	
Round 10	2	5	1	1	1	5	2																	
Round 1	2	4	1	1	1	1	1	1	4	2														
Round 2	2	4	1	1	1	1	1	1	4	2														
Round 3	2	3	1	1	1	1	1	1	1	3	2													
Round 4	2	3	1	1	1	1	1	1	1	3	2													
Round 5	2	2	1	1	1	1	1	1	1	1	2	2												
Round 6	2	2	1	1	1	1	1	1	1	1	1	2												
Round 7	2	1	1	1	1	1	1	1	1	1	1	1	2											
Round 8	2	1	1	1	1	1	1	1	1	1	1	1	1	2										
Round 9	2	1	1	1	1	1	1	1	1	1	1	1	2											
Round 20	2	2	1	1	1	1	1	1	1	3	2													
Round 1	2	3	1	1	1	1	1	1	3	2														
Round 2	2	3	1	1	1	1	4	2																
Round 3	2	4	1	1	1	1	4	2																
Round 4	2	5	1	1	1	5	2																	
Round 5	2	5	1	1	1	5	2																	
Round 6	2	6	1	6	2																			
Round 7	2	6	1	6	2																			
Round 8	2	5	1	1	1	5	2																	
Round 9	2	4	1	3	1	4	2																	
Round 30	2	1	5	1	3	2																		
Round 1	2	2	1	7	1	2	2																	
Round 2	2	1	1	9	1	1	2																	
Round 3																								
Round 4																								

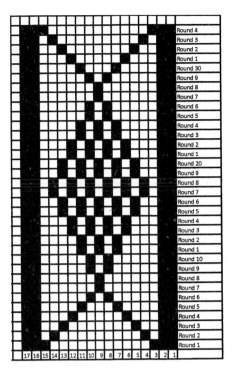

Column combination open single moss
diamond and closed double moss diamond,
17 sts and 33 rds.

Bottom chart table:

	K	P	K	P	K	P	K	P	K	P	K	P	K	P	K	P	K	P
Round 1	8	1	8															
Round 2	8	1	8															
Round 3	7	1	1	1	7													
Round 4	7	1	1	1	7													
Round 5	6	1	1	1	1	1	6											
Round 6	6	1	1	1	1	1	6											
Round 7	5	1	1	1	1	1	1	1	5									
Round 8	5	1	1	1	1	1	1	1	5									
Round 9	4	1	1	1	1	1	1	1	1	1	4							
Round 10	4	1	1	1	1	1	1	1	1	1	4							
Round 11	3	1	1	1	1	1	1	1	1	1	1	1	3					
Round 12	3	1	1	1	1	1	1	1	1	1	1	1	3					
Round 13	2	1	1	1	1	1	1	1	1	1	1	1	1	1	2			
Round 14	2	1	1	1	1	1	1	1	1	1	1	1	1	1	2			
Round 15	1	1	1	1	1	1	1	1	1	1	1	1	1	1	1	1	1	
Round 16	1	1	1	1	1	1	1	1	1	1	1	1	1	1	1	1	1	
Round 17		1	1	1	1	1	1	1	1	1	1	1	1	1	1	1	1	1

Reverse double moss triangle,
17 sts and 18 rds.

Star, 23 sts and 38 rds; chevron, 19 sts and 9 rds; half-flag, 9 sts and 10 rds. *Below:* the pattern above the welt.

Mrs Hutton's pattern begins with the half flag immediately after the welt. Six inches are worked plain and then the wave pattern is formed, after which the major pattern is worked.

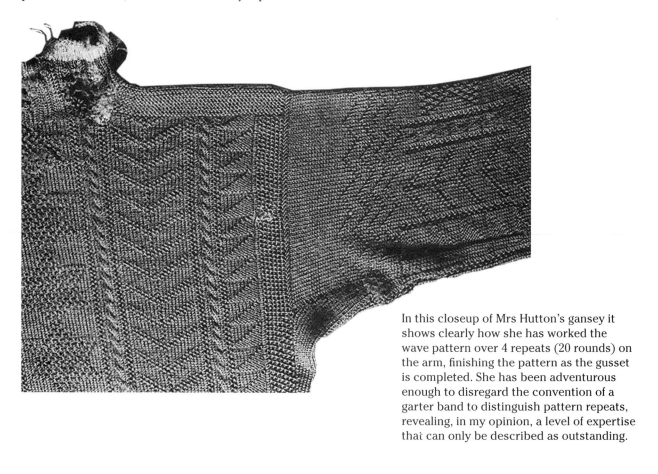

In this closeup of Mrs Hutton's gansey it shows clearly how she has worked the wave pattern over 4 repeats (20 rounds) on the arm, finishing the pattern as the gusset is completed. She has been adventurous enough to disregard the convention of a garter band to distinguish pattern repeats, revealing, in my opinion, a level of expertise that can only be described as outstanding.

Mrs Hutton of Goole

Heapy, 13 sts and 12 rds

	K	P	K
Round 1	12	1	
Round 2	11	2	
Round 3	10	3	
Round 4	9	4	
Round 5	8	5	
Round 6	7	6	
Round 7	6	7	
Round 8	5	8	
Round 9	4	9	
Round 10	3	10	
Round 11	2	11	
Round 12	1	12	

Vertical half flag, 9 sts & 9 rds.

	K	P	K	P	K	P	K
Knit round							
		Purl round					
Knit round							
Round 1	1	1	9	1			
Round 2	1	1	8	2			
Round 3	1	1	7	3			
Round 4	1	1	6	4			
Round 5	1	1	5	5			
Round 6	1	1	4	6			
Round 7	1	1	3	7			
Round 8	1	1	2	8			
Round 9	1	1	1	9			
Round 10	1	11					
Round 1	1	1	9	1			
Round 2	1	1	8	2			
Round 3	1	1	7	3			
Round 4	1	1	6	4			
Round 5	1	1	5	5			
Round 6	1	1	4	6			
Round 7	1	1	3	7			
Round 8	1	1	2	8			
Round 9	1	1	1	9			
Round 20	1	11					

Horizontal half flag, 9 sts & 9 rds.

	K	P	K	P	K	P
purl round						
knit 2rds.						
Round 1	1	10	1	10	1	10
Round 2	2	9	2	9	2	9
Round 3	3	8	3	8	3	8
Round 4	4	7	4	7	4	7
Round 5	5	6	5	6	5	6
Round 6	6	5	6	5	6	5
Round 7	7	4	7	4	7	4
Round 8	8	3	8	3	8	3
Round 9	9	2	9	2	9	2
Round 10	10	1	10	1	10	1

Wave pattern, 12 sts & 32 rds.

	K	P	K	P	K	P	K
Round 1	knit one round						
Round 2	4	1	7				
Round 3	3	1	1	5	1	1	
Round 4	2	1	5	1	1	1	
Round 5	2	1	3	1	3	1	2
Round 6	1	1	5	1	1	1	3
Round 7	1	7	1	4			
Round 8	4	1	7				
Round 9	3	1	1	5	1	1	
Round 10	2	1	5	1	1	1	
Round 1	2	1	3	1	3	1	2
Round 2	1	1	5	1	1	1	3
Round 3	1	7	1	4			
Round 4	4	1	7				
Round 5	3	1	1	5	1	1	
Round 6	2	1	5	1	1	1	
Round 7	2	1	3	1	3	1	2
Round 8	1	1	5	1	1	1	3
Round 9	1	7	1	4			
Round 20	4	1	7				
Round 1	3	1	1	5	1	1	
Round 2	2	1	5	1	1	1	
Round 3	2	1	3	1	3	1	2
Round 4	1	1	5	1	1	1	3
Round 5	1	7	1	4			
Round 6	4	1	7				
Round 7	3	1	1	5	1	1	
Round 8	2	1	5	1	1	1	
Round 9	2	1	3	1	3	1	2
Round 30	1	1	5	1	1	1	3
Round 1	1	7	1	4			
Round 2	knit one round						
Round 3	purl one round						

Heavy chevron, 19 sts & 10 rds.

	K	P	K	P	K	P	K
Round 1	9	1	9				
Round 2	8	3	8				
Round 3	7	5	7				
Round 4	6	2	1	1	2	6	
Round 5	5	2	2	1	2	2	5
Round 6	4	2	3	1	3	2	4
Round 7	3	2	4	1	4	2	3
Round 8	2	2	5	1	5	2	2
Round 9	1	2	6	1	6	2	1
Round 10	1	1	7	1	7	1	1

Phoebe Carr of Thorne

The traditional star, diamond and cable pattern is taken from a gansey knitted by Mrs Phoebe Carr of Thorne. Mrs Carr was one of the last knitters of keelmen's ganseys, and was well known for the quality of her work.

	K	P	K	P	K	P	K	P	K	P	K	P	K	P	K	P	K	P	K	P	K	P	K	P	K
Round 1	12	1	12																						
Round 2	12	1	12																						
Round 3	11	1	1	1	11																				
Round 4	11	1	1	1	11																				
Round 5	10	1	1	1	1	1	10																		
Round 6	10	1	1	1	1	1	10																		
Round 7	9	1	1	1	1	1	1	1	9																
Round 8	9	1	1	1	1	1	1	1	9																
Round 9	8	1	1	1	1	1	1	1	1	1	8														
Round 10	8	1	1	1	1	1	1	1	1	1	8														
Round 11	7	1	1	1	1	1	1	1	1	1	1	1	7												
Round 12	7	1	1	1	1	1	1	1	1	1	1	1	7												
Round 13	6	1	1	1	1	1	1	1	1	1	1	1	1	1	6										
Round 14	6	1	1	1	1	1	1	1	1	1	1	1	1	1	6										
Round 15	5	1	1	1	1	1	1	1	1	1	1	1	1	1	1	1	5								
Round 16	5	1	1	1	1	1	1	1	1	1	1	1	1	1	1	1	5								
Round 17	4	1	1	1	1	1	1	1	1	1	1	1	1	1	1	1	1	1	4						
Round 18	4	1	1	1	1	1	1	1	1	1	1	1	1	1	1	1	1	1	4						
Round 19	3	1	1	1	1	1	1	1	1	1	1	1	1	1	1	1	1	1	1	1	3				
Round 20	3	1	1	1	1	1	1	1	1	1	1	1	1	1	1	1	1	1	1	1	3				
Round 21	2	1	1	1	1	1	1	1	1	1	1	1	1	1	1	1	1	1	1	1	1	1	2		
Round 22	2	1	1	1	1	1	1	1	1	1	1	1	1	1	1	1	1	1	1	1	1	1	2		
Round 23	1	1	1	1	1	1	1	1	1	1	1	1	1	1	1	1	1	1	1	1	1	1	1	1	1
Round 24	1	1	1	1	1	1	1	1	1	1	1	1	1	1	1	1	1	1	1	1	1	1	1	1	1
					5					10					15					20					25

Large double moss diamond, 25 sts and 48 rds.
Continue in reverse rd 22 to rd 1.

	K	P	K	P	K	P	K	P	K	P	K	P	K	P	K	P	K	P	K	P	K	P	K
Round 1	11	1	11																				
Round 2	11	1	11																				
Round 3	10	1	1	1	10																		
Round 4	10	1	1	1	10																		
Round 5	9	1	1	1	1	1	9																
Round 6	9	1	1	1	1	1	9																
Round 7	8	1	1	1	1	1	1	1	8														
Round 8	8	1	1	1	1	1	1	1	8														
Round 9	7	1	1	1	1	1	1	1	1	1	7												
Round 10	7	1	1	1	1	1	1	1	1	1	7												
Round 11		1	1	1	1	1	1	1	1	1	1	1	1	1	1	1	1	1	1	1	1	1	1
Round 12		1	1	1	1	1	1	1	1	1	1	1	1	1	1	1	1	1	1	1	1	1	1
Round 13	1	1	1	1	1	1	1	1	1	1	1	1	1	1	1	1	1	1	1	1	1	1	1
Round 14	1	1	1	1	1	1	1	1	1	1	1	1	1	1	1	1	1	1	1	1	1	1	1
Round 15	2	1	1	1	1	1	1	1	1	1	1	1	1	1	1	1	1	1	1	1	2		
Round 16	3	1	1	1	1	1	1	1	1	1	1	1	1	1	1	1	1	1	3				
Round 17	3	1	1	1	1	1	1	1	1	1	1	1	1	1	1	1	1	1	3				
Round 18	4	1	1	1	1	1	1	1	1	1	1	1	1	1	1	1	1	4					

Star Pattern, 23 sts and 36 rds.
Continue in reverse order.

Mrs Phoebe Carr of Thorne: double moss, 8 sts and 4 rds; star, 23 sts and 38 rds; diamond, 23 sts and 46 rds; cable every 5th rd at arrows.

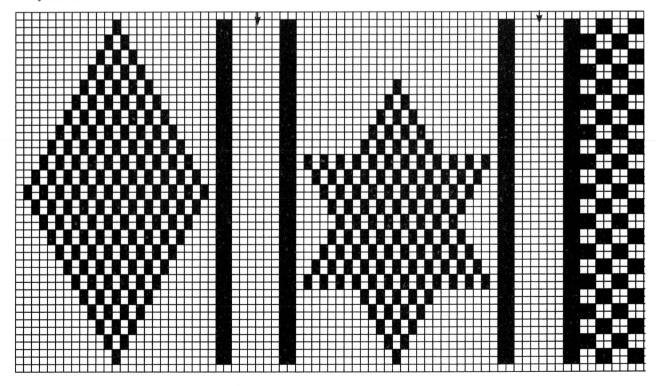

Phoebe Carr of Thorne

Three swatch samplers explore the use of a large central motif, cable, double cable and simple seeding columns.

Swatch 1 is a full half round with central diamond surrounded by star repeats edged with double moss.

Swatch 2 is a Central Star edged by open and closed diamond and chevrons with reverse 'heapies' knitted to the garter bands that would begin the yoke.

Swatch 3 is a full half round where reverse 'heapies' edge a horizontal Hen's Claw, and where the verticals display a large Central Star, chevron and closed diamonds separated by single and triple seeding columns.

The Fisher Gansey Patterns of North East England

Fishermen of North Shields Tyne and Wear. These ganseys display a minimum of pattern variation, most often double moss combinations over the yoke after knitting garter rows to separate the lower plain knitting. Note the 'twists' (cables at the shoulders to 'tighten the fit').

Introduction

The North East is unique in knitting terms, since this area more than most has a knitting heritage that is part of life for everybody. Through the legacy of the depression years, knitting has permeated the whole of society here in the north: it was one obvious solution to help ease the poverty of unemployment that struck this industrial and rural area. It is ironic that the current revival of interest should coincide with another acute depression. Today there are more efficient methods of keeping warm. The revival of interest is an effort to maintain the tradition and widen its appeal now that the fishing industry—which in the past has been responsible for the survival of local traditions—is in decline.

Among the general populace there is still the attitude that knitting is practised as a substitute for purchasing the 'real thing' in the shops and the present-day increase in prices is greeted with horror and incredulity. This factor is turned on its heel for many of us. The richer we are, the more likely are we to surround ourselves with truly handmade artifacts, perhaps as a means of possessing in some way the labour, the love and the beauty they radiate. A badge of success, as it were; a short cut to the quality of life and unfortunately a hollow one at that.

The major wool merchants and spinners all have their bases in Yorkshire and the North East. But although knitting is a way of life here, the knowledge of the craft's tradition has largely gone unnoticed, since it has always been assumed that the only supply of patterns has been through these wool merchants. The creation of personal patterns has been left, as is so often the case, to the fishing communities.

Before we look at the patterns of the fishing communities of the North East, it is worth noting that I have been unable to find any connection between them and contract knitting. As I have already said, it was usually through this commercial practice that knitting traditions were maintained. In all the other districts I have visited I have always been able to find a direct link between contract work and gansey knitting, either by personal memory of those I met, or through archival material in the form of sales documents, census forms and old photographs.

Contract Knitting

The most likely reason for such a lack of entrepreneurial activity along this stretch of the coast was that there was already established an extremely large rural population in the Dales of Cumbria and Yorkshire that had earned its living by knitting since the 1600s, continuing without a break until the 1850s. This contract knitting was on a vast scale. It was literally the only form of income for thousands of families: everyone was connected with it, man, woman and child. This is how Daniel Defoe saw it in 1724:

> Here you begin to find a manufacturer on foot:— the knitters work whilst they walk, tending the sheep, going to market etc., the wool and the knitting attached to their clothes and as before, all was clothing, and all the people 'claithing'; here you see all the people great and small, a knitting; and at Richmond you have a market for woollen and yarn stockings which they make coarse and ordinary . . .
>
> *(Tour through England and Wales)*

To give you further indication of this activity I refer to the documentary evidence collected by Marie Hartley and Joan Ingilby and published in 1951. *The Old Hand-Knitters of the Dales* is the definitive work on contract knitting and their research and interest was timely. They were able to speak to the last of these knitters, now long since passed on:

> Mrs Martin of Gayle and Mrs Martha Dinsdale were two of the last of the knitters. They remembered men and women sitting outside their front doors 'wapping away' [the local term for knitting]. 'We were fain to deu it', said Mrs Dinsdale, 'ther' wer' nowt else'. She knitted sailors' jerseys with long sleeves, some high necked and some open necked, for which she was paid 6 shillings for six.
>
> Mrs Crabtree recalled that her mother could knit a jersey or frock, as they were called, in a day, and was paid a shilling for it. Some of the jerseys had a diamond at either side of the front and back in 'hit and missiit' [one plain, one purl]; some were in cable stitch and others had a square of ribbed knitting from the neck downwards gradually decreasing in a V. They received better payment for the jersey in fancy stitches.

The knitting of these jerseys was a late development in contract work, the bulk of the work being socks. Over time, of course, there was bound to be a demand for other types of knitting and the knitters of the Dales are most remembered for their patterned gloves, introduced towards the end of their history. Knit up in two natural shades, they followed a basic design alternating dark and light colours with, in some cases, spots on the palms and fingers, an elaborate pattern on the back of the hand, a band of pattern round the base followed by a wristband with the name of the owner and, lastly, a fringe, later superseded by knitting a striped welt. During the last century jerseys, called speckled frocks, were also knitted. They were made up from natural and brown wool knitted alternately over the body.

Gloves knitted by Mary Allen in 1911 for the family of the Revd Curwen, Vicar of Dent (from the Marie Hartley and Joan Ingilby collection).

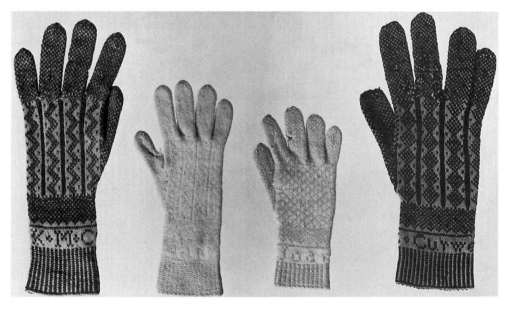

Gloves knitted by A. Pearson 1919 from Mark Hentley and Joan Ingelby collection.

The Journey

The villages of the North East lie between the rivers Humber and Tweed—the old boundaries of Northumberland. They vary tremendously, from the major ports of Hull, Grimsby, Whitby and North Shields, to the smaller towns of Scarborough and Seahouses, down to the self-sufficient communities of Filey, Redcar, Cullercoats and Newbiggin. As the photographs on these pages reveal, each community had a character all its own, and within the tradition of gansey making this difference continued.

But the stretch of coastline between Staithes in Yorkshire and Cullercoats in Northumberland has in the last century come heavily under the influence of industrialisation. The villages and towns that once owed their living to fishing now offer only token support to their original heritage. For many families, the industrial way of life has offered them easier and more lucrative incomes. This is particularly so in Saltburn, Marske, Redcar, Hartlepool and South Shields. It is difficult to imagine that these places were once fishing villages. Among the true fishermen the traditions are dying out; most of the men have their ganseys made up by the fisherwives of Staithes and Whitby and consequently their patterns reflect that area.

Many of the fishermen in these communities earn extra income by working in the steel plants and mines during the winter, and the reverse occurs with what the fulltime fishermen call 'weekenders'—men from the industrial areas who come down to the coast and hunt the inshore waters for cod and lobsters. The true fishermen consider this activity a real threat to their livelihoods, especially recently with the introduction of conservation policies.

McGarry Kelly from Whitby repairing a lobster pot. His pattern comprises a moss stitch over the majority of the gansey with the exception of the arms which show evidence that they have both been renewed: an easy task when they are knit from the shouler to the wrist. Compare this pattern to the pattern on the gansey he is wearing in the photograph on page 21

66

PATRINGTON AND WITHERNSEA

My journey northwards began at the major ports of Hull and Grimsby and, as I suspected, the search for patterns was particularly hard here since the old communities have been broken up through modern development. I had to travel further north to the villages of Patrington and Withernsea, where the fishermen are mainly inshore men, catching cod, salmon, crabs and lobsters in season, whose lifestyle is related to that of the fishermen at the turn of the century. In these two villages many of the fisherwives still retain the memory of knitting ganseys for their menfolk, though it was extremely difficult to find examples.

The pattern illustrated is in the possession of the Women's Institute at York. It was knitted by Mrs Forster many years ago and is considered by everyone to be the pattern exclusive to these two villages. It reflects influence from Scotland through the visiting herring fleet, and from Norfolk through the movement of many families from Sheringham at a time when the whole population of this coast was under expansion, some migrating as far as Whitby and Scarborough. Their influence is still felt in Withernsea by their introduction of new fishing techniques and in particular by the kind of boats they used. This area of the coast was normally fished in the Whitby 'coble', until the Sheringham men brought their 'hobblers'. Both were inshore fishing boats and capable of beach landing, but the hobbler had the advantage of being wider and lighter, with the added ability to beach broadside, which meant that the boat simply drifted up with the tide while the men sorted and gutted their fish.

There are no knitters now. Most families moved away years ago or gained other employment when it was possible. The youngsters are not so lucky today; in desperation many of them are turning back to the hard life of inshore fishing.

When I visited in 1982 they had just brought in the biggest catch ever landed—3,000 cod. Charlie Burns with whom I talked said it reminded him of the old days when they fished for mackerel: 'We could catch 200 or 300 mackerel before we came ashore in less than an hour, and now if you catch two or three you've done well'. It is to be hoped that their renewed interest in fishing will extend to the knitting of ganseys again.

Cleaning fish on the North East coast *c.* 1900.

Mrs Forster's pattern.

MRS FORSTER'S PATTERN
Knitted by Mrs Lester in 56 hrs.

Size: The size of the gansey if worked as indicated measures
for a 44-inch (112 cm) chest.
Wool: 5-ply worsted wool, 20 x 50 gm.
Needles: One set of five 35 cm, No. 12 (2¾ mm) double-pointed pins.
Tension: 7 stitches and 10 rows to 1 inch (2.5 cm).

Cast on evenly over four needles in thumb method for 280 sts using wool double. K2, P2 for 4 inches (10 cm), keeping the wool double for the first five rounds. After working the welt, continue in plain knitting for 12 inches (30 cm) increasing evenly to 320 sts. The pattern now begins. Work three rounds of purl stitch to divide the plain knitting from the pattern.

ROUND 1: P1, K18, P2, K6, (P2, K2) 4 times, P2, K6, P2, K18, P2, K6, P2, K6, P2, K18, P2, K6, P2, (K2, P2) 4 times, K6, P2, K18, P1.
This completes one half round. Repeat from beginning.
ROUND 2: As 1st.
ROUND 3: P1, K18, P2, K6, P4, (K2, P2) 3 times, P2, K6, P2, K18, P2, K6, P2, K6, P2, K18, P2, K6, P4, (K2, P2) 3 times, P2, K6, P2, K18, P1.
To complete half round. Repeat from beginning.
ROUND 4: As 3rd.
ROUND 5: As 1st.
ROUND 6: P21, C6, (P2, K2) 4 times, P2, C6, P22, C6, P2, C6, P22, C6, P2, (K2, P2) 4 times, C6, P21.

The pattern continues with double moss as set out—the cable, and the purl line on the ladder pattern is worked every sixth round.

Work the pattern until you have cabled twice. The gusset now begins. You will notice that you have knit a purl stitch at the beginning and the end of each half round. Knit one plain stitch between these two stitches on the next round (322 sts). On the next and every 4th round make one plain stitch each side of the centre stitch you have just worked and continue until this plain section is 19 sts wide. This forms half the gusset under the arms. Slip these gusset stitches and the purl stitches and the stitches for the back onto a holder and work up the front in pattern on *two* needles to your required height. Put these

Cable every 5th rd at arrows.

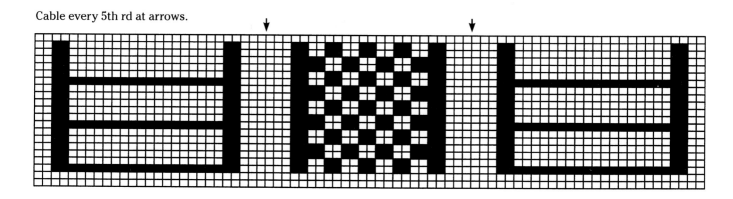

stitches onto a holder. Leave the gusset stitches and the purl stitches on a holder and continue as for the front up the back.

Place shoulder seams together and knit through the front and back loops together for 50 sts on each shoulder. Knit along loops and cast off.

The neck

Pick up the centre stitches and K2, P2 for 3 inches (7.5 cm) or as required, casting off ribwise using the wool double.

The sleeves

141 sts are picked up and patterned as the yoke with the cables centred on the shoulder ridge. Work the ladder pattern each side of centre cables and knit the remaining stitches, including the gusset in plain knitting.

Decrease 1 st either side of the seam stitches on the next and following 4th rounds until the gusset is worked out. Decrease every 6th round until 96 sts—then back to every 4th until 68 sts (adjust for width and length here).

The cuff

K2, P2 for 3 inches (7.5 cm) or as preferred. Cast off ribwise with wool doubled. The pattern on the arm should only be knit to just before the elbow. Knit the rest of the arm in plain knitting.

FLAMBOROUGH

The village of Flamborough sits on the cliff tops on the stretch of coastline known as Flamborough Head, set well back away from the two dramatic landing coves hundreds of feet below. My visit to this community was a refreshing experience because, after Patrington and Withernsea, I had begun to think that my quest for gansey patterns was going to be very difficult. But here was a true fishing community: as soon as I arrived I noticed fishermen wearing their ganseys.

I arrived at lunchtime and explained why I was visiting; by evening word must have got around, because at the local pub anyone *not* wearing a gansey was out of place! I fortunately was wearing mine—decorated with a pattern from my own village of Cullercoats in Northumberland—and it served as a good starting point in getting to know everyone. It would take me too long to tell you all I heard so, in deference to the wonderful knitters I met, I have chosen to concentrate on two families: Miss Ada and Miss Edie Major (the oldest ladies in the village) and Mrs Stephenson's family, who were kind enough to put me up.

When I visited the Misses Major they were on with their weekly baking—mountains of scones, cakes and pies literally filled the kitchen and the dining room. I asked, with my mouth full of delicious cake, whether it was possible that the two of them could eat all that cooking and if they were making it for some special occasion, such as a church fête. 'Oh no! We do this every week and give it to all our neighbours', they said, as they rushed around busily—and both of them now in their eighties! Their pattern is the only one they have knitted all their lives.

I stayed with Mrs Stephenson while in Flamborough, and one afternoon, 11th February 1982, she organised all her family and in-laws to come round for a gansey session; over sherry and cakes we discussed the patterns they had knitted all their lives. Their basic configuration was similar to the Misses Major's, though no matter what pattern they did, it always included a panel of hearts down the centre and back. This panel would be flanked with cables, ladder stitch, net mask (diamonds), basket stitch—whatever took their fancy. One of her daughters explained that her hearts were smaller than her mother's because that was the way she had been taught as a child.

Mrs Stephenson's other daughter Christine remarked, 'My husband liked Flamborough ganseys before I knew him and when I first saw him in one I thought, Oh no, will I ever learn!' Mrs Stephenson explained, 'Christine had never knitted at all but she took to it like a duck to water'. She continued that she was the same herself. She had come from a trawling family in Hull and she had learnt to knit to please her husband: 'It was the same for everybody. When the girls started courting fishermen they wanted to learn'. I asked how they felt about the work of knitting the

Lifeboat being launched off Flamborough Head.

70

ganseys and they said that they were as proud to knit them as the men were proud to wear them. I remarked on the fact that fishing was dying out and asked what would be the fate of the patterns. Mrs Stephenson was of the opinion that rather than let gansey knitting die, teaching someone else was preferable. It was a great shame, she said, that

there was this break up of the community; her own family could be traced back through the church marriage register to the 1500s. On the wall and in faded photographs in her albums were records of all her family wearing the same gansey pattern, going back for five generations.

Ms Edie Major knitting a miniature gansey with extra fine needles.

The Misses Major's pattern.

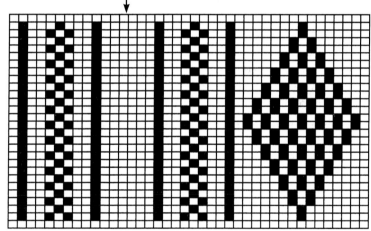

Misses Major: Centred double moss diamond, 15 sts & 27 rds is flanked by a 'fives' seeding column set in a plain knit background edged with single purl, and then flanked with a cable column turned every 5th rd at arrow. See matrix instructions on page 73.

Note in this gansey, knitted by Miss Ada Major, that she has left out cables on the arm so that the gansey can be worn under a jacket.

Ms Ada Major knitting in the round.

John and Master Peter Stephenson.

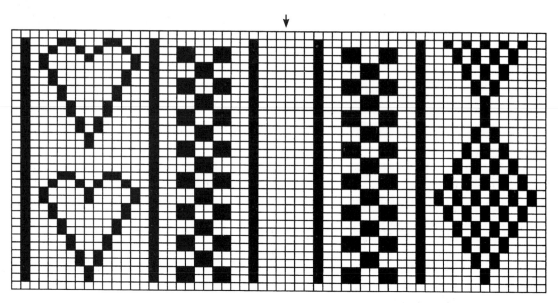

Peter's 18th birthday: heart, 13 sts & 17 rds, 2 vertical double
moss columns, 12 sts centred by cable column, 6 sts cabled every
5th rd and edged with diamond, 13 sts & 22 rds..

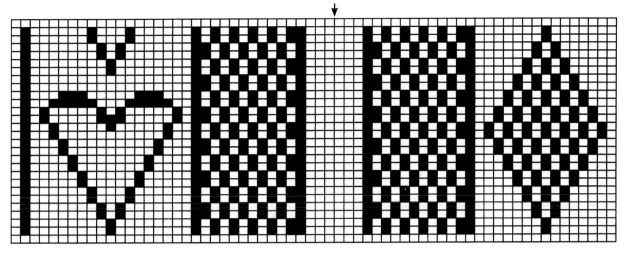

Mrs Stephenson: heart, 17 sts & 20 rds 2 vertical moss columns, 12 sts centred by cable column 6 sts cabled every 5th rd and edged with diamond, 15 sts and 27 rds.

Heart, 17 sts and 19 rds.

	P	K	P	K	P	K	P	K	P	K	P
Round 1	8	1	8								
Round 2	8	1	8								
Round 3	7	1	1	1	7						
Round 4	7	1	1	1	7						
Round 5	6	1	1	1	6						
Round 6	6	1	1	1	6						
Round 7	5	1	1	1	1	5					
Round 8	5	1	1	1	1	5					
Round 9	4	1	1	1	1	4					
Round 10	4	1	1	1	4						
Round 1	3	1	1	1	3						
Round 2	3	1	1	1	3						
Round 3	2	1	11	1	2						
Round 4	2	1	5	1	5	1	2				
Round 5	1	1	5	3	5	1	1				
Round 6	1	1	5	1	1	1	5	1	1		
Round 7	2	5	3	5	2						
Round 8	3	3	5	3	3						
Round 9	17										
Round 20											

Centre moss column, 12 sts & 4 rds.

	K	P	K	P	K	P	K	P	K	P	K	P
Round 1	2	1	1	1	1	1	1	1	1	1		
Round 2	2	1	1	1	1	1	1	1	1	1		
Round 3	1	1	1	1	1	1	1	1	1	1	2	
Round 4	1	1	1	1	1	1	1	1	1	1	2	

Diamond, 15 sts and 27 rds.

	P	K	P	K	P	K	P	K	P	K	P	K
Round 1	6	1	6									
Round 2	6	1	6									
Round 3	5	1	1	1	5							
Round 4	5	1	1	1	5							
Round 5	4	1	1	1	1	1	4					
Round 6	4	1	1	1	1	1	4					
Round 7	3	1	1	1	1	1	1	1	3			
Round 8	3	1	1	1	1	1	1	1	3			
Round 9	2	1	1	1	1	1	1	1	1	1	2	
Round 10	2	1	1	1	1	1	1	1	1	1	2	
Round 1	1	1	1	1	1	1	1	1	1	1	1	1
Round 2	1	1	1	1	1	1	1	1	1	1	1	1
Round 3	2	1	1	1	1	1	1	1	1	1	2	
Round 4	2	1	1	1	1	1	1	1	1	1	2	
Round 5	3	1	1	1	1	1	1	1	2			
Round 6	3	1	1	1	1	1	1	1	2			
Round 7	4	1	1	1	1	1	4					
Round 8	4	1	1	1	1	1	4					
Round 9	5	1	1	1	5							
Round 20	5	1	1	1	5							
Round 1	6	1	1	1	6							
Round 2	6	1	1	1	6							

Peter's heart, 13 sts and 14 rds, plus 3 knit rds before repeat

	K	P	K	P	K	P	K	P	K	P	K
Round 1	6	1	6								
Round 2	6	1	6								
Round 3	5	1	1	1	5						
Round 4	5	1	1	1	5						
Round 5	4	1	3	1	4						
Round 6	4	1	3	1	4						
Round 7	3	1	5	1	3						
Round 8	3	1	5	1	3						
Round 9	2	1	7	1	2						
Round 10	2	1	7	1	2						
Round 1	1	1	4	1	4	1	1				
Round 2	1	1	4	1	4	1	1				
Round 3	2	1	2	1	1	1	2	1	2		
Round 4	3	2	3	2	3						

Centre double moss columns, 12 sts and 4 rds and 6 st cable panel.

	K	P	K	P	K	P	K	P	K	P	K	P	K	P	K	P
Round 1	1	2	2	2	2	2	1	6	1	2	2	2	2	2	1	
Round 2	1	2	2	2	2	2	1	6	1	2	2	2	2	2	1	
Round 3	1	4	2	4	1	6	1	4	2	4	1					
Round 4	1	4	2	4	1	6	1	4	2	4	1					

Peter's diamond, 13 sts and 22 rds.

	K	P	K	P	K	P	K	P	K	P	K	P
Round 1	6	1	6									
Round 2	6	1	6									
Round 3	5	1	1	1	5							
Round 4	5	1	1	1	5							
Round 5	4	1	1	1	1	1	4					
Round 6	4	1	1	1	1	1	4					
Round 7	3	1	1	1	1	1	1	1	3			
Round 8	3	1	1	1	1	1	1	1	3			
Round 9	2	1	1	1	1	1	1	1	1	1	2	
Round 10	2	1	1	1	1	1	1	1	1	1	2	
Round 1	1	1	1	1	1	1	1	1	1	1	1	1
Round 2	1	1	1	1	1	1	1	1	1	1	1	1
Round 3	2	1	1	1	1	1	1	1	1	1	2	
Round 4	2	1	1	1	1	1	1	1	1	1	2	
Round 5	3	1	1	1	1	1	1	1	2			
Round 6	3	1	1	1	1	1	1	1	2			
Round 7	4	1	1	1	1	1	4					
Round 8	4	1	1	1	1	1	4					
Round 9	5	1	1	1	5							
Round 20	5	1	1	1	5							
Round 21	6	1	1	1	6							
Round 22	6	1	1	1	6							

Close up of Peter's 18th birthday gansey, a wonderful example of multiple vertical columns and 'rig and fur' shoulders (looks like ridges and furrows of a newly ploughed field).

Mrs Stephenson's pattern.

Mrs John Stephenson hard at work on her latest gansey.

FLAMBOROUGH PATTERN

Size: The size of the gansey if worked as indicated measures for a 42 inch (107 cm) chest.

Wool: 5-ply worsted wool.

Needles: One set of five No. 12 (2¾ mm) double-pointed pins.

Tension: 7 stitches and 10 rows to 1 inch (2.5 cm).

Cast on 282 sts evenly over four needles using wool double in the thumb method, K2, P2 for 4 inches (10 cm) keeping the wool double for the first five rounds. Knit eight rounds of plain knitting where you establish two purl sts on both sides of the gansey. This is a seam line and runs throughout the body and arms forming a basis for the gussets under the arm and the point of division for knitting the armholes. The pattern now begins.

ROUND 1: *P2, K1, (P1, K1) 4 times, P2, K13* repeat * to * four times, P2, K1, (P1, K1) 4 times. Repeat from beginning to end to complete one round.

ROUND 2: *P2, K2, (P1, K1) 3 times, K1, P2, K13* repeat from * to * 4 more times, P2, K2, (P1, K1) 3 times, K1. Repeat from beginning to end to complete one round.

ROUND 3: *P2, K1, (P1, K1) 4 times, P2, K6, P1, K6* repeat from * to * 4 more times, P2, K1, (P1, K1) 4 times. Repeat from beginning to end to complete one round.

ROUND 4: *P2, K2, (P1, K1) 3 times, K1, P2, K5, P1, K1, P1, K5* repeat from * to * 4 more times, P2, K2, (P1, K1) 3 times, K1. Repeat from beginning to end to complete one round.

ROUND 5: *P2, K1 (P1, K1) 4 times, P2, K4, (P1, K1) 3 times, K3* repeat from * to * 4 more times, P2, K1, (P1, K1) 4 times. Repeat from beginning to end to complete one round.

ROUND 6: *P2, K2, (P1, K1) 3 times, K1, P2, K3, (P1, K1) 4 times, K2* repeat from * to * 4 more times, P2, K2, (P1, K1) 3 times, K1. Repeat from beginning to end to complete one round.

ROUND 7: *P2, K1, (P1, K1) 4 times, (P1, K1) 5 times, K1* repeat from * to * 4 more times, P2, K1, (P1, K1) 4 times. Repeat from beginning to end to complete one round.

ROUND 8: *P2, K2, (P1, K1) 3 times, K1, P2, K1, (P1, K1) 6 times*, repeat from * to * 4 times, P2, K2, (P1, K1) 3 times, K1. Repeat from beginning to end to complete one round.

ROUND 9: *P2, K1, (P1, K1) 4 times, P2, K2, (P1, K1) 5 times, K1* repeat from * to * 4 more times, P2, K1, (P1, K1) 4 times. Repeat from beginning to end to complete one round.

ROUND 10: As 6th.

ROUND 11: As 5th.

ROUND 12: As 4th.

ROUND 13: As 3rd.

ROUND 14: As 2nd.

This completes the pattern. Continue round 15 as round 1. Repeat the pattern until 3 inches (7.5 cm) below your underarm measurement. At this point you must make the increase for the gussets under the arm. Continuing in pattern on the next round increase one stitch in centre of the two purl stitches. This is the beginning of the gusset. Increase one stitch each side of this centre knit stitch on the next and every 4th round until 19 sts wide.

This is grandfather coxswain John Robert Stephenson. He was the last coxswain of the South Leeming lifeboat before it was taken away. He was bowman, second coxswain, coxswain and was on the boat in 1916 when she capsized.

Kenneth Stephenson, 1958; heart net mesh open diamond. Note the restricted use of cables at the neck and shoulder edge. The pattern sequence is intense in contrast to his son John's gansey, which has a wide column sequence.

Flamborough fisherman wearing cork lifebelt (as a member of the lifeboat crew) His gansey is knit in double moss columns of diamonds,, with wide moss seeding. Echoes of the pattern can be seen in the gansey of Ada Major and Mrs Stephenson.

At this point divide for the front and back to continue in pattern over two needles by slipping gusset stitches and stitches for the back onto a holder. Work front in pattern until work measures to your overall length, keeping the outside purl stitch and single knit stitch as the arm edge. Finish on complete pattern segment. Place centre 39 sts and stitches for shoulder onto a holder and knit other shoulder in 2 rows plain, 2 rows purl for 10 rows—leave on holder. Repeat this for other shoulder (this forms neck shaping). Repeat for back. Cast off the shoulders together on the inside.

The sleeves

Pick up evenly around armhole. 140 sts including gusset. Purl 1 st each side of gusset—*i.e.* picked up stitches.

SLEEVE PATTERN:

6 full diamond patterns down then stocking stitch.

P1, K25, P2, K13, P2, K1, (P1, K1) 4 times, P2, K13—*i.e.* 6 sts one side of centre shoulder seam, 1 stitch directly on seam and 6 sts down other side, centre shoulder seam, 1 stitch directly on seam and 6 sts down other side, P2, K1, (P1, K14) 4 times, P2, K13, P2, K25, P1, K19 gusset stitches.

Decrease one stitch either side of seam stitches every 4th round until gusset worked out. Then decrease on every 6th round until sleeve measures 12 inches, (30 cm) then back to every 4th round until 16 inches (41 cm), then every 3rd round until 18¼ inches (46 cm). Work ¼ inch extra stocking stitch, then 3½ inches (9 cm) rib, making sleeve measurement 22 inches total or to required length. Cast off in rib with wool doubled.

The neck

Pick up evenly 39 sts each from back and front together with stitches from shoulder edge (124 sts total). K1, P1, rib for neck worked into back of all rib stitches for 2½ inches (6 cm) or as preferred. Cast off loosely ribwise.

John Stephenson wearing a gansey that closely resembles the pattern sequence on the gansey of his father, Kenneth. This gansey displays beautifully the short arm length which the fishermen required in order that their lower arms did not break out with salt water 'plooks' due to their skin being in almost constant contact with seawater.

Note also the extra wide welt, which provided extra warmth when tucked down their (traditional) button-fronted trousers!

R. R. Stephenson, the Mainprize boy, and R. Major showing off their Board of Trade medals for bravery for saving lives, 17th February 1894.

These richly patterned ganseys have been left for readers to decode.

FILEY

Continuing my journey north to Filey, I found that the tradition still survives here among the older generation. There were many examples, even though the fishing has stopped and the village has expanded into a flourishing township through its development as a resort. The fishermen still wear ganseys and are extremely proud of their tradition. They were most helpful in introducing the knitters who still continue making them—Mrs Hunter, Mrs Haxby, Mrs Johnson and Mrs Wilkinson—who gladly passed on their techniques and patterns.

The tradition here is to use tiny configurations of the classic patterns—cables, open and closed diamonds and Marriage Lines in particular. The arms are almost always knit in a pattern named after Betty Martin—a good guide to the ganseys' origin. As in Flamborough, Filey traditions were greatly influenced by folk from Scotland and Norfolk and as a result their patterns are many and varied.

The group photograph on page 78 shows some of these variations and the dedicated knitter should find it great fun to decipher and construct the many configurations. Two of them have been worked out and notated. Mrs Hunter's pattern, given in full, is typical of the Filey tradition. It is a piece of perfect craftmanship: the combination of rope, ladder and open diamond configurations make it one of the finest.

77

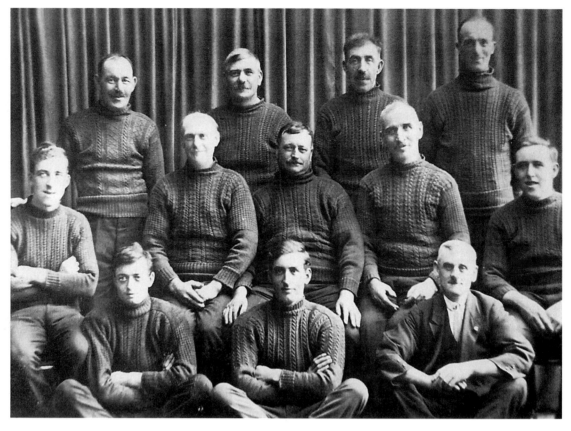

Fishermen at Pye Nest, Filey, 1926.

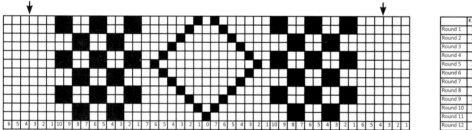

	K	P	K	P	K	P	K	P	K	P	K	P	K	P	K
Round 1	2	2	2	2	9	1	9	2	2	2	2				
Round 2	2	2	2	2	8	1	1	1	8	2	2	2	2		
Round 3	2	2	2	2	5	1	3	1	5	2	2	2	2	2	
Round 4	2	2	2	2	2	4	1	5	1	4	2	2	2	2	2
Round 5	2	2	2	2	5	1	7	1	5	2	2	2	2		
Round 6	2	2	2	2	4	1	9	1	4	2	2	2	2		
Round 7	2	2	2	2	2	1	11	1	1	2	2	2	2	2	2
Round 8	2	2	2	2	2	1	9	1	2	2	2	2	2	2	
Round 9	2	2	2	2	5	1	7	1	5	2	2	2	2		
Round 10	2	2	2	2	6	1	5	1	6	2	2	2	2		
Round 11	2	2	2	2	2	5	1	3	1	5	2	2	2	2	2
Round 12	2	2	2	2	2	6	1	1	1	6	2	2	2	2	2

Filey group—back left: Double moss 10 sts & 4 rds and diamond repeats
13 sts & 14 rds are placed centre and edged by cables which together are
repeated to complete the half round.

	K	P	K	P	K	P	K	P	K	P	K	P	K	P	K
Round 1	2	6	12	6	2	2	2	2	2	2					
Round 2	2	6	2	8	2	6	2	2	2	2					
Round 3	2	6	2	8	2	6	2	4	2	2	2	2			
Round 4	2	6	12	6	2	4	2	2	2	2					

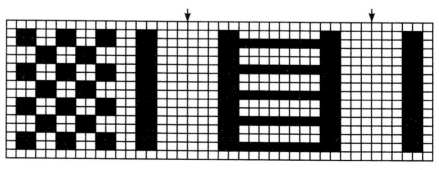

Filey group, back 2nd from left: Double moss 10 sts & 4 rds and ladder 8 sts
& 3 rds verticals are edged with cabling every 5th rd at arrows, each column
seeded by 2 purl sts.

MRS HUNTER'S PATTERN

Knitted by Mrs Hunter in 68 hrs.
Open diamond, ladder and rope pattern with Betty Martin sleeve.

Size: The size of the gansey if worked as indicated measures for a 42-inch (107 cm) chest.
Wool: 5-ply worsted wool.
Needles: One set of five No. 12 (2¾ mm) double-pointed pins.
Tension: 7 stitches and 10 rows to 1 inch (2.5 cm).
Abbreviations: Cable 6 (C6): Slip 3 sts to back of work, knit 3, knit off cable needle.

Cast on evenly over four needles with double wool 280 loops and continue in K2, P2 for 4½ (11 cm) inches keeping the wool double for five rounds (makes for increased strength and tension). Change to stocking stitch and continue in the round increasing evenly over the four needles on the next eight rounds until 364 sts. The pattern for the body now begins. Note - K2, P2 and P2, K2 at the beginning and end of each round will make a seam line which will read K2, P4, K2 as the rounds progress *(see instructions for knitting the gusset).*

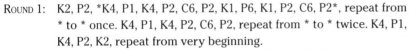

ROUND 1: K2, P2, *K4, P1, K4, P2, C6, P2, K1, P6, K1, P2, C6, P2*, repeat from * to * once. K4, P1, K4, P2, C6, P2, repeat from * to * twice. K4, P1, K4, P2, K2, repeat from very beginning.

ROUND 2: K2, P2, *K3, P1, K1, P1, K3, P2, K6, P2, K8, P2, K6, P2*, repeat from * to * once. K3, P1, K1, P1, K3, P2, K6, P2, repeat from * to * twice. K3, P1, K1, P1, K3, P2, K2, repeat from very beginning.

ROUND 3: K2, P2, *K2, P1, K3, P1, K2, P2, K6, P2, K8, P2, K6, P2*, repeat from * to * once. K2, P1, K3, P1, K2, P2, K6, P2, repeat from * to * twice. K2, P1, K3, P1, K2, P2, K2, repeat from very beginning.

ROUND 4: K2, P2, *K1, P1, K5, P1, K1, P2, K6, P2, K8, P2, K6, P2*, repeat from * to * once. K1, P1, K5, P1, K1, P2, K6, P2, repeat from * to * twice. K1, P1, K5, P1, K1, P2, K2, repeat from very beginning.

ROUND 5: K2, P2, *P1, K7, P3, K6, P2, K8, P2, K6, P2*, repeat from * to * once. P1, K7, P3, K6, P2, repeat from * to * twice. P1, K7, P3, K2, repeat from very beginning.

ROUND 6: As 4th.
ROUND 7: As 3rd.
ROUND 8: As 2nd.
ROUND 9: As 1st.

This completes the pattern. Repeat the pattern until required height.

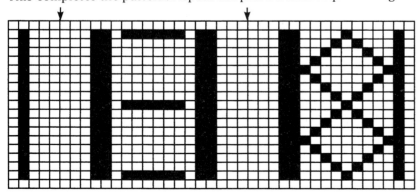

Mrs Hunter's pattern.

Mrs Hunter: open diamond, 9 sts and 8 rds; ladder, 8 sts and 8 rds; cable every 5th rd at arrows.

79

Instructions for knitting the gusset

Three inches (7.5 cm) below your underarm measurement begin the increases for the gusset as follows: at the centre of your seam line each side of the gansey (K2, P4, K2), make a knit stitch at the centre of the seam: *ie* K2, P2, (K1), P2, K2 on this round and then on every following 4th round make 1 knit stitch each side of the centre knit stitch. (The gusset will now have 3, 5, 9 stitches as you work up every 4 rounds.) Increase in this manner until the gusset is 19 stitches wide.

Continue pattern in the round without increasing on the gusset until 20 patterns total are worked. Now divide for front and back by slipping the gusset and seam stitches and stitches for back onto a holder. Continue working with two needles for 10 more patterns (adjust for size) completing the last pattern fully. Knit 2 rows purl. Leave these stitches on a stitch holder except for 56 sts which form one shoulder. Knit 21 rows of moss stitch (1st row, K1, P1; 2nd row, P1, K1) and leave on holder. Repeat back as front and shape opposite shoulder as before. Graft corresponding shoulder panel edges to front and back on the inside of the garment.

The neck

Pick up evenly around neck edge 160 sts in K2, P2 rib and continue for 3 inches (7.5 cm) and then cast off using wool double.

The sleeves

Pick up evenly 140 sts including gusset. Knit in pattern decreasing 1 st either side of seam every 4th round until gusset is worked out. Then continue to decrease every 6th round to 96 sts—then back to every 4th until 68 sts remain. Knit a few extra rounds to required length before K2, P2, for 3 inches (7.5 cm) for the cuff. Cast off using wool double.

SLEEVE PATTERN (BETTY MARTIN):
ROUND 1: Knit.
ROUND 2: Knit.
ROUND 3: K2, P2, repeat to end.
ROUND 4: K2, P2, repeat to end.
Continue in pattern for 90 rounds and then continue in stocking stitch. 160 sts remain. Knit straight if further length required and then begin cuff. K2, P2, for 2½ inches (6 cm). Cast off ribwise.

SCARBOROUGH

This elegant spa town is made up of two bays: the harbour bay, with the old fishing village spreading underneath the splendid castle ruins on one side and the fine Victorian and Edwardian buildings dominated by the spa on the other; and the commercial bay, with its shops, hotels and boarding houses. Once a society resort for the express purpose of 'taking the waters', it still retains in many parts the genteel atmosphere of its past.

Today, the town caters for the modern tourist with a proliferation of amusement arcades and modern developments along the seafront, while its Victorian heritage has been turned to advantage by the successful promotion of the town as a conference centre. But the old harbour and its fishing village continue in much the same way as they have always done, with a thriving fishing industry and a haven for boats from all over the east coast.

It was difficult to find any gansey patterns that were generally considered exclusive to Scarborough, since the influence of other areas was very great. There was a display of fishermen's clothes in the local museum and the gansey there had more affinity with Filey than Scarborough.

Mrs Rewster, a local fisherwife, had many of these patterns. She explained that the Scarborough pattern was generally considered to be the one given here, since it was the oldest anyone could remember. It had been knitted by her family for three generations. It has no welt, being cast on and knit in two rounds of purl and two rounds of plain to make a horizontal garter band. The rest of the body is knit plain, with the exception of the yoke pattern which is in double moss stitch, with a ladder stitch configuration at the shoulder edges.

Scarborough from the harbour.

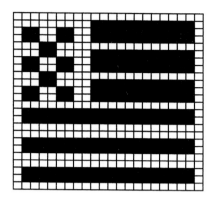

Mrs Rewster's pattern.

MRS REWSTER'S PATTERN
Knitted by Mrs Pickering in 38 hrs.

Size: The size of the gansey if worked as indicated measures for a 38/40-inch (97/101 cm) chest.
Wool: 5-ply worsted wool.
Needles: One set of five No. 12 (2¾ mm) double-pointed pins.
Tension: 7 stitches and 10 rows to 1 inch (2.5 cm).

Cast on 280 sts over four needles (70/needle) in thumb method using the wool double. Continue in single wool. Knit 2 rounds, purl 2 rounds. Repeat these four rounds four more times (20 rds). At the same time establish 2 purl stitches each side of the gansey to mark the half round. They are carried up the sides and mark the point to form a gusset and the point of division to work the front and back yokes. Continue in plain knitting for 12 inches (30 cm), your first round being P2, K138, P2, K138 beginning on the seam stitch.

The yoke pattern begins by purling 2 rounds and knitting 2 rounds. Repeat these four rounds twice more (12 rds). At the same time the gusset increases begin by knitting 1 plain st in the centre of the 2 purl seam sts both sides of the gansey. This forms the beginning of the gusset. On the next and every following 4th round increase 1 plain st both sides of the centre stitch until the gusset is 19 sts wide. The pattern continues as you are working the gusset.

ROUND 1: K2, P12, K2, (P2, K2) to last 16 sts—K2, P12, K2. Then work the gusset to complete the half round. Repeat.
ROUND 2: As 1st.
ROUND 3: K16, (P2, K2) to last 16 sts—K16. Then the gusset. Repeat.
ROUND 4: As 3rd.

Continue to increase the gusset and work this pattern until gusset is 19 sts wide. Divide the work by placing the gusset stitches and the stitches for the back onto a holder and continue in pattern up the front (138 sts) using two needles, until you measure 24 inches (61 cm) at the neck edge. (Adjust here for your size.) Leave centre 50 sts and 44 sts for the shoulder on a holder and work remaining stitches for 10 rows of 1 row plain and 2 rows garter. Leave on holder. Pick up 44 sts for other shoulder and repeat the 10 rows. Leave on holder. Rejoin wool and work the back as the front. Graft shoulders together by casting off together to form a ridge on the outside of the work. Pick up 118 sts for the neck and K1, P1 (working into the back of the rib stitches) for 2½ inches (6 cm).

The sleeves
Pick up 105 sts around the arm and 19 sts on the gusset (124). The sleeves are knitted in stocking stitch throughout, decreasing on the gusset every 4th round until it is worked out. Continue decreasing every 6th round until 96 sts, then every 5th until 68 sts (adjust here for width and length). The cuff is ribbed as the neck for 3 inches (7.5 cm), casting off in double wool ribwise. You may of course like to add some decoration to the top third of the arm, by echoing the pattern on the chest, 12 rounds of garter bands, then 12 rounds of double moss, finishing with 12 rounds of garter band. The other alternative is to work the ladder pattern by working the garter bands and then K2, P2 for 12 rounds, ending with the garter bands.

WHITBY

The fishing port of Whitby lies on the River Esk, its houses and harbour tucked beneath the cliffs and overlooked by the priory. Its livelihood is derived from fishing and from tourism which vie in gentle antagonism from opposite sides of the harbour. Most of the fishermen live in the oldest quarter, beneath the priory, in the pleasant little alleyways and yards off Church Street. Here the old fishing traditions are kept alive and gansey making is no exception.

Mrs Cole, Mrs Laidler and Mrs Richardson still knit the traditional patterns. Mrs Noble, Mrs Peart and Mrs Elders were able to give valuable insights into the tradition, although they could no longer knit because of infirmity. Mrs Laidler explained, 'This one [a moss stitch diamond separated by ropes] is a traditional pattern which has come into vogue during the last thirty years. Me father taught me to knit because me mother died—he used to sit in front of the fire and tell me what to knit. The most traditional for Whitby is this [cable and ladder columns] . . . about 3 purl rounds and 3 knit rounds. It wasn't the diamond—that came when the Scotch fishing fleets came. Before that it was this ladder. . . . Mind you, me father preferred a real plain one . . . like a lot of fishermen. . . . Me granda's were always plain with a couple of twists at the shoulder to keep it in shape'.

Mrs Noble added, 'No, it wasn't the diamond like you see today, it was what is called a ladder pattern. The moss and the diamond came from the Scottish when they came for the herring . . . they used to knit on eight short needles. They taught me the anchor and the chevron and they did a plait instead of a cable. There was another one from Scotland—the half flag—me mother used to do that one without any ropes'.

Whitby harbour (*Frank Meadow Sutcliffe*).

Mrs. Cole's pattern: All-over step and cable verticals with polo neck.

Mrs Cole has kindly knitted up her pattern which is the oldest pattern in Whitby.

MRS COLE'S PATTERN

Knitted by Mrs Cole in 53 hrs.

Size: The size of the gansey if worked as indicated measures for a 40/42-inch (107/112 cm) chest.
Wool: 5-ply worsted wool.
Needles: One set of five No. 12 (2¾ mm) double-pointed pins.
Tension: 7 stitches and 10 rows to 1 inch (2.5 cm).

Cast on 314 sts. Knit K1, P1 rib for 2½ inches (6 cm) then continue in the following pattern.

Front and back

ROUND 1:   *P2, K6, P2, K11*, repeat from * to * 6 times ending P2, K6, P2.
ROUND 2::   As 1st.
ROUND 3::   As 1st.
ROUND 4::   *P2, K6, P2, K1, P9, K1* repeat from * to * 6 times ending P2, K6, P2.
ROUND 5:   As 4th.
ROUND 6::   *P2, C6, P2, K1, P9, K1* repeat from * to * 6 times ending P2, C6, P2.
These six rounds form 1 pattern. Repeat 17 times.

The gusset

°P1, K1, P3, K3, P2, *K11, P2, K6, P2*, repeat from * to * 5 times ending P2, K3, P3, K1°. Repeat from ° to ° once. Repeat this round 3 times.

Keeping pattern correct, increase one knit stitch on either side of inside of the outside purl sts on every 4th round until 13 sts have been worked across the centre of the gusset. Now place the following 21 sts and stitches for back onto a stitch holder to form half the gusset, *i.e.* K2, P2, K6, P1, K6, P2, K2.

Divide for front and back

Now working on two needles, continue in pattern as follows:
K1, *P2, K11, P2, K6, P2* 6 times ending K11, P2, K1. Continue for 11 patterns (adjust for size) and then work 3 more rows of pattern or continue until required height. Leave front on needle and repeat for back.

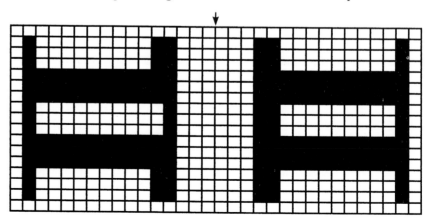

Mrs Cole's pattern: Ladder, 9 sts and 6 rds; cable every 6th rd at arrow.

84

The shoulders and neck

Place centre 31 sts on stitch holder, leaving 56 sts on front and back for right shoulder on two needles. Left shoulder is as right shoulder.

Insertion of shoulder saddle strap

With contrast wool cast on 27 sts on 1 needle using thumb method (this wool is to be pulled out later leaving 27 sts ready to be picked up for neck). With main colour knit 1 row. Now place these 27 sts onto the same needle as right front shoulder (neck edge). Using back right shoulder needle as 2nd needle, insert saddle strap as follows:

Knit 1st stitch of right hand back shoulder. Turn.

1ST ROW: Purl across 27, P2 tog (1 from saddle strap and 1 from shoulder)

2ND ROW: K2 tog tb1, K3 ('saddle strap' P2, K1, P9, K1, P2) K3, K2 tog tb1. Turn.

3RD ROW: P5 (K2, P1, K9, P1, K2) P3, P2 tog. Turn.

4TH ROW: K1, K2 tog tb1, K2, (P2, K1, P9, K1, P2) K2, K2 tog, K2 tog tb1. Turn.

5TH ROW: P3, (K2, P11, K2) P3, P2 tog. Turn.

6TH ROW: K1, K2 tog tb1, K1, (P2, K11, P2) K1, K2 tog, K2, tog tb1. Turn.

7TH ROW: P3, (K2, P11, K2), P2, P2 tog. Turn.

8TH ROW: K1, K2 tog tb1 (P2, K1, P9, K1, P2) K2 tog, K2 tog tb1. Turn.

This completes shaping for neck gusset.

9TH ROW: K1, P2, (K2, P1, K9, P1, K2) P2, K1.

Continue in this way, taking one stitch from each alternate side until all shoulder stitches are knitted. Leave remaining 21 sts on safety pin.

The sleeves

Using four needles, pick up 122 sts evenly around armhole, including 21 sts of gusset and 21 sts of saddle strap, retaining purl stitch as seam stitch.

1ST ROW: P1, K6, P2, K2, P2, *K11, P2, K6, P2* repeat from * to * 3 times ending K11, P2, K2, P2, K6.

Continue in pattern as before decreasing 1 st each side of centre gusset (13 sts) every 6th row for 10 complete patterns, then change to stocking stitch continuing to decrease 1 st either side of seam line every 6th row until 60 stitches remain. Rib in K1, P1, for cuff for 3½ inches (6 cm). Cast off ribwise in double wool.

The collar

Pick up 31 sts from stitch holder on front of neck, 27 sts from right shoulder strap 31 sts from back of neck and 27 sts from left shoulder strap (116 sts). Rib in K1, P1, for 6½ inches.

Mrs Laidler's Whitby pattern.

MRS LAIDLER'S PATTERN

Knitted by Mrs Laidler in 53 hrs.

In Mrs Laidler's pattern, one can see that the Scottish influence is quite prominent. It is interesting to note the shoulder flap: instead of the normal method of knitting it in the same direction as the body, it has been knit up at right angles, the stitches of the front and back picked up as one works from the neck edge to the shoulder. The advantage of this method is that the pattern can be continued down the arm without a break.

Size: The size of the gansey if worked as indicated measures for a 40/42-inch (107/112 cm) chest.
Wool: 5-ply combed wool worsted.
Needles: One set of five No. 12 (2¾ mm) double-pointed pins.
Tension: 7 stitches and 10 rows to 1 inch (2.5 cm).

The body

Cast on 300 loops evenly over four needles and K1, P1 for 3½ inches (9 cm) for the welt. Keeping one purl stitch each side of the work knit plain for 12 inches (30 cm) or to 3 inches (7.5 cm) below your underarm measurement. Your 1st round will be P1, K149, P1, K149. After the plain stitches are worked it is now the beginning of the gusset and it is at this point that the pattern begins. Increase 1 st each side of purl seam, *i.e.* K3 and increase on every 3rd round until 20 sts wide plus seam stitches.

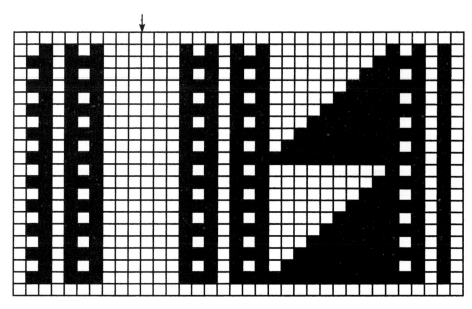

Mrs Laidler: half flag, 10 sts and 10 rds; cable every 5th rd at arrow.

ROUND 1: *(P1, K1) 4 times, P9, (K1, P1) 4 times K*, repeat 3 times more ending (P1, K1) 4 times, P9, (K1, P1) 4 times.

ROUND 2: *P3, K1, P3, K2, P8, K1, P3, K1, P3, K6*, repeat 3 times more ending P3, K1, P3, K2, P8, K1, P3, K1, P3.

ROUND 3: *(P1, K1) 4 times, K2, P7, (K1, P1) 4 times, K6*, repeat 3 times more ending (P1, K1) 4 times, K2, P7, (K1, P1) 4 times.

ROUND 4: *P3, K1, P3, K4, P6, K1, P3, K1, P3, K6*, repeat 3 times more ending P3, K1, P3, K4, P6, K1, P3, K1, P3.

ROUND 5: *(P1, K1) 4 times, K4, P5, (K1, P1) 4 times, K6*, repeat 3 times more ending (P1, K1) 4 times, K4, P5, K1, P3, K1, P3.

ROUND 6: *P3, K1, P3, K6, P3, K1, P3, K1, P3, C6*, repeat 3 times more ending P3, K1, P3, K6, P4, K1, P3, K1, P3.

ROUND 7: *(P1, K1) 4 times, K6, P3, (K1, P1) 4 times, K6*, repeat 3 times more ending (P1, K1) 4 times, K6, P3, K1, P3, K1, P3.

ROUND 8: *P3, K1, P3, K8, P2, K1, P3, K1, P3, K6*, repeat 3 times more ending P3, K1, P3, K8, P2, K1, P3, K1, P3.

ROUND 9: *(P1, K1) 4 times, K8, P1, (K1, P1) 4 times, K6*, repeat 3 times more ending (P1, K1) 4 times, K8, P3, K1, P3.

ROUND 10: *P3, K1, P3, K9, P1, K1, P3, K1, P3, K6*, repeat 3 times more ending P3, K1, P3, K8, P1, K1, P3, K1, P3.

ROUND 11: As 1st.

ROUND 12: As 2nd.

Continue in this manner for three complete patterns. At this point you now begin the division for the armholes by slipping gusset and stitches for the back onto a holder and continuing up the front in pattern until your required height. Leave these stitches on a holder and repeat for back (leaving gusset on holder).

The shoulders and neck

For left shoulder place centre 39 sts on stitch holder leaving 55 sts on front and back for right shoulder on two needles. Right shoulder is as the left.

Insertion of shoulder saddle strap

You will now have four needles in position. Cast on, on 1 needle in contrast wool for 34 sts in thumb method (this wool is to be pulled out later leaving 34 sts ready to be picked up for the neck). With main colour knit one row. Now place these 34 sts onto same needle as right front shoulder at the neck edge. Use the back shoulder needle to work with. Insert saddle strap as follows.

Knit first stitch of left hand back shoulder.

1ST ROW: Purl across 34, P2 tog (1 from saddle strap and 1 from shoulder).

2ND ROW: (1 from each) K1, K2 tog tb1, K3, (K1, P1) 4 times, K6, (P1, K1) 4 times, K3, K2 tog tb1. Turn.

3RD ROW: P5, (P1, K3, P1, K3, P6, K3, P1, K3, P1) P4, P2 tog. Turn.

4TH ROW: K1, K2 tog tb1, K2, (P1, K1) 4 times more, K6, (K1, P1) 4 times, K2, K2 tog tb1. Turn.

5TH ROW: P4, (P1, K3, P1, K3, P6, K3, P1, K3, P1) P3, P2, tog. Turn.

6TH ROW: K1, K2 tog tb1, K1, (P1, K1) 4 times, C6, (K1, P1) K1, K2 tog, K2 tog tb1. Turn.

7TH ROW: P3, (P1, K3, P1, K3, P6, K3, P1, K3, P1) P2, P2 tog. Turn.

8TH ROW: K1, K2 tog tb1, (P1, K1) 4 times, K6, (K1, P1) 4 times, K2 tog, K2 tog tb1. Turn.

9TH ROW: P2, (P1, K1) 4 times, P6, (K1, P1) 4 times, P2, K1

Continue in this way, taking 1 st from each alternate side until all shoulder stitches are knitted. Leave remaining stitches on safety pin ready to be picked up for the arm.

The sleeves

Using four needles pick up 129 sts evenly around armhole including 21 sts of gusset and stitches of saddle strap retaining purl stitch.

1ST ROW: P1, K36, (P1, K1) 4 times, P9, (K1, P1) 4 times, K6 (P1, K1) 4 times, P9, (K1, P1) 4 times, K36.

Continue in pattern as before except 19 sts on either side of sleeve stitches. They are knitted plain. Decrease 1 st each side of centre gusset every 4th row until gusset worked out. Then continue to decrease every 6th round to 96 sts—then back to every 4th until 60 sts remain. Knit straight if further length required. Rib in K1, P1 for 3½ inches (9 cm). Cast off ribwise in double wool.

The collar

Cast on 6 sts. Pick up 17 sts (half) from saddle, 39 sts from front neck, 28 sts from right shoulder saddle, 39 sts from back and 17 sts from other half of 1st saddle strap. Knit 20 sts garter stitch placing buttonholes every 4th row (3) and remainder in K1, P1 until last 14 sts knit with garter stitch. Knit 2 extra rows and cast off in rib.

STAITHES

Staithes *(Frank Meadow Sutcliffe)*.

The next village on my journey northwards was the tiny fishing village of Staithes. Tucked deep in the base of the cliffs that stretch all along the coast, this tiny community still retains all its charm and character, due largely to its inaccessibility. Indeed, not long ago the accent of the fisherfolk was different from those people who lived on the clifftop, not half a mile away.

The fishing tradition is as strong here as anywhere, and so are the customs: the village is well known for the distinctive 'Staithes' bonnet worn by the womenfolk.

As in Whitby, the modern gansey has changed from the old days. The men now prefer more elaborate designs than their fathers, who wanted their ganseys plain with only a little decoration on the shoulder.

Miss Verrill's pattern is a popular one throughout Britain, especially in Cornwall where most of the patterns are made up of horizontal bands.

MISS VERRILL'S PATTERN

Knitted by Mr Wilson in 40 hrs.

Size: The size of the gansey if worked as indicated measures for a 38-inch (97 cm) chest.
Wool: 5-ply worsted wool.
Needles: One set of five No. 12 (2¾ mm) double-pointed pins.
Tension: 7 sts and 10 rows to 1 inch (2.5 cm).

Cast on 280 sts using thumb method evenly over four needles and knit 2 rounds plain, 2 rounds purl. Repeat these 4 rounds 6 times. This forms the welt in this gansey. Continue in stocking stitch until work measures 12 inches (30 cm) keeping a seam line of P1, K1, K137, P1, K1, P1, K137, P1. The gusset increase now begins as well as the pattern. On the first round of the pattern increase by 1 st on centre knit stitch, making 2 knit sts in centre with purl stitch each side. Increase 1 st each side of the centre stitches every 4th round until 20 stitches worked. The yoke pattern is as follows.

*2 rounds purl, 2 rounds plain. *Repeat once.

ROUND 1: K2, P2, repeat to end.
ROUND 2: Knit.
ROUND 3: P2, K2, repeat to end.
ROUND 4: Knit.

Repeat these four rounds five times for each panel.

One pattern is 28 rounds.

When gusset stitches are worked, you now divide for front and back by slipping gusset stitches including the purl stitches and stitches for back onto a stitch holder.

Continue in pattern on two needles making the first and last 3 stitches in garter stitch. Work until there are 5 patterns.

Knit first section of the sixth pattern.

Neck shaping (adjust to size)

Leave 87 sts for neck and shoulder on a holder. Knit 12 rows of 2 rows purl, 2 plain on other shoulder, finishing on a plain row, leave these stitches on a stitch holder. Repeat for the corresponding shoulder leaving neck stitches on the holder. Repeat back as front. Cast off shoulders together on the right side forming a ridge.

The neck

Pick up 108 sts evenly around neck edge and K2, P2 for 3 inches (7.5 cm) finishing with 1 plain, 2 purl, 1 plain round. Cast off using wool double (ribwise).

The sleeves

The sleeves are picked up evenly including the gusset (128 sts). The pattern for the arm is 2 rounds plain, 2 rounds purl (keeping the gusset plain). Repeat these four rounds again. Work next 2 inches (5 cm) plain knitting, and the following pattern for 20 rounds.

ROUND 1: P2, K2 (repeat to end of round).
ROUND 2: Knit.
ROUND 3: K2, P2.
ROUND 4: Knit.

End the pattern with two rounds purl and continue for the rest of the sleeve in plain knitting. At the same time as working the pattern decrease one stitch each side of the centre of the gusset every 4th row. Continue decreasing until 70 sts remain—knit straight to required length. For the cuff K2, P1 for 3 inches (7.5 cm) casting off in rib using the wool double.

Miss Verrill: Garter and moss stitch panel repetition over the yoke from gusset to end of 5th repetition.

CULLERCOATS

Cullercoats Bay.

Travelling northwards along the coast from Staithes, it is necessary to go past Redcar, Hartlepool and beyond the mouth of the River Tyne before industrialisation gives way to an urban and rural economy and fishing is again a way of life. In the once major port of North Shields there are elements of industrialisation; the fishing industry has declined so much here that most of the fishermen using the port come from other areas to work on the trawlers, and many of these men do not come from fishing families. As a consequence they have little respect for their heritage. It is only among the older generation that any interest is shown and these fishing families now tend to retail fish rather than catch it.

One has to turn to the tiny fishing communities where there is still evidence of the old families. My own home village of Cullercoats clearly illustrates this trend. It was not long ago that only five or six families made up the community, owning between them the largest inshore fishing fleet on the whole North East coast. In its heyday over one hundred cobles beached above the hightide mark. Today only two or three boats work regularly from the bay—the remaining fishermen prefer to harbour their boats at Blythe. Most of the families are still in Cullercoats, the younger generations moving into retailing or the merchant side of the trade.

Because the families are still there, the contact with their tradition remains even though many of them now have no contact with the sea. In the past these traditions have been so strong that any outside intrusion has been met with swift and effective retaliatory action. The story of how the local Seamen's Mission started in the mid-19th century illustrates this protectiveness admirably.

As in most other fishing communities, religion is taken seriously and the men were looking forward to the arrival of a new vicar. Unfortunately, in a surge of enthusiasm for his new job, he insisted when he arrived that the men wear shirts, ties and jackets and the women coats and hats while they attended church. He was unaware of the tradition that the community wore their traditional Sunday best to church—the men their ganseys and the women their shawls and pleated skirts. Unmindful of their custom, he was offended that they should worship in what he thought were work-clothes. The community was as unbending in attitude as the vicar and, to a man, stopped attending church. Neither side would relent. The vicar had to turn to the new community arriving at the housing estates that were built as an overflow from the city of Newcastle, while the fishing community built its own church. To this day the atmosphere remains, with the church at one end of the street and the mission at the other.

Needless to say, gansey making is very popular and most fishermen have a substantial collection. The tradition has, however, suffered in that the younger generation, as in most other places, is more interested in knitting fashion garments. Esther Reed's pattern is considered to be the pattern exclusive to Cullercoats—it was the pattern most commented on by the fishermen and the one they were most interested in obtaining. In fact, this pattern can be seen quite readily up and down the coast. Its popularity is due to the simple yet very decorative configuration of horizontal bands of 'Bird's Eye' and garter stitch. The pattern was obtained from Mrs Stone who was given it by Esther Reed before she died so that it would not be forgotten. She need not have worried since the archives in the local library revealed this excellent photograph taken in 1890 showing Mr and Mrs Taylor in their Sunday best (*see next page*).

Fisherwives sorting fish, North Shields quayside, 1884.

CULLERCOATS GANSEY, 1890

Size: 32-34, 36-38, 40-42, 44-46, 48-50 inches (80-86, 92-96, 102-107, 112-117, 122-127 cm.)
Wool: 5-ply worsted
Needles: 1 set No. 12 (2.75 mm) pointed at both ends
Tension: 7 stitches and 10 rows to 1 inch (2.5 cm).

Cast on 224 (240, 252, 268, 280) sts, using rope edge method (using wool double and two needle method, knitting between each stitch). Divide stitches equally onto 4 needles and P2, K2 for 4 inches (10 cm), keeping wool double for first 5 rounds.

Knit 9-10-11-12-12 inches (23-25-28-31-31 cm) in plain keeping 2 purl stitches at each side of garment making a seamline.

Your first round will be: plain 110 (119-124-132-138), P2, 110 (117-124-132-138) plain. Keep seamline continuous throughout. Now start pattern after you have worked to height according to your size.

*Round 1: Purl
Round 2: Plain.
Repeat these two rounds three more times.
Then for the Bird's Eye pattern:
Round 1: K2, P2; repeat to end.
Round 2: Knit
Round 3: P2, K2; repeat to end.
Round 4: Knit.
Repeat these 4 round 5 more times.

Esther Reed's pattern, worn by Mr Taylor accompanied by his wife in her Sunday best, 1890.

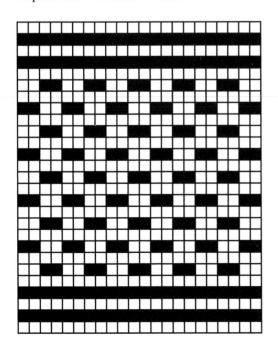

Esther Reed: garter and Bird's Eye panel repeated vertically. Knitted by Mrs Carlin in 34 hrs.

92

Repeat pattern from * and at the same time start the gusset; increase in the first round by making knit stitches in the centre of the seam stitches (both sides of the gansey). These 2 sts are the centre for the gusset, which is worked throughout in plain. Increase 1 st each side of the gusset (on the inside of the purl) every 3rd round until you have worked 7 increases.

Knit round and now divide for the front and back by placing the gusset stitches on the seam stitches and stitches for the back onto a holder.

For the Front

Continue working the pattern over two needles until you have completed 3 panels and 24 rows of the 4th panel.

Row 25: Knit 30 (34-37-41-44), Knit 50 and leave on holder for neck, knit 30 (34-37 -41-44). Knit 3 rows for shoulder and leave 30 (34-37-41-44) sts on st.holder.
Repeat for other shoulder.

Back

With the right side facing rejoin and work as front. With wrong side facing place shoulders together and cast off stitches together.

Neck

Pick up stitches over shoulders, 50 along front and 50 along back. Work in K2, P2 for 1.5 inches (4 cm) and cast off using wool double.

Sleeves

Pick up stitches evenly around armhole (including gusset and seam stitches).

For the first 7 decreases, decrease 1 st each side of gusset.

Using the following pattern decrease either side of seam stitch every 6th row till 60 sts remain (adjust to length).

Round 1: Knit
Round 2: Purl
Repeat 3 times
Round 9: Knit
Round 10: K2, P2, rep.
Round 11 : Knit
Repeat these 4 rounds 5 times
Round 33: Knit
Round 34: Purl
Repeat these two rounds 3 times
Round 41: Knit

Continue knitting plain and decreasing until 60 sts. remain. K2, P2 for 2.5 inches (6 cm) for cuff and cast off ribwise using wool double.

CULLERCOATS ROCKET BRIGADE GANSEY

Knitted by Mrs Moore in 60 hrs.

Nearly every village at the turn of the century had a lifeboat station and a Rocket rescue crew. It was a privilege to be appointed a permanent member of the crew and for the fisherwife it was an opportunity to show off her skills in knitting a special Rocket gansey for her man to wear on duty. Tom Lisle's gansey features the Hen's Claw and moss stitch from a traditional Cullercoats pattern. It is most effective and quite unique.

Where garment is knit over two needles, knit and purl stitches are to be reversed on all wrong side rows.

Size: The size of the gansey if worked as indicated measures for a 38/40-inch (97/102 cm) chest.
Wool: 5-ply worsted wool, 20 x 50 gm.
Needles: One set of five 35 cm, No. 12 (2¾ mm) double-pointed pins.
Tension: 7 stitches and 10 rows to 1 inch (2.5 cm).

Cast on evenly over four needles 260 sts in thumb method using the wool double. K2, P2 for 4 inches (10 cm), keeping the wool double for the first five rounds. Knit stocking stitch for 4½ inches (11 cm), establishing 2 purl sts on each half round. These stitches form the 'seam' line which runs up the sides of the gansey to form the beginning of the gusset under the arm and the point of division for working the front and back. The pattern now begins. Purl two rounds and work 20 rounds in moss stitch *(K1, P1)* repeat * to * to end of round. *P1, K1* repeat * to * to end of round. Repeat these two rounds. Purl one round and knit one round. The herringbone pattern now begins.

Round 1: *P1, K8 (P1, K9) to last nine sts—P1, K8, P2 (side seam)*. Repeat to complete round.

Round 2: *K1, P1, K8 (P1, K9) repeat to last 8 sts—P1, K7 (P2 for the seam)*. Repeat completely * to *.

Round 3: *K2, P1, K8 (P1, K9) repeat to last 7 sts—P1, K6 (P2 for the seam)*. Repeat completely * to *.

Round 4: *K3, P1, K8 (P1, K9) repeat to last 6 sts—P1, K5 (P2 for the seam)*. Repeat completely * to *.

Round 5: *K4, P1, K8 (P1, K9) repeat to last 5 sts—P1, K4 (P2 for the seam)*. Repeat completely * to *.

Round 6: *K5, P1, K8 (P1, K9) repeat to last 4 sts—P1, K3 (P2 for the seam)*. Repeat completely * to *.

Round 7: *K6, P1, K8 (P1, K9) repeat to last 3 sts—P1, K2 (P2 for the seam)*. Repeat completely * to *.

Round 8: *K7, P1, K8 (P1, K9) repeat to last 2 sts—P1, K1 (P2 for the seam)*. Repeat completely * to *.

Round 9: *K8, P1, K8 (P1, K9) repeat to last 3 sts—P3 (including seam sts)*. Repeat completely * to *.

Round 10: *K9, P1, K8 (P1, K9) repeat to end P2 for the seam.

Round 11: Purl to end.

Round 12: *K9, P1, K8 (P1, K9) repeat to last 9 sts—K8, P1, then P2 side seam*. Repeat completely * to *.

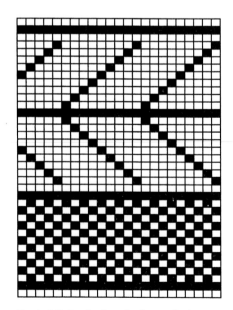

Tom Lisle in his Rocket crew gansey, wearing his Rocket belt and medal for gallantry.

Rocket Brigade: herringbone, 9 sts and 21 rds.

94

Round 13: *K8, P1, K8 (P1, K9) repeat to last 10 sts—K8, P1, K1, then P2 side seam*. Repeat completely * to *.

Round 14: *K7, P1, K8 (P1, K9) repeat to last 11 sts—K8, P1, K2, then P2 side seam*. Repeat completely * to *.

Round 15: *K6, P1, K8 (P1, K9) repeat to last 12 sts—K8, P1, K3, then P2 side seam*. Repeat completely * to *.

Round 16: *K5, P1, K8 (P1, K9) repeat to last 13 sts—K8, P1, K4, then P2 side seam*. Repeat completely * to *.

Round 17: *K4, P1, K8 (P1, K9) repeat to last 14 sts—K8, P1, K5, then P2 side seam*. Repeat completely * to *.

Round 18: *K3, P1, K8 (P1, K9) repeat to last 15 sts—K8, P1, K6, then P2 side seam*. Repeat completely * to *.

Round 19: *K2, P1, K8 (P1, K9) repeat to last 16 sts—K8, P1, K7, then P2 side seam*. Repeat completely * to *.

Round 20: *K1, P1, K8 (P1, K9) repeat to last 17 sts—K8, P1, K8, then P2 side seam*. Repeat completely * to *.

Round 21: *P1, K8, P1 (P1, K9) repeat to last 18 sts—K8, P1, K9, then P2 side seam*. Repeat completely * to *.

Round 22: Knit.

Purl one round and moss stitch 21 rounds.

Pattern 22 rounds of herringbone.

Pattern the moss stitch for 22 rounds (purl one round, moss 21) at the same time the increases for the gusset begin. Increase one knit stitch in the centre of the two seam stitches both sides and increase one knit stitch both sides of this centre stitch on the next and every 4th round until gussets are 19 sts wide. At this point place the gusset stitchess and the back onto a holder and continue in pattern over two needles up the front.

To make it clear, the garment is:
1 moss panel
1 herringbone panel
1 moss panel
1 herringbone panel
1 moss panel—when the gusset begins
1 herringbone panel—round two is the beginning of working front.
1 moss panel
1 herringbone pattern
1 moss panel ending shoulder on the 19th row, (adjust here for your own length) next part left on 10th row of moss panel (adjust here for your own length).
Leaving gusset stitches on holder, work the back as the front.

The neck
Pick up 124 sts in K2, P2 rib. Work for 3 inches (7.5 cm), the last round with wool double. Cast off in rib with wool double.

The shoulders
Place shoulders together and cast off on the inside together.

The sleeves

Pick up 140 sts inclusive of gusset stitches and work two rounds in plain knitting. Purl one round and work 21 rounds in moss stitch. Purl 2 rounds. At the same time decrease one stitch each side of gusset every 4th round until gusset is worked out. Continue to decrease every 6th round until 96 sts—then back to every 4th until 68 sts (adjust here for width and length). The rest of the sleeve is knit plain after the purl rounds. K2, P2 for 3 inches for the cuff. Cast off in rib with wool double.

Newbiggin main street, 1890s.

NEWBIGGIN

This village in Northumberland still retains all the hallmarks of a fishing community, unlike Cullercoats where the character of the village has been altered by redevelopment. Here, in Newbiggin, the old fishermen's cottages can still be found lining the seafront.

Many fishermen still work out of here in the old inshore tradition, the cobles lying on the sands above the hightide mark. There is no slipway for launching the boats and the sea is quite shallow. Before the days of the tractor, the boats had to be manhandled into the water and dragged out again in the evening, the men up to their waists in water. Often their wives used to launch the boats and carry their men out on their backs so that they did not have to spend the day soaked to the skin.

The life of the fisherwife was very hard, perhaps even harder than her husband's. She had to maintain a house and a family, bait the lines (on average some 300 hooks a day), gut all the fish that came in at the end of the day, sell the fish and still find time to knit ganseys.

Today there is only one lady still practising knitting regularly, although as usual there are a number of ladies who still retain the knowledge, such as Mrs Taylor. Her son showed me a gansey he wore that was knitted in 1931. It looked as good as new and was a piece of perfect craftsmanship.

MRS ROWE'S PATTERN NO. 1
Knitted by Mrs Rowe in 60 hrs.

Mrs Rowe still knits in the old tradition and for her the working of the pattern has religious significance. She knits church windows, cross and diamond patterns with what she calls 'Jesus stitches' to equalise the pattern. The Newbiggin pattern in common use, however, is the classic Marriage Line, traditionally said to reflect the ups and downs of life. It contains the buttoned neck which is now found everywhere on this part of the coastline and Mrs Rowe was kind enough to knit up the pattern for me.

Size: The size of the gansey if worked as indicated measures for a 42-inch (107 cm) chest.
Wool: 5-ply worsted wool.
Needles: One set of five No. 12 (2¾ mm) double-pointed pins.
Tension: 7 sts and 10 rows to 1 inch (2.5 cm).

Cast on evenly over four needles in thumb method using wool double, 280 loops and continue for 4½ inches (11 cm) in K2, P2 keeping the wool double for the first five rounds. (This makes for increased strength and tension.) Change to stocking stitch and continue in the round increasing evenly on each needle over the next eight rounds until 348 loops. (Increase 1 stitch every 33 stitches.) The pattern now begins, keeping a seam line of a centre purl stitch and two knit stitches either side, front and back.

ROUND 1: **P1, K2**, *P1, K1, P1, K2, P1, K10, (P1, K1) 3 times, P2, K1, P1, K2, P1, C6* repeat from * to * 3 times, P1, K1, P1, K2, P1, K10, (P1, K1) 3 times, P2, K1, P1, K2, P1, **K2**. Repeat from very beginning to end.

ROUND 2: P1, K2, *P1, K2, P1, K1, P1, K9, (P1, K1) 5 times, K1, P1, K1, P1, K6* repeat from * to * 3 times, P1, K2, P1, K1, P1, K9, (P1, K1) 5 times, K1, P1, K1, P1, K2. Repeat from very beginning to end.

ROUND 3: P1, K2, *P1, K1, P1, K2, P1, K8, (P1, K1) 4 times, K1, P1, K1, P1, K2, P1, K6* repeat from * to * 3 times, P1, K1, P1, K2, P1, K8, (P1, K1) 4 times, K1, P1, K1, P1, K2, P1, K2. Repeat from very beginning to end.

ROUND 4: P1, K2, *P1, K2, P1, K1, P1, K7, (P1, K1) 4 times, K2, P1, K2, P1, K1, P1, K6* repeat from * to * 3 times, P1, K2, P1, K1, P1, K7, (P1, K1) 4 times, K2, P1, K2, P1, K1, P1, K2. Repeat from very beginning to end.

ROUND 5: P1, K2, *P1, K1, P1, K2, P1, K6, (P1, K1) 4 times, K3, P1, K1, P1, K2, P1, K6* repeat from * to * 3 times, P1, K1, P1, K2, P1, K6, (P1, K1) 4 times, K3, P1, K1, P1, K2, P1, K2. Repeat from very beginning to end.

ROUND 6: P1, K2, *P1, K2, P1, K1, P1, K5, (P1, K1) 4 times, K4, P1, K2, P1, K1, P1, K6* repeat from * to * 3 times, P1, K2, P1, K1, P1, K5, (P1, K1) 4 times, K4, P1, K2, P1, K1, P1, K2. Repeat from very beginning to end.

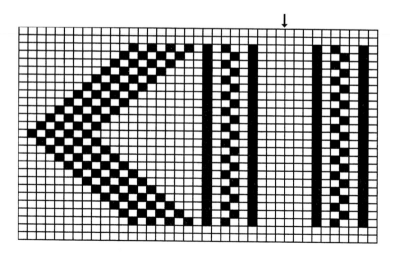

Marriage Line, 18 sts and 20 rds; cable every 6th rd at arrow

Newbiggin pattern 1, knitted by Mrs Rowe.

ROUND 7: P1, K2, *P1, K1, P1, K2, P1, K4, (P1, K1) 4 times, K5, P1, K1, P1, K2, P1, C6* repeat from * to * 3 times. P1, K1, P1, K2, P1, K4,(P1, K1) 4 times. K5, P1, K1, P1, K2, P1, K2. Repeat from very beginning to end.

ROUND 8: P1, K2, *P1, K2, P1, K1, P1, K3, (P1, K1) 4 times, K6, P1, K2, P1, K1, P1, C6* repeat from * to * 3 times. P1, K2, P1, K1, P1, K3,(P1, K1) 4 times, K6, P1, K2, P1, K1, P1, K2. Repeat from very beginning to end.

ROUND 9: P1, K2, *P1, K1, P1, K2, P1, K2, (P1, K1) 4 times, K7, P1, K1, P1, K2, P1, K6* repeat from * to * 3 times, P1, K1, P1, K2, P1, K2, (P1, K1) 4 times, K7, P1, K1, P1, K2, P1, K2. Repeat from very beginning to end.

ROUND 10: P1, K2, *P1, K2, (P1, K1) 6 times, K8, P1, K2, P1, K1, P1, K6* repeat from * to * 3 times, P1, K2, (P1, K1) 6 times, K8, P1, K2, P1, K1, P1, K2. Repeat from very beginning to end.

ROUND 11: P1, K2, *P1, K1, P1, K2, P1, (P1, K1) 4 times, K9, P1, K1, P1, K2, P1, K6* repeat from * to * 3 times, P1, K1, P1, K2, P1, (P1, K1) 4 times, K9, P1, K1, P1, K2, P1, K2. Repeat from very beginning.

ROUND 12: To round 20 repeat pattern in reverse order, round 12 as round 10, round 13 as round 9, and so on until round 20 (cable on round 13).

This completes the pattern. Remember to cross the cable every 6 rounds as the cable does not repeat equally.

Continue in pattern until 3 inches (7.5 cm) below your underarm measurement then begin increases for underarm gusset by increasing one stitch either side of centre panel stitch, increasing on next and every 4th round until 19 sts wide, plus seam stitches.

Divide for working back and front on two needles, by slipping gusset and seam stitches and stitches for back onto a holder and repeat back as front from * to *. Pattern now begins on the purl stitch of the border. Continue in pattern until work measures 25 inches total (64 cm) (or to required height). Finish on a complete pattern.

The shoulder
Continue working on shoulder over 57 sts for 10 rows of moss stitch—(1st row K1, P1), (2nd row K1, P1) leaving other shoulder and neck loops on stitch holder. Now leave the shoulder on pins after working these 10 rows. Repeat back as front from * to * and work opposite shoulder in moss stitch. Graft shoulder straps onto their opposite sides on the inside of the garment.

The neck

To work in a 3 button neck. Cast on 6 sts and pick up evenly around the neck edge and shoulder straps. Knit 17 sts garter stitch placing buttonholes every 4th row (3). Knit remainder in K1, P1, until last 11 stitches, which are knitted in garter stitch. Cast off with doubled wool.

The sleeves

Pick up evenly on four needles 140 sts around armhole, including 25 gusset and seam stitches. Knit in Betty Martin pattern decreasing 1 st either side of seam line every 4th round until gusset is worked out. Change to decrease every 6th round to 96 sts then back to every 4th round until 68 sts remain. Knit straight if further length required. Rib in K2, P2 for 3 inches (7.5 cm). Cast off ribwise in double wool.

BETTY MARTIN SLEEVE PATTERN:
ROUND 1: Knit.
ROUND 2: Knit.
ROUND 3: K2, P2, repeat to end.
ROUND 4: K2, P2, repeat to end.

Repeat these 4 rounds over 90 rounds about one third of sleeve, then continue for the rest of the sleeve in stocking stitch.

A local fishwife has met her husbands 'coble' as it was being beached (on the right of photograph—the coble rests just above high water mark).

She will return to the boat many times—here she is lugging long line and netting; passing numerous houseboats as she makes her way back home.

MRS ROWE'S PATTERN NO. 2

Mrs Rowe's pattern No. 2. Knitted by
Mrs. Ballatine in 58 hours.

29 sts and 32 rnds. Cable on 1st and every 6th following.

	K	P	K	P	K	P	K	P	K	P	K	P	K	P	K	P	K	P	K	P	K
Round 1	1	1	2	2	1	1	1	1	2	1	6	1									
Round 2	2	1	1	1	1	1	9	1	2	1	1	1	6	1							
Round 3	1	1	2	2	1	1	8	1	1	1	2	1	6	1							
Round 4	2	1	1	1	1	1	1	1	7	1	2	1	1	1	6	1					
Round 5	1	1	2	2	1	1	1	1	6	1	1	1	2	1	6	1					
Round 6	2	1	1	1	1	1	1	1	1	1	5	1	2	1	1	1	6	1			
Round 7	1	1	2	2	1	1	1	1	1	1	4	1	1	1	2	1	C	1			
Round 8	2	1	1	1	1	1	1	1	1	1	1	3	1	2	1	1	1	6			
Round 9	1	1	2	2	1	1	1	1	1	1	1	1	2	1	1	1	2	1	6		
Round 10	2	1	1	1	1	1	1	1	1	1	1	1	1	1	1	1	2	1	1		
Round 11	1	1	2	2	1	1	1	1	1	1	1	1	1	2	1	1	1	2	1	6	

Round 12 as round 10. Round 13 as round 9. Continue in reverse in this manner, cabling on every 6th round (round 13 and 19) to round 21.

	K	P	K	P	K	P	K	P	K	P	K	P	K	P	K	P	K	P	K	P	K	P
Round 22	2	1	1	1	10	2	2	1	1	1	6	1										
Round 23	1	1	2	1	9	1	1	1	1	1	2	1	6	1								
Round 24	2	1	1	1	8	1	1	2	2	1	1	1	6	1								
Round 25	1	1	2	1	7	1	1	1	1	1	2	1	C	1								
Round 26	2	1	1	1	6	1	1	1	1	2	2	1	1	1	6	1						
Round 27	1	1	2	1	5	1	1	1	1	1	1	1	1	2	1	6	1					
Round 28	2	1	1	1	4	1	1	1	1	1	2	2	1	1	1	6	1					
Round 29	1	1	2	1	3	1	1	1	1	1	1	1	1	1	2	1	6	1				
Round 30	2	1	1	1	2	1	1	1	1	1	1	1	2	2	1	1	1	6	1			
Round 31	1	1	2	1	1	1	1	1	1	1	1	1	1	1	1	1	2	1	6	1		
Round 32	2	1	1	2	1	1	1	1	1	1	1	1	2	2	1	1	1	6	1			

Round 33 as round 31. Round 34 as round 30. Continue in reverse in this manner to round 42 cabling every 6th round.

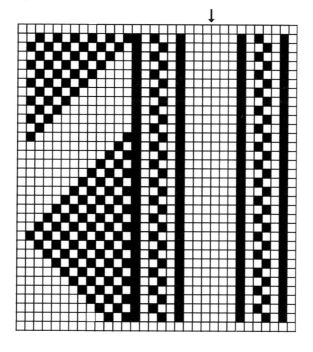

AMBLE

This thriving little fishing town lies on the river Coquet which runs off the Cheviots. It is here that the inshore fishing boat, the coble, is constructed along Norwegian lines, a tradition brought to this coast many centuries ago. Norwegian influence can still be felt through the traditional Northumberland dialect. Like gansey making, the tradition of boat building is suffering from the overall decline in inshore fishing. It will soon disappear, not from lack of interest but from lack of the dedication necessary to learn this most taxing of crafts. There is more money to be made in the smelting factories that are close at hand.

Gansey making has suffered a similar fate. The fishermen buy imitations from Fraserburgh, not from preference but because there is only one family still active. The Armstrong family had plenty of samples made over the last thirty years. As is usual, it is the elders in the family who still knit but they have not passed on their crafts, not because of any lack of interest from daughters, but because they have had only sons. Vertical panels of open and closed diamonds, separated by a double cable, with a horizontal Hen's Claw pattern make up Mrs Redford Armstrong's gansey.

MRS REDFORD ARMSTRONG'S PATTERN

Knitted by Mrs Lytton in 50 hrs.

Vertical panels of open and closed diamonds, separated by a double cable, with a horizontal Hen's Claw pattern.

Size: The size of the gansey, if worked as indicated measures for a 40/42-inch (102/107 cm) chest.
Wool: 5-ply worsted wool, 1 kilo.
Needles: One set of five No. 12 (2¾ mm) double-pointed pins.
Tension: 7 stitches and 10 rows to 1 inch (2,5 cm).

Cast on over four needles in thumb method 280 loops using wool double. Knit 3½ inches (7.5 cm) in K2, P2, keeping wool double for five rounds. After working welt continue in plain and increase over 6 rounds until 306 sts. Increases from 280 sts to 306.

Half rounds—P2, K16, increase 1 st by picking up loop between stitches and knitting into the back of it, K35, increase 1 st, K35, increase 1 st, K35, increase 1 st, K16. 4 sts increased.

Next round knit keeping purl side stitches.

Next round increase one of 4 sts.

Next round knit.

Next round increase one of 5 sts.

Next round knit.

13 sts increased in each half round–26 in all.

1st pattern now begins.

ROUND 1:   *P3, (K5, P1) 23 more times, K6*. Repeat from * to *.
ROUND 2:   *P2, K1, (P1, K5) 24 more times*. Repeat from * to *.
ROUND 3:   *P2, K2, (P1, K5) 23 more times, P1, K4*. Repeat.

Mrs Redford Armstrong's pattern: horizontal herringbone, 6 sts and 11 rds; open and closed diamonds, 13 sts and 23 rds; cable every 5th rd at arrows.

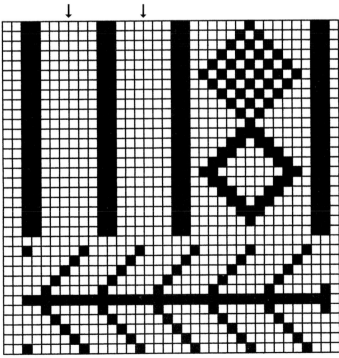

Round 4: *P2, K3, (P1, K5) 23 more times, P1, K3*. Repeat.

Round 5: *P2, K4, (P1, K5) 23 more times, P1, K2*. Repeat.

Round 6: *P2, (K5, P1) 24 times, K1*. Repeat.

Round 7: Purl.

Rounds 8 to 13: As rounds 6 to 1 (pattern in reverse).

Continue in plain and increase evenly over the next seven rounds until 348 sts, keeping the 2 purl stitches as a seam line dividing the front from the back. Increases from 306 to 348.

Half rounds—P2, K29, increase 1 st, K30, increase 1 st, K31, increase 1 st, K30, increase 1 st, K31—4 sts increased.

Next round knit.

Next half round increase—P2, K14, increase 1 st, K15, increase 1 st, K31, increase 1 st, K33, increase 1 st, K31, increase 1 st, K15, increase 1 st, K16—6 sts increased.

Next round knit.

Next half round—P2, K15, increase 1 st, K16, increase 1 st, K31, increase 1 st, K35, increase 1 st, K31, increase 1 st, K17, increase 1 st, K16—6 sts increased.

Next round knit.

Next half round increase—P2, K33, increase 1 st, K31, increase 1 st, K19, increase 1 st, K18, increase 1 st, K31, increase 1 st, K35—5 sts increased. 21 sts increased half round.

The second pattern now begins. The purl sitches become knit stitches.

Round 1: K2, (P2, K13, P2, C6, P2, C6) repeat 4 more times ending P2, K13, P2, repeat from beginning.

Round 2: K2, (P2, K6, P1, K6, P2, K6, P2, K6) repeat 4 more times ending P2, K6, P1, K6, P2, repeat from beginning.

Round 3: K2, (P2, K5, P3, K5, P2, K6, P2, K6) repeat 4 more times ending P2, K5, P3, K5, P2, repeat from beginning.

Round 4: K2, (P2, K4, P2, K1, P2, K4, P2, K6, P2, K6) repeat 4 more times P2, K4, P2, K1, P2, K4, P2, repeat from beginning.

Round 5: K2, (P2, K3, P2, K3, P2, K3, P2, K6, P2, K6) repeat 4 more times P2, K3, P2, K3, P2, K3, P2, repeat from beginning.

Round 6: K2, (P2, K2, P2, K5, P2, K2, P2, K6, P2, K6) repeat 4 more times P2, K2, P2, K5, P2, K2, P2, repeat from beginning.

Round 7: K2, (P2, K1, P2, K7, P2, K1, P2, C6, P2, C6) repeat 4 more times P2, K1, P2, K7, P2, K1, P2, repeat from beginning.

Rounds 8 to 13: As rounds 6 to 1 (pattern in reverse).

Round 14: As 2nd.

Round 15: K2, (P2, K5, P1, K1, P1, K5, P2, K6, P2, K6) repeat 4 more times P2, K5, P1, K1, P1, K5, P2, repeat from beginning.

Round 16: K2, (P2, K4, (P1, K1) 3 times, K3, P2, K6, P2, K6) repeat 4 more times, P2, K2, (P1, K1) 3 times, K3, P2, repeat from beginning.

Round 17: K2, (P2, K3, (P1, K1) 4 times, K2, P2, K6, P2, K6) repeat 4 more times. P2, K3, (P1, K1) 4 more times. P2, K3, (P1, K1) 4 times, K2, P2, repeat from beginning.

Round 18: K2, (P2, K2, (P1, K1) 5 times, K1, P2, K6, P2, K6) repeat 4 more times. P2, K2, (P1, K1) 5 times, K1, P2, repeat from beginning.

Round 19: K2, (P2, K1, (P1, K1) 6 times, P2, C6, P2, C6) repeat 4 more times. P2, K1, (P1, K1) 6 times, P2, repeat from beginning.

Round 20: As 18th.

Rounds 21 to 24: As rounds 17 to 14.

This completes pattern.

Return to round 1 and continue in pattern until 3 inches (7.5 cm) below underarm measurement (12 inches/30.5 cm). Continuing in pattern increase 1 st each side of the centre stitch dividing the front from the back on the next and every 4th round until gusset is 18 sts wide. At this point divide for front and back to work in pattern over two needles by slipping gusset stitches and stitches for back onto a holder. Continue in pattern until work measures to your overall length. Finish on complete pattern and leave on holder.

The shoulder and neck

Pattern the first 59 sts leaving rest on holder. Continue in pattern for 5 rows and leave on holder, include neck stitches (54). Pattern other shoulder. Leave on holder. Leave gusset stitches on holder and pick up back stitches and knit as front. Place shoulders together and cast off together with right side facing thus forming a ridge.

For the neck: Pick up in rib (K1, P1) (128 sts) and work for 5 inches (13 cm). Cast off in rib with double wool.

The sleeves

Pick up evenly 140 sts including gusset. Knit in pattern for first 8 inches (20 cm), thereafter plain, decreasing 1 st either side of seam every 4th round until gusset worked out. Then continue to decrease every 6th round to 96 sts, then back to every 4th until 60 sts remain. Knit a few extra rounds to required length before K2, P2 for 3 inches (7.5 cm) for the cuff. Cast off using wool double.

Craster, 1890.

CRASTER

The little village of Craster lies halfway between Amble and Seahouses, tucked away on a minor road that leads to Dunstanborough Castle. It was once an extremely insular community and only recently had a harbour built, mainly for the export of local stone. It now provides a base for the keel boats that have made this village famous for its kippers.

'Sunday Best' ganseys were regarded by most fishermen as part of their suits; for many, the only time in their lives they would ever wear a shirt and tie was on their wedding day. As the words of the old sea-shanty have it, 'He wore no shirt upon his back, but wool unto his skin'.

The pattern that follows was found for me by Mrs Beverage whose mother, Mrs Nelson, knitted it in 1920. It is very subtle, with a zigzag ('Marriage Line') knit in alternate double moss. There are no cables, and the divisions between the vertical panels of zigzag are achieved by deep lines made up of three purl stitches, the centre of which is knit plain every other round. The neck has been shaped at the front in this example, but you could make the more traditional high neck if you prefer, by working the front yoke in exactly the same way as the back.

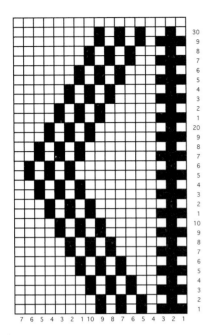

Craster 14 st triple zigzag with 3 st purl seeding

MRS ANNIE JANE NELSON'S PATTERN
Knitted by Mrs Moat in 55 hrs.

Size: The size of the gansey if worked as indicated measures for a 41-inch (104 cm) chest.
Wool: 5-ply worsted wool.
Needles: One set of five No. 12 (2¾ mm) double-pointed pins, circular 100 cm.
Tension: 7 stitches and 10 rows to 1 inch (2.5 cm).

Cast on thumb method 280 sts and distribute evenly over four needles using the wool double. K2, P2 for 4 inches (10 cm) keeping the wool double for the first five rounds. Change to plain knitting and over the next six rounds increase evenly until there are 306 sts. The pattern now begins. The first stitch of each half round forms the 'seam line', which runs up the body and down the arms, forming a basis for the gusset under the arms and the points of division for the armholes. (Mark these stitches with a length of contrast wool to remind you of their position exactly on the half round.)

Your first round will be:
P3 (K1, P1, K1, P1, K1, P1, K8), repeat * to * 8 more times. To complete round repeat from the beginning. The pattern sequence is as follows. Seeding: 3 sts & 2 rounds. Zigzag: 14 sts & 30 rounds.

Continue in pattern until you are three inches (7.5 cm) below the armpit measurement. At this point you must make the increase under the arms to form the gusset. Increase one knit stitch both sides of the centre stitch you have marked on the next and every 4th round until the gusset is 19 sts wide. At this point divide for front and back by slipping gusset stitches and stitches for the back onto a holder and continue in pattern over two needles up the front to finish on a complete pattern segment. Work over 57 sts in moss stitch leaving rest on holder. This forms the shoulder. Continue for 10 rows, the last row knit. Leave on holder and include neck stitches. Repeat moss stitch for the other shoulder. Leave on holder. Leaving gusset stitches, rejoin wool and work the back as the front. Place shoulders together with right side facing and cast off together, forming a ridge.

The neck
Pick up stitches and work K2, P2 for 2½ inches (6 cm) or as preferred. Cast off using wool double.

The sleeves
Pick up gusset stitches and around armhole. Pattern around arm, placing the centre panel between the zigzags at the ridge point on the shoulder. Knit plain extra stitches under the arm. At the same time decrease one stitch both sides of the gusset on the next and every 4th round until worked out. Decrease either side of seam every 6th round until 96 sts, then every 4th until 60 sts remain. (Adjust to length.)

The cuff
K2, P2 for 3 inches (7.5 cm). Cast off using wool double (ribwise).

Plain working ganseys, c.1890.

Fisherwives gutting herring,
Seahouses quayside, 1880.

SEAHOUSES

About eighty fishermen work out of the village of Seahouses, a centre for kippers and herrings. It was no surprise to find many patterns here, since the village's reputation for gansey knitting is well established.

Miss Esther Rutter and Mrs Laidlaw were the main gansey knitters of Seahouses, both now no longer alive. They have, however, left behind them many examples of their work and the patterns have been passed around the community. Knitting was Miss Rutter's means of livelihood and her patterns were seen all along the coast.

The pattern shown here is one of many she knitted for her brother, Henry Rutter. It effectively exploits the classic double moss stitch. She has formed a central pattern of double moss stitch edged by vertical panels of plain knitting and ladder pattern. It is a useful pattern for a novice to attempt since it is very simple and contains all the hallmarks of traditional knitting.

There are the buttoned neck, the gussets and the shoulder strap placed to enable the pattern to be carried down the arm. Whitby and Staithes in Yorkshire are the only other places to knit in this way, most other places making their neck and shoulder shapings by simply knitting extra rows and casting off the seams together.

Mrs Laidlaw's daughter-in-law showed me some ganseys she had knitted using her mother's patterns. She explained that it was impossible to get the proper wool for gansey knitting; she considered this was the main reason for the death of the tradition along this stretch of the coast.

Mrs Laidlaw's pattern echoes one of the major configurations found further up the coast in the villages of the 'Scottish Fleet'. She was taught it by one of the fisherwives who visited her while travelling down the coast with the herring fleet. It is a very effective combination of the Tree of Life pattern and the purl half diamond.

MISS ESTHER RUTTER'S PATTERN
Knitted by Mrs Banks in 50 hrs.

Size: The size of the gansey if worked as indicated measures for a 40/42-inch (102/107 cm) chest.
Wool: 5-ply combed worsted wool.
Needles: One set of five No. 12 (2¾ mm) double-pointed pins.
Tension: 30 stitches and 36 rows to 4 inches (10 cm).

Cast on thumb method 292 sts and distribute evenly over four needles using the wool double. and K2, P2 for 3½ inches (9 cm) for the welt, keeping the wool double for the first five rounds. The pattern begins immediately and includes a seam line of two purl stitches, which forms the basis for a gusset under the arms and divides the front from the back.

ROUND 1: *P1 (K6, P3) 4 more times, P1, K4, P1, (P2, K2) 10 times, P3, K4, P1 (P3, K6) 4 more times, P1*. Repeat from * to * to complete round.
ROUND 2: As 1st.
ROUND 3: *P1, (K6, P3) 4 more times, P1, K4, P1 (K2, P2) 10 times, K2, P1, K4, P1, (P3, K6) 4 more times, P1*. Repeat from * to * to complete round.
ROUND 4: *P1, K45, P1, C4, P1, (K2, P2) 10 times, K2, P1, C4, P1, K45, P1*. Repeat from * to *.
ROUND 5: *P1, K45, P1, K4, P1, (P2, K2) 10 times, K2, P1, K4, P1, K45, P1*. Repeat from * to *.
ROUND 6: *P1, K45, P1, K4, P1 (P2, K2) 10 times, P2, P1, K4, P1, K45, P1*. Repeat from * to *.

This sets the pattern—the cable is crossed every 4th round. The centre panel is revealed as a double moss pattern surrounded with tight cable and panels of ladder stitch

The left shoulder and neck
Place centre 32 sts on stitch holder, leaving 56 sts on front and back for left shoulder on two needles. Continue in pattern until work measures 3 inches (7.5 cm) below underarm height. At this point the gusset begins by increasing one knit stitch each side of purl seam (both sides of the gansey) on the next and every 4th round until gusset is 18 sts

wide. (The gusset remains plain while you continue in pattern over the rest of the gansey.) When the gusset is worked to this point you must now divide the work to pattern up the front and the back over two needles to shape the armholes. Slip the gusset stitches and the stitches for the back onto a holder and continue to pattern the front using two needles until the work measures to your overall height. Leave on needle and repeat for the back.

The right shoulder and neck
Place centre 32 sts on stitch holder, leaving 56 sts on front and back for right shoulder on two needles. Left shoulder as for right shoulder. You will now have four needles in place. For the insertion of a shoulder strap to enable pattern to be continued down the arm cast on 29 sts on a needle using contrast wool in thumb method. (This wool is to be pulled out later leaving sts ready to be picked up for the neck.) With main wool knit one row. Now place these 29 sts onto the needle on the right front shoulder at the

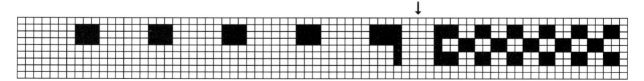

Miss Esther Rutter's pattern: cable every 4th rd at arrow.

neck edge. Using back right shoulder needle as the second needle insert saddle strap as follows.

Knit first stitch of right hand back shoulder. Turn.
1st row: Purl across 29 sts, P2 together—one from strap and one from shoulder. Turn.
2nd row: K1, K2 tog tbl, K3, (saddle strap—(P2, K2) 4 times, P2, K3, K2 tog, K2 tog tbl. Turn.
3rd row: P5, K2, P2 (P2, K2) 4 times, P2, P4, P2 tog. Turn.
4th row: K1, K2 tog tbl, K1 (P2, K2) 4 times, K2) K2, K2 tog, K2 tog tbl. Turn.
5th row: P4 (P2, K2) 4 times, K2) P3, P2 tog. Turn.
6th row: K1, K2 tog tbl, K1 (P2, K2) 4 times, P2) K1, K2 tog, K2 tog tbl. Turn.
7th row: P3 (P2, K2) 4 times, P2) P2, P2 tog. Turn.
8th row: K1, K2 tog tbl (P2, K2) 4 times, K2) K2 tog, K2 tog tbl. Turn.
9th row: P2 (P2, K2) 4 times, K2) P1, P2 tog.

Continue in this way taking one stitch from each alternate side until all shoulder stitchess are knitted. Leave remaining stitches on safety pin, 22 sts.

The sleeves
Using four needles pick up evenly 138 sts (49 for armhole, 22 for shoulder strap, 49 for back armhole, and 18 for gusset.) Continue the saddle strap pattern on the arm and work in pattern around the top half of the sleeve. Work rest of stitches in plain knitting retaining purl stitch as seam stitch.

Continue in pattern decreasing 1 st each side of seam line every 4th round until gusset is worked out. Change to decrease every 6th round to 96 sts then back to every 4th round until 60 sts remain. The pattern is worked for eight inches (20 cm) and the rest of the arm is knitted plain. Make relevant adjustments to size. The cuff is worked K2, P2 for 3 inches and cast off in rib, using the wool double.

The collar
A three button collar lying on the left. Cast on 6 sts (for a flap)—pick up half the stitches from the left saddle strap and all the way round the neck. Knit the cast on stitches and half the saddle in garter stitch, placing three button holes (every 4th row). Knit the remainder in K1, P1 until the last half of left saddle strap which you also knit in garter stitch. Knit two extra rows and cast off in rib, using the wool double.

MRS LAIDLAW'S PATTERN

Mrs Laidlaw's pattern: Tree of Life, 19 sts and 33 rds; moss stitch and purl half-diamond, 21 sts and 12 rds.

	K	P	K	P	K	P	K	P	K	P	K	P	K	P	K	P	K	P	K	P	K	P
Round 1	2	1	2	1	1	1	31	1														
Round 2	2	1	2	1	1	2	29	2														
Round 3	1	1	2	1	2	3	12	1	1	1	12	3										
Round 4	1	1	2	1	2	4	10	2	1	2	10	4										
Round 5	2	1	2	1	1	5	8	2	3	2	8	5										
Round 6	2	1	2	1	1	6	6	2	5	2	6	6										
Round 7	1	1	2	1	2	7	4	2	2	1	1	1	2	2	4	7						
Round 8	1	1	2	1	2	6	4	2	2	2	1	2	2	2	4	6						
Round 9	2	1	2	1	1	5	4	2	2	2	3	2	2	2	4	5						
Round 10	2	1	2	1	1	4	4	2	2	2	5	2	2	2	4	4						
Round 11	1	1	2	1	2	3	5	1	2	2	2	1	1	1	2	2	2	1	5			
Round 12	1	1	2	1	2	2	8	2	2	2	1	2	2	2	8	2						
Round 13	2	1	2	1	1	1	8	2	2	2	3	2	2	2	8	1						
Round 14	1	1	2	1	2	1	7	1	2	2	5	2	2	1	7	2						
Round 15	1	1	2	1	1	3	8	2	2	1	1	2	2	8	3							
Round 16	1	1	2	1	2	4	6	2	2	2	1	2	2	2	6	4						
Round 17	2	1	2	1	1	5	5	1	2	2	3	2	2	6	5							
Round 18	2	1	2	1	1	6	6	2	5	2	6	6										
Round 19	1	1	2	1	2	7	4	2	2	1	1	1	2	2	4	7						
Round 20	1	1	2	1	2	6	5	1	2	2	1	2	2	1	5	6						
Round 21	2	1	2	1	1	5	8	2	3	2	8	5										
Round 22	2	1	2	1	1	4	8	2	5	2	8	4										
Round 23	1	1	2	1	2	3	9	1	2	1	1	1	2	1	9	3						
Round 24	1	1	2	1	2	2	12	1	1	2	12	2										
Round 25	2	1	2	1	1	1	12	1	2	3	2	12	1									
Round 26	2	1	2	1	1	2	11	1	5	1	11	2										
Round 27	1	1	2	1	2	3	12	1	1	1	1	12	3									
Round 28	1	1	2	1	2	4	10	2	1	2	10	4										
Round 29	2	1	2	1	1	5	8	2	3	2	8	5										
Round 30	2	1	2	1	1	6	7	1	5	1	7	6										
Round 31	1	1	2	1	2	7	6	2	3	2	6	7										
Round 32	1	1	2	1	2	6	8	2	1	2	8	6										
Round 33	2	1	2	1	1	5	10	1	1	1	10	5										
Round 34	2	1	2	1	1	4	25	4														
Round 35	1	1	2	1	2	3	27	3														
Round 36	1	1	2	1	2	2	29	2														
Round 37	2	1	2	1	1	1	31	1														

The Scottish Fishing Fleet

Scottish 'Zulus' leaving harbour.

In my researches around the countryside, I found that the influence of Scotland on English ganseys has been significant. It seems that even before the turn of the century the knitters of Scotland passed on their patterns to the people in the villages they visited on their yearly migration following the herring fleet. It could be argued that the humble herring has been responsible for the dissemination of patterns throughout the British Isles. As you will see, the Scottish knitters were more creative and adventurous and their patterns much more exciting. It seems there has been little or no influence northwards from England.

Most people, when thinking of Scotland, nearly always identify with the west coast—The Isles of Skye, Fort William, Glencoe, Loch Lomond. The east coast generally misses out, apart from the fame brought to it in the last few years by the oil industry. It is sad that this is so: the east coast has a character and a beauty all of its own, as you will see from the photographs in this book. The buildings and the atmosphere are the same; the only thing that has changed is time. Tourism has hardly touched this part of Scotland; indeed, they have a saying in the villages along this coast that they do not get tourists, only visitors. The difference is significant. It is from many such visits that this collection of patterns has been put together.

Unloading at the quayside, 1890.

In order to gather background material and immerse myself in the historical atmosphere of the region, it was first necessary to visit the Country Life Archives at the Scottish National Museum of Antiquities in Edinburgh. It is worth outlining the historical development of knitting in Scotland to give you an idea of the atmosphere of the areas in question.

As in most other rural areas, the traditional economies of farming and fishing were supplemented by contract knitting; and we find the first mention of knitting in Scotland in 1564 when the registrar of the Privy Council mentions the making of stockings for retail. There can be no doubt that socks were knitted at home in much earlier times.

In Scotland, contract knitting was on a large scale—the years 1750 to 1795 were the most prosperous for the industry. For example, in 1777 there were twenty-two mercantile houses engaged in stocking knitting around Aberdeen. One of these houses, the proprietor of which was a Mr Pyper, had four hundred knitters on its books.*

This practice of supplementing income was a double-edged sword in that the traditional economies became neglected as people came to prefer the easier method of earning a modest income. Then, with changes in fashion, the knitting market dropped—and the people to suffer were those who had given up their traditional livelihoods. The closing of continental markets due to war and the introduction

* I. H. Grant, *An Old Scottish Handicraft Industry*, 1921, pp. 277–89

of the Hawick framed stocking industry in 1771 knocked the bottom out of this income. Agricultural improvements brought a cut-down in labour and by 1845 only eleven of the poorest parishes of the original forty-four in Aberdeenshire knitted stockings on any scale.

The following account of the industry in 1895 was given by the Provost of Inverness, Alexander Ross, in the County Accounts for that year:

'The trade in plaidings, shawls and stockings has always been an important one; it still continues to be so, and, at the annual exhibitions and sales, forms the bulk of articles vended. In the seventeenth century the trade in both linen and woollen goods was so brisk, and the domestic products of these so considerable, that much was exported over the seas by the Aberdeen merchants, and, according to all accounts, much of the rent was paid by the industry of the women folks in these home-mades.

'So great was the proficiency attained by the country women in knitting, that as much as 20s was paid for a pair of stockings. The system of giving out wool and linen to be spun by the country people attained to a great trade in the seventeenth and eighteenth centuries, but with the introduction of cheap factory-made goods it has gradually fallen. In Aberdeenshire it became a very important industry. Round Inverness and in various parts of Ross-shire, the same system prevailed, and a very large number of old women were occupied spinning the threads'.

'Shetland and the Fair Isle seem now to be the only part of the kingdom where this knitting has continued to flourish. In Aberdeenshire the industry appears comparatively to have collapsed, though efforts are now being made to revive it. The decay may have been caused, for we find great complaints made about the inequality—the short measurement, careless weaving, shrinkage etc.

'Women of all ages were seen every-where, walking from place to place busily employed knitting, for which they gave up all other employement, even men and boys were engaged . . . because of the ease with which they gain moderate subsistence. But this branch of manufacture, from a change in consumer tastes and the introduction of the stocking frame, has been for some time past on the decline; and it is possible that in a few years time it will be completely demolished.'

(J. Anderson. Agriculture, Aberdeen 1794)

A herring 'skaning' (gutting) crew, 1890, in front of the hundreds of barrels they have packed for export to the continent and to Russia. They have protected their fingers with bands of cloth, supplied by the Fishermen's Mission, to prevent them being cut by the knives and the cuts exacerbated by the salt in which the fish were packed.

A Scottish fishing crew.

'While I accuse men of indolence, I should do great injustice to the women if I did not exempt them from the charge, by whose industry and diligence their families are, in a great measure, supported.'

(The minister of Glenmuick. Inverness Statistical Accounts, 1895)

'An Act was passed by George II, which provided, under penalties, that all serges and fingrams shall be of equal work and fineness from one end of the piece to the other, "also, that all stockings that shall be made in Scotland shall be wrought and made of three threads, and one sort of wool and worsted, and of equal work and fineness throughout, free from left loops, hanging hairs, burnt, or mended holes, and of such shapes and respectively as the pattern which shall be marked by the several Deans of Guild of the chief burghs of the respective counties".

'Notwithstanding this, it is said that the Aberdeen exports became so insufferably bad that the Hollander would not buy the goods at any price. In spite of this falling off of foreign trade, the Braemar Highlanders still made a considerable quantity of saleable home-mades and continued well into the present century to send down to Forfarshire, as far as Dundee and Arbroath, quantities of goods home-made, in the shape of hosiery and such like, and it would almost appear that the present Shetland hosiery is but a survival of an old Scottish industry which took a great hold of the country during the seventeenth and latter half of the last century, but which machinery has rendered unremunerative, and so has destroyed'.

So even in those days there was already a well-established folk tradition. It seems likely that the commercial exploitation of women knitting was an extension of an already existing tradition. The dark blue ganseys that the fishermen wore were not seen as having any worthwhile commercial possibilities since the Fair Isle patterns were more interesting visually, and by then the development of knitting frame technology had superseded the need for hand knitting. Fashion demanded pullovers without patterns, and the frame industry and the subsequent growth in mass production techniques finished the craft of knitting for contract on any scale. Knitting, therefore, continued mainly as a family and community activity, the fisherwives knitting socks for local sale and ganseys for their menfolk.

These images of Scottish fishermen from the district of Fife display on their ganseys a rich mixture of pattern sequencing which has not been deciphered. Close examination should reward your efforts at forming your personal sequence.

Fishermen, St Monans, Fife (1914), enjoying a joke during a hair shaving session.

Fife fishermen pose in their finest ganseys (occasion unknown).

A group of fishing families.

The Journey

From Eyemouth on the Scottish border—where my research begins—
the lifestyle is predominantly inshore fishing, with share boatmen
working the Firth of Forth. On the far (northern) side, the fishing
trade has developed into one of Britain's major industries, though
one that is now in steady decline. The beach landings and the coble
boats have given way to complex harbour systems and keel boats—
nowadays massive seine netters capable of catching tons of fish at
a time. They have a greater catch and distance potential and were
built in their hundreds by the big merchants to catch one fish in
particular—the herring.

In the industry's heyday from the turn of the century to the mid-war
years, the boats followed the herring migration down the east coast of
Scotland and England as far as Yarmouth and Lowestoft. Russian and
Continental markets demanded great quantities of herring—so much
so that the fishermen and their families were away for eight months
of the year. The womenfolk were an essential part in this industry and
needless to say they took their knitting and their patterns with them.
It was their job to gut and pack the fish which their menfolk landed,
and the women brought their knitting to do in the few quiet moments
between landing catches.

Anstruther harbour.

ANSTRUTHER

My search for patterns began in earnest at the Scottish Fisheries Museum at Anstruther in Fife. There was no better place to start, as the museum had set out in graphic detail the history and development of all aspects of the industry and life of the fisherfolk of Scotland. It was also the best place to be introduced to the fishing community, as I had found on many previous occasions that to arrive in an area unannounced wasted a lot of time. It was also a little forward for a stranger in a very close community to bang on doors in the mid-evening rain asking questions about the whereabouts of women knitting traditional patterns. Firstly there was the oddness of the request, and secondly the fact that a man was asking questions about knitting! There still exists the opinion that knitting is exclusively women's work. There is nothing quite like the look on the face of a burly fisherman, sitting over his pint and his dominoes, when interrupted by a question that indicates that you fancy the pattern on his gansey!

Mary Murrey was the first lady to be introduced. She is a local fisherwife whose ready turn of phrase and colourful illumination brought back to life her memories of the old ways. It was soon apparent that due to the collective nature of the Scottish fishing industry—the banding together of boats from many ports on the yearly herring migration—insularity between communities did not exist. The patterns, derived from village to village, were everyone's property; indeed, people took great pride in their ability to 'pinch' one another's patterns, and incorporate them into their own.

The patterns Mary Murrey described were knit up on 'a smooth round wool' (probably Seafields 5-ply worsted) and the pattern configurations were small enough not to include a seam stitch on each half round. The pattern was repeated all round, and great fun was made of any girl who knit up her repeats unequally. As in most other areas, the arms were knit extraordinarily short to stop the wool chafing the skin and causing 'plooks' (salt water boils which scar very nastily). Silk scarves were also worn around the necks to stop chafing—in this part of Scotland they were known as 'ponjees', an obvious derivative of Punjab, their city of origin. Mary explained that the patterns from her area are simple in comparison with the 'norlands' ganseys from further up the coast—and this was found to be true, especially compared with the Hebrides and the 'Foula Froaks' of the Shetlands.

The museum in Anstruther had one or two fine examples of ganseys, but my intention was to find knitters who still practised the craft, in order to see what patterns they were making. Mrs Murrey introduced her friends Mrs Shannon and Mrs Gardner of Cellardyke who were avid knitters. They knitted very simple patterns, usually a repeat of one configuration, which set the tone for the rest of Scotland as far up as Fraserburgh, where the patterns began to be more elaborate.

Most of the knitting was made up in 4-ply because, until recently, the old 5-ply worsted was not available in this part of the country. The use of finer yarns, with more stitches to the inch, made the gansey patterns very intense, with a greater number of pattern repeats. The two ladies knitted up the most popular patterns, though it was apparent that they were not as adventurous as their predecessors, being quite happy to leave large areas plain.

A Fife fishing crew wearing plain working ganseys.

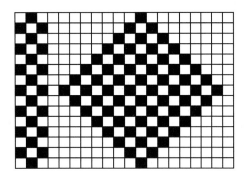

	k	p	k	p	k	p	k	p	k	p	k	p	k	p	k	p	k	p	k	p	k
Round 1	8	1	9	1	1																
Round 2	7	1	1	1	7	1	1	1													
Round 3	6	1	1	1	1	1	7	1	1												
Round 4	5	1	1	1	1	1	1	1	5	1	1	1									
Round 5	4	1	1	1	1	1	1	1	1	1	5	1	1	1							
Round 6	3	1	1	1	1	1	1	1	1	1	1	1	3	1	1	1					
Round 7	2	1	1	1	1	1	1	1	1	1	1	1	1	1	3	1	1				
Round 8	1	1	1	1	1	1	1	1	1	1	1	1	1	1	1	1	1	1	1	1	1
Round 9	2	1	1	1	1	1	1	1	1	1	1	1	1	1	3	1	1				
Round 10	3	1	1	1	1	1	1	1	1	1	1	1	3	1	1	1					
Round 11	4	1	1	1	1	1	1	1	1	1	5	1	1	1							
Round 12	5	1	1	1	1	1	1	1	5	1	1	1									
Round 13	6	1	1	1	1	1	7	1	1												
Round 14	7	1	1	1	7	1	1	1													
Round 15	8	1	9	1	1																

Moss stitch closed diamond with 'fives' seeding,
15 +2 sts x 15 rds plus 3 sts x 2 rds.

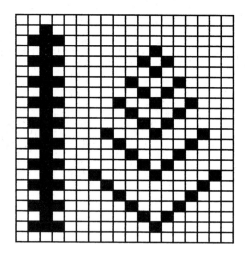

	k	p	k	p	k	p	k	p	k
Round 1	6	1	7	3					
Round 2	5	1	1	1	7	1			
Round 3	4	1	3	1	5	3			
Round 4	3	1	5	1	5	1	1		
Round 5	2	1	7	1	3	3			
Round 6	1	1	4	1	4	1	3	1	1
Round 7	5	1	1	1	6	3			
Round 8	4	1	3	1	6	1	1		
Round 9	3	1	1	1	5	4	3		
Round 10	2	1	3	1	3	1	4	1	1
Round 11	5	1	1	1	6	3			
Round 12	4	1	3	1	6	1	1		
Round 13	3	1	2	1	2	1	4	3	
Round 14	5	1	1	1	7	1	1		
Round 15	6	1	8	1	1				
Round 16	14	3							
Round 17	15	1	1						

Tree of Life with 'fives' seeding,
11 sts + 2 x 17 rds plus 3 sts x 2 rds and 20 rds.

	K	P	K	P	K
Round 1		1	1	1	13
Round 2	1	1	1	1	12
Round 3	2	1	1	1	11
Round 4	3	1	1	1	10
Round 5	4	1	1	1	9
Round 6	5	1	1	1	8
Round 7	6	1	1	1	7
Round 8	7	1	1	1	6
Round 9	8	1	1	1	5
Round 10	9	1	1	1	4
Round 1	10	1	1	1	3
Round 2	11	1	1	1	2
Round 3	12	1	1	1	1
Round 4	11	1	1	1	2
Round 5	10	1	1	1	3
Round 6	9	1	1	1	4
Round 7	8	1	1	1	5
Round 8	7	1	1	1	6
Round 9	6	1	1	1	7
Round 20	5	1	1	1	8
Round 1	4	1	1	1	9
Round 2	3	1	1	1	10
Round 3	2	1	1	1	11
Round 4	1	1	1	1	12

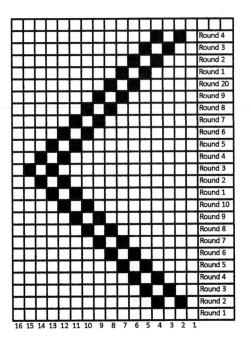

'Road to Crovie', 17 sts and 24 rds.

These photographs of fishermen from Anstruther give an opportunity to closely examine the patterns decorating their ganseys.

Lizzie Guthrie knitting on the
quayside at St Monance, Fife, 1913.

CRUDEN BAY

From Anstruther my journey up the coast continued through St
Andrews and across the Firth of Tay to Dundee, and then up the
coastline to the Auchmithie, Aberdeen and Cruden Bay area.

Cruden Bay has an interesting pattern attributed to it. It is an open
diamond with a cross in the centre repeated in columns six times
over front and back, evening out by repeating the first seven stitches
at the end of each half round. Notice the 'rig and fur' pattern on the
shoulder straps which have been cast off together on the outside.

CRUDEN BAY PATTERN

Size: The size of the gansey if worked as indicated measures for a 41-inch chest.
Wool: 5-ply worsted wool.
Needles: One set of five No. 12 (2¾ mm) extra-long, double-pointed pins, circular twin pins size 12.
Tension: 7 stitches and 10 rows to 1 inch.

Cast on in thumb method 288 sts and distribute evenly over four needles using the wool double. K2, P2 for 4 inches, keeping the wool double for the first five rounds. The pattern now begins.

Your first round will be:

* (P1, K2, P1, K2, P1, K8, P1, K8) repeat * to * 5 more times.

* Repeat from * to * to complete round 1.

The second purl stitch on your first round will be the 'seam' line at both sides of the gansey on the half round and will run throughout the body and arms, forming a basis for the gussets under the arm and the points of division for the armholes. It would be well if you marked this stitch with a length of contrast wool to remind you of your position.

Continue in pattern until 3 inches below your underarm measurement. At this point you must make the increase for the gusset under the arm. Continuing in pattern on the next round increase one knit stitch each side of the centre purl stitch marked with contrast wool. This is the beginning of the gusset which is knit in plain knitting. Increase one knit stitch each side every 4th round until the gusset is 19 sts wide. You are now ready to divide for the front and back, continuing in pattern over two needles up to your required height. Slip the gusset stitches and the stitches for the back onto a holder and work front to

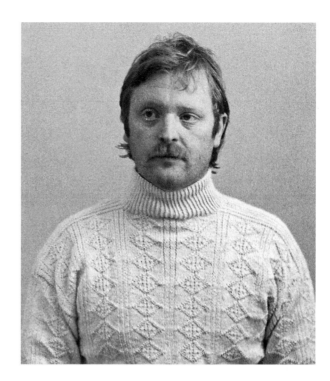

required height, finishing on a complete pattern section. Knit the last 5 rows (3 purl rows and 2 plain rows).

The shoulders

Place centre 39 stitches and stitches for shoulder onto a holder and knit the remaining stitches on the needle in the 'rig and fur' pattern sequence, *ie.* 2 rows plain-facing, 2 rows purl-facing *(see Fig. 13, page 28)* for 10 rows. Place these stitches and the centre stitches onto a holder and repeat the rig and fur pattern for the other shoulder. Place all the stitches onto a holder and pick up stitches for the back and repeat as front. Place shoulders together and cast off together on the outside making a ridge.

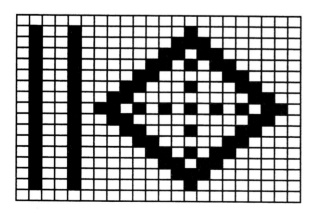

Cruden Bay open diamond with centre cross, 17 sts and 15 rds + seeding.
The pattern is repeated in columns six times in one half round with the seeding repeated on the end of each half round to even pattern.

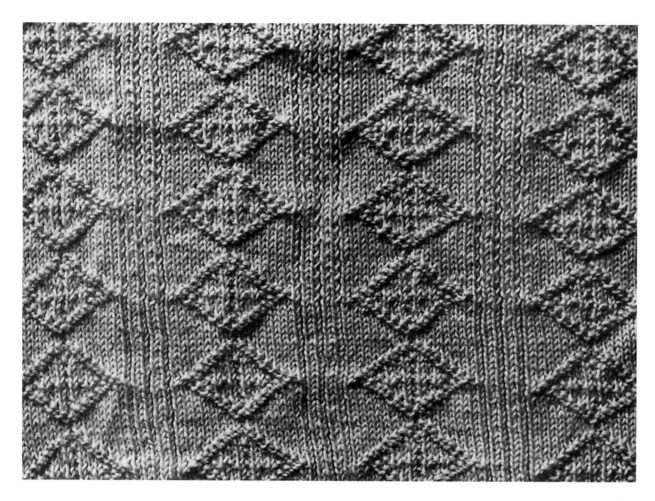

The sleeves

Pick up evenly around the armhole including the gusset stitches. Purl 1 st each side of gusset. Decrease one stitch each side of gusset every 4th round until gusset is worked out. Then decrease on every 6th round until the sleeve has 96 sts, then every 4th round until 60 sts, knit straight until required length. K2, P2 for 3 inches for the cuff. Cast off ribwise.

THE SLEEVE PATTERN: Place tip of diamond at the ridge point of the shoulder and edge of the diamond each side with the plain and purl columns. Knit around the rest of the arm in plain knitting. Work this pattern down 8 inches of the arm, knit 2 rounds of purl and then continue down the rest of the arm in plain knitting.

The neck

Pick up stocking stitch evenly around neck edge and knit collar in K1, P1, working into the back of all rib sts for 3 inches or as preferred. Cast off loosely ribwise.

No sewing up is necessary—your gansey is now finished.

BODDAM

Searching for archive material in national institutions is one way of collecting material, yet nothing can match researching 'in the field'. Introductions in Aberdeen led to a little village, Boddam, just outside Peterhead, and to a Mr and Mrs Stevens, who enthusiastically produced and discussed their large collection, showing off their favourites.

In her first pattern, Kate Stevens has introduced a combination of vertical columns and reversed the normal process of knitting a diamond in moss stitch. She has chosen to knit the surround in moss stitch and let the diamond stand out by virtue of its contrast. She has used a chevron pattern connected by a purl stitch column which has turned the pattern into a vertical herringbone. It is more usual to see this pattern worked horizontally. The two main patterns are separated by a wide ladder pattern, and the shoulder strap has been worked in moss stitch.

MRS STEVEN'S PATTERN NO. 1

Chevron with centre purl stitch (13 sts and 6 rds); seeding (7 sts and 2 rds);
plain diamond with moss surround (13 sts and 12 rds).

	K	P	K	P	K	P	K
Round 1	5	3	5				
Round 2	4	1	1	1	1	1	4
Round 3	3	1	2	1	2	1	3
Round 4	2	1	3	1	3	1	2
Round 5	1	1	4	1	4	1	1
Round 6		1	5	1	5	1	

	K	P	K	P
Round 1	7			
Round 2	1	1	1	1

Seeding.

Chevron with
centre purl stitch.

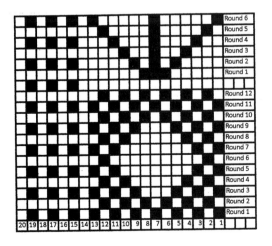

	K	P	K	P	K	P	K	P	K	P	K	P	K	P
Round 1		1	1	1	1	1	1	1	1	1	1	1	1	1
Round 2	1	1	1	1	1	1	1	1	1	1	1	1	1	
Round 3		1	1	1	1	1	3	1	1	1	1	1		
Round 4	1	1	1	1	5	1	1	1	1					
Round 5		1	1	1	7	1	1	1						
Round 6	1	1	9	1	1									
Round 7		1	1	1	7	1	1	1						
Round 8	1	1	1	1	5	1	1	1	1					
Round 9		1	1	1	1	1	3	1	1	1	1	1		
Round 10	1	1	1	1	1	1	1	1	1	1	1	1	1	
Round 11		1	1	1	1	1	1	1	1	1	1	1	1	1
Round 12	1	1	1	1	1	1	1	1	1	1	1	1	1	

Plain diamond with moss stitch surround.

The second pattern is very decorative: a Wheat Ear cable separates a simple open diamond column from a beautifully worked Tree of Life configuration. Mrs Stevens has put in the shoulder strap most ingeniously: she has worked the diamond to complement the main pattern, separating the strap from the yoke by a series of garter rows cast off on the inside.

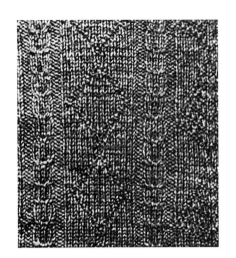

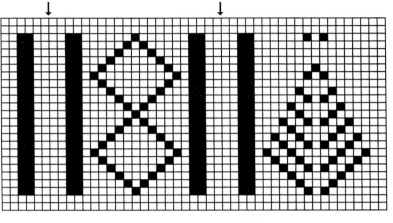

	K	P	K	P	K
Round 1	6	1	6		
Round 2	5	1	1	1	5
Round 3	4	1	3	1	4
Round 4	3	1	5	1	3
Round 5	2	1	7	1	2
Round 6	1	1	9	1	1
Round 7	2	1	7	1	2
Round 8	3	1	5	1	3
Round 9	4	1	3	1	4
Round 10	5	1	1	1	5
Round 11	6	1	6		
Round 12	5	1	1	1	5
Round 13	4	1	3	1	4
Round 14	3	1	5	1	3
Round 15	2	1	7	1	2
Round 16	1	1	9	1	1
Round 17	2	1	7	1	2
Round 18	3	1	5	1	3
Round 19	4	1	3	1	4
Round 20	5	1	1	1	5
Round 21	6	1	6		

	K	P	K	P	K	P	K	P	K
Round 1	6	1	1	1	6				
Round 2	5	1	3	1	5				
Round 3	4	1	5	1	4				
Round 4	3	1	2	1	1	1	2	1	3
Round 5	2	1	2	1	3	1	2	1	2
Round 6	1	1	2	1	5	1	2	1	1
Round 7	3	1	2	1	1	1	2	1	3
Round 8	2	1	2	1	3	1	2	1	2
Round 9	4	1	5	1	4				
Round 10	3	1	2	1	1	1	2	1	3
Round 11	5	1	3	1	5				
Round 12	4	1	5	1	4				
Round 13	6	1	1	1	6				
Round 14	5	1	3	1	5				
Round 15	15								
Round 16	6	1	1	1	6				
Round 17	7	1	7						
Round 18	15								
Round 19	15								
Round 20	15								
Round 21	6	1	1	1	6				

Vertical open diamond, 13 sts and 21 rds; Tree of life, 15 sts and 21 rds; cable 2 sts left, 2 sts right, every 4th rd at arrows.

A Scottish lifeboat crew.

MRS STEVEN'S PATTERN NO. 3

Mrs Stevens' third gansey is a development of the zigzag. She has used the 9-stitch diamond as the basis, repeating one side three times, and has then reversed it, resulting in this very effective small Marriage Line. The seeding pattern separating the main repeat is made up of two columns of purl stitch separating two double stitch cables worked every fifth row, with a very effective herringbone pattern over the shoulder strap.

Triple zigzag, 17 sts & 8 rds.

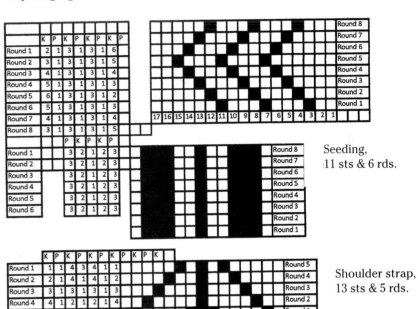

	K	P	K	P	K	P	K	P
Round 1	2	1	3	1	3	1	6	
Round 2	3	1	3	1	3	1	5	
Round 3	4	1	3	1	3	1	4	
Round 4	5	1	3	1	3	1	3	
Round 5	6	1	3	1	3	1	2	
Round 6	5	1	3	1	3	1	3	
Round 7	4	1	3	1	3	1	4	
Round 8	3	1	3	1	3	1	5	

	P	K	P	K	P
Round 1	3	2	1	2	3
Round 2	3	2	1	2	3
Round 3	3	2	1	2	3
Round 4	3	2	1	2	3
Round 5	3	2	1	2	3
Round 6	3	2	1	2	3

Seeding, 11 sts & 6 rds.

	K	P	K	P	K	P	K	P	K	P	K
Round 1	1	1	4	3	4	1	1				
Round 2	2	1	4	1	4	1	2				
Round 3	3	1	3	1	3	1	3				
Round 4	4	1	2	1	2	1	4				
Round 5	5	1	1	1	1	1	5				

Shoulder strap, 13 sts & 5 rds.

MRS STEVEN'S PATTERN NO. 4

The fourth pattern is a pleasant combination of the open diamond and the classic Marriage Line configuration, separated by a 9-stitch ladder pattern.

	K	P	K	P	K	P	K	P	K	P	K	P	
Round 1	7	1	7										Round 13
Round 2	6	1	1	1	6								Round 12
Round 3	5	1	1	1	1	1	5						Round 11
Round 4	4	1	1	1	1	1	1	1	4				Round 10
Round 5	3	1	1	1	3	1	1	1	3				Round 9
Round 6	2	1	1	1	5	1	1	1	2				Round 8
Round 7	1	1	1	1	7	1	1	1	1				Round 7
Round 8	2	1	1	1	5	1	1	1	2				Round 6
Round 9	3	1	1	1	3	1	1	1	3				Round 5
Round 10	4	1	1	1	1	1	1	1	4				Round 4
Round 11	5	1	1	1	1	1	5						Round 3
Round 12	6	1	1	1	6								Round 2
Round 13	7	1	7										Round 1

Double moss open diamond, 15 sts & 14 rds.

	K	P	K	P	K
Round 1	9	1	1	1	1
Round 2	8	1	1	1	2
Round 3	7	1	1	1	3
Round 4	6	1	1	1	4
Round 5	5	1	1	1	5
Round 6	4	1	1	1	6
Round 7	3	1	1	1	7
Round 8	2	1	1	1	8
Round 9	1	1	1	1	9
Round 10	2	1	1	1	8
Round 11	3	1	1	1	7
Round 12	4	1	1	1	6
Round 13	5	1	1	1	5
Round 14	6	1	1	1	4
Round 15	7	1	1	1	3
Round 16	8	1	1	1	2

	P	K	P	K	P
Round 1	2	1	3	1	2
Round 2	2	5	2		
Round 3	2	5	2		
Round 4	2	1	3	1	2

Double moss Marriage Line, 13 sts & 16 rds and ladder pattern, 9 sts & 4 rds.

A gutting crew.

Quayside and warehouses at Peterhead.

PETERHEAD

The major port of Peterhead is important for its proximity to the oil and fishing fields, and as an administrative centre for the inland area. Among the books and artifacts in the local archives was a photographic collection compiled by one of the jobbing photographers of the area, who ran a studio at the turn of the century. Interestingly enough, the collection did not reflect in any detail the local fishing industry. It became evident that the photographer preferred his clients to be the local institutions—banks, public buildings, large stores and eminent politicians—reflecting, one suspects, the prosperity of a fast-rising middle class, photographers included.

Mrs Cow, one of the library assistants, came to the rescue and explained that she was from a fishing family and was herself an avid knitter of ganseys. It was not long, therefore, before I was knee deep in ganseys from her neighbours' and her own collections.

As expected, the patterns were similar to those of Mrs Stevens of Boddam, except that the Tree of Life occurred in greater numbers, either on its own or with the moss stitch diamond. The variations shown give some indication of the various seeding columns separating the major patterns. The cable, so popular on the east coast of England, hardly ever occurred other than as a tiny two stitch double cable.

129

Tree of Life, 13 sts and 16 rds; open diamonds, 13 sts and 10 rds; 2 st cables ever 4th rd at arrows.

	K	P	K	P	K
Round 1	13				
Round 2	5	1	1	1	5
Round 3	4	1	3	1	4
Round 4	3	1	5	1	3
Round 5	2	1	7	1	2
Round 6	1	1	9	1	1
Round 7	5	1	1	1	5
Round 8	4	1	3	1	4
Round 9	3	1	5	1	3
Round 10	2	1	7	1	2
Round 11	5	1	1	1	5
Round 12	4	1	3	1	4
Round 13	3	1	5	1	3
Round 14	5	1	1	1	5
Round 15	4	1	3	1	4
Round 16	13				
Round 17	5	1	1	1	5

Tree of Life, 13 sts and 17 rds.

	K	P	K	P	K	P	K	P	K	P	K	P	K
Round 1	6	1	6										
Round 2	5	1	1	1	5								
Round 3	4	1	1	1	1	1	4						
Round 4	3	1	1	1	1	1	1	1	3				
Round 5	2	1	1	1	1	1	1	1	1	1	2		
Round 6	1	1	1	1	1	1	1	1	1	1	1	1	1
Round 7	2	1	1	1	1	1	1	1	1	1	2		
Round 8	3	1	1	1	1	1	1	1	3				
Round 9	4	1	1	1	1	1	4						
Round 10	5	1	1	1	5								
Round 11	6	1	6										
Round 12	13												

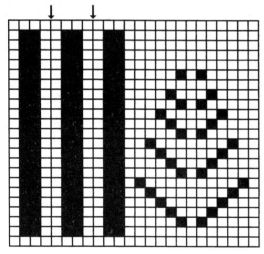

Diamond, 13 sts and 12 rds.

A Peterhead keel boat crew.

Common seeding patterns used in this
area as minimum pattern separators.

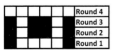

			cable			cable			Round 4
									Round 3
			cable			cable			Round 2
									Round 1

		P	K	P	K	P	K	P	
Round 1		2	2	2	2	2	2		Round 1
Round 2		2	C	2	C	2			Round 2

Seeding 1, 10 sts. Cabled every
alternate round.

					Round 4
					Round 3
					Round 2
					Round 1

		P	K	P	K	P	K	P	
Round 1		1	4	1					Round 1
Round 2		1	1	2	1	1			Round 2
Round 3		1	1	2	1	1			Round 3

Seeding 2, 6 sts and 3 rd.

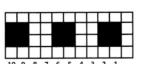

10 9 8 7 6 5 4 3 2 1

		P	K	P	K	P	K	P	
Round 1		8							Round 1
Round 2			2	1	2	1	2	Round 2
Round 3			2	1	2	1	2	Round 3

Seeding 3, 8 sts and 3 rds.

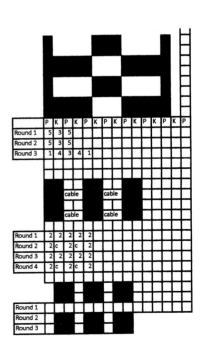

		P	K	P	K	P	K	P	K	P	K	P	K	P	K	P
Round 1		5		3		5											
Round 2		5		3		5											
Round 3		1		4		3		4		1							

| | | | cable | | | cable | | | |
| | | | cable | | | cable | | | |

		P	K	P	K	P	K	P	
Round 1		2	2	2	2	2			
Round 2		2	c	2	c	2			
Round 3		2	2	2	2	2			
Round 4		2	c	2	c	2			

			Round 1
			Round 2
			Round 3

131

MORAY FIRTH

Lily McKay's Horizontal Trellis

Refer to page 29 for Lily's description of how to knit a gansey.

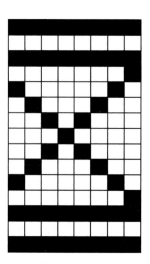

	P	K	P	K	P	K
Round 1	Purl round					
Round 2	Knit round					
Round 3	Purl round					
Round 4	1	7				
Round 5		1	1	5	1	
Round 6		2	1	3	1	1
Round 7		3	1	1	1	2
Round 8		4	1	3		
Round 9		3	1	1	1	2
Round 10		2	1	3	1	1
Round 11		1	1	5	1	
Round 12	1	7				
Round 13	Purl round					
Round 14	Knit round					
Round 15	Purl round					

Fraserburgh harbour.

INVERALLOCHY

An introduction to Billy Edwards and his wife in Inverallochy, near Fraserburgh, revealed many more patterns. Sadly, Mrs Edwards was blind and no longer made up her patterns, but she was enthusiastic in their description and soon had Mr Edwards posing in his best in the garden—which, incidentally, led right onto the sands. It would be impossible to live any closer to the shore. The whole village was set out in this manner, as though the beach were the garden, and the sea the main highway.

Mrs Edwards' pattern repeats the classic zigzag. Where it departs from the norm is that the seeding between the main patterns takes on equal importance. The 'Marriage Lines' have been separated by four 2-stitch cables. As is usual for these 'modern' ganseys, the arms are knit plain for the purpose of wearing a jacket.

MRS EDWARDS' PATTERN NO. 1

Marriage Lines,15 sts and 20 rds; 2 st cables every 4th rd at arrows.

	K	P	K	P	K	P	
Round 1	1	1	1	1	1	11	Round 1
Round 2	2	1	1	1	1	10	Round 2
Round 3	3	1	1	1	1	9	Round 3
Round 4	4	1	1	1	1	8	Round 4
Round 5	5	1	1	1	1	7	Round 5
Round 6	6	1	1	1	1	6	Round 6
Round 7	7	1	1	1	1	5	Round 7
Round 8	8	1	1	1	1	4	Round 8
Round 9	9	1	1	1	1	3	Round 9
Round 10	10	1	1	1	1	2	Round 10
Round 11	11	1	1	1	1	1	Round 11
Round 12	10	1	1	1	1	3	Round 12
Round 13	9	1	1	1	1	3	Round 13
Round 14	8	1	1	1	1	4	Round 14
Round 15	7	1	1	1	1	5	Round 15
Round 16	6	1	1	1	1	6	Round 16
Round 17	5	1	1	1	1	7	Round 17
Round 18	4	1	1	1	1	9	Round 18
Round 19	3	1	1	1	1	9	Round 19
Round 20	2	1	1	1	1	10	Round 20

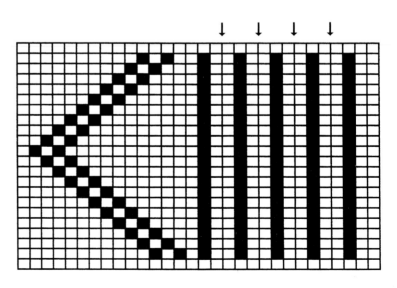

MRS EDWARD'S PATTERN NO. 2

Mrs Edward's second pattern is an elegant trellis and ladder configuration, creatively completed by echoing the major pattern on the shoulder panels

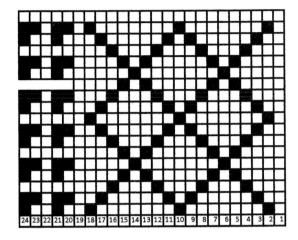

Billy Edwards.

	K	P	K	P	K	P	K	P	K	P	K	P	K	P	K
Round 1	1	1	7	1	7	1	1				1	1	2	1	1
Round 2	2	1	5	1	1	1	5	1	2			2	1	2	
Round 3	3	1	3	1	3	1	3	1	3		5				
Round 4	4	1	1	1	5	1	1	1	5		1	1	2	1	1
Round 5	5	1	7	1	5							2	1	2	
Round 6	4	1	1	1	5	1	1	1	5		5				
Round 7	3	1	3	1	3	1	3	1	3		1	1	2	1	1
Round 8	2	1	5	1	1	1	5	1	2			2	1	2	

Trellis, 19 sts & 8 rds with seeding variation, 5 sts & 3 rds.

Billy and Mrs Edwards' seeding patterns employed between major patterns,

Twist cable every other round

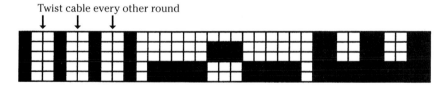

P	K	P	K	P	K	P	K	P	
1	2	1	2	1	2	1	2	1	Round 1
									Round 2
									Round 3
									Round 4
									Round 5

Basket stitch: 2 knit sts cable and purl, 13 sts and 1 rd.

P	K	P	K	P
5	3	5		
5	3	5		
1	4	3	4	1
1	4	3	4	1

Ladder, 13 sts and 4 rds.

	P	K	P	K	P
Round 1	10				
Round 2	10				
Round 3	2	2	2	2	2
Round 4	2	2	2	2	2
Round 5	2	2	2	2	2

Ladder, 10 sts and 5 rds.

Billy Edwards, detail of shoulder panel.

	K	P	K	P	K	P	K	P	K	P	K	P	K	P	K	P	K	P	K
Round 1	9	1	9																
Round 2	8	1	1	1	8														
Round 3	7	1	3	1	7														
Round 4	6	1	1	1	1	1	1	1	6										
Round 5	5	1	3	1	3	1	5												
Round 6	4	1	1	1	1	1	1	1	1	1	1	1	4						
Round 7	3	1	3	1	3	1	3	1	3										
Round 8	2	1	1	1	1	1	1	1	1	1	1	1	1	1	1	1	2		
Round 9	1	1	3	1	3	1	3	1	3	1	1								
Round 10	2	1	1	1	1	1	1	1	1	1	1	1	1	1	1	1	2		
Round 11	3	1	3	1	3	1	3	1	3										
Round 12	4	1	1	1	1	1	1	1	1	1	1	1	4						
Round 13	5	1	3	1	3	1	5												
Round 14	6	1	1	1	1	1	1	1	6										
Round 15	7	1	3	1	7														
Round 16	8	1	1	1	8														

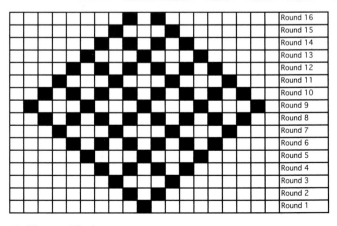

Trellis diamond, 19 sts x 16 rds

BANFF PATTERN

Double moss diamond columns 18 sts & 16 rds with a centre set of three 'fives' columns, 15 sts & 2 rds

Size: The size of this gansey if worked as indicated measures for a 38/40-inch chest.
Wool: 5-ply worsted wool.
Needles: One set of five No. 12 (2¾ mm) double pointed pins (14″ long) or circular needle (40″).
Tension: 7 sts and 10 rows to the inch.

Cast on 294 sts evenly over 4 needles using the wool double in the thumb method. K2, P2 for 4" keeping the wool double for the first five rounds. On completion of the welt, knit the first 8 rounds of the body in plain knitting and establish 1 knit st at each side of the gansey on the half round; mark with a length of contrast wool. This will be your seam line and it runs throughout the body and down the arms, forming a basis for the gusset under the arm and the point of division for knitting the armholes. It is also good practice to mark centre back and centre front stitches to help establish your pattern. The pattern now begins.

Your first round will be: 3 sets of 'fives" (P1, K1, P1, K3, P1, (**K1**), P1, K3, P1, k1, P1) (15 sts.), where the bold K1 is the stitch you identified as the half round. Then start the double moss diamond, K8, P2, K8 (18 sts.). Now repeat from begining 3 more times: P1, K1, P1, K3, P1, K1, P1, K3, P1, K1, P1, K8, P2, K8 (33 sts) P1, K1, P1, K3, P1, K1, P1, K3, P1, K1, P1, K8, P2, K8 (33 sts) P1, K1, P1,K3, P1, K1, P1, K3, P1, K1, P1, K8, P2, K8 (33 sts) to complete half round. Repeat completely, to complete one round. Continue in pattern, following the chart below until 3″ (7 cm) below your underarm measurement.

The gusset increases now begin, by increasing one knit stitch both sides of the marked centre stitch, on the next and every 4th round until the gusset is 19 sts wide. At this point divide for front and back by slipping gusset stitches and stitches for back onto a holder. Continue in pattern over two needles up the front to the required height. Finish on a complete pattern. Work over 57 sts in double moss stitch, leave rest of stitches on holder. This forms the shoulder. Continue for 10 rows. Knit the last row. Leave on holder and include

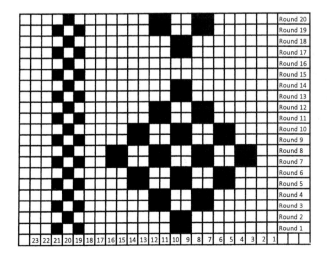

137

51 sts for the neck. Work the double moss on the other shoulder. Leave all stitches on holder. Pick up the stitches for the back, leaving the gusset stitches on a holder; rejoin wool and work up in pattern as the front including the shoulders. Place shoulders together and cast off together on the inside.

The sleeves

Pick up 140 sts evenly around armhole (more if necessary), including the gussets. Pl at each side of gusset. Decrease 1 st either side of the gusset every 4th round until the gusset is worked out. Decrease 1 st on each side every 6th round until 96 sts; then every 4th round until 60 sts (adjust for width and length if necessary).

The pattern is worked for the first 8″ down the arm ending with 2 rounds of purl. The rest of the arm is knit plain. Place the tip of the diamond at the centre of the shoulder and pattern both sides with the moss stitch columns. Knit round the rest of the arm in plain knitting to keep the arm from being too bulky.

The cuff

K2, P2 for 3" and cast off loosely ribwise.

The neck

Pick up evenly centre stitches and the shoulder saddles—124/126 sts (adjust as needed). K1, P1 rib, working into the back of all rib stitches for 5″ or as preferred. Cast off loosely ribwise.

Crovie village in the Bay of Gamrie, Banffshire, showing the typical layout of a fishing community at the shore's edge. The houses have given up the beautiful sea views—for comfort and security, the gable ends face the onslaught of rain, wind and heavy seas.

FRASERBURGH

Fraserburgh owes its living to fishing and there was no difficulty finding gansey knitters, although it was necessary to visit the smaller villages surrounding Fraserburgh since it was the older generation that practised and they lived away from the port. Introductions and directions led to the parish of Gamrie in Banffshire, and to the delightful villages of Gordonstoun and Crovie in the Bay of Gamrie, each built around 1730 for about 100 inhabitants.

In Gordonstoun and Crovie the two Mrs Wests and Christine Wiseman showed me their collections. They remarked how nice it was to see someone else interested in their craft, and explained that they were now using patterns collected in a delightful book they had been given. Imagine the surprise on all sides when it was discovered that the book was my own! It made the day, and over lunch they told of their lives as fisherwives and their history of knitting.

The patterns in their collection were extensive and the influence widespread. They took their craft seriously and all were able to knit extremely fast using knitting belts, making up on average about 'two cuts' a night, 4 oz. The patterns they made now included a lot of Aran stitches, so we had to delve deep into their cupboards to find the earliest patterns they could remember doing. Those are the ones shown here.

These early patterns were all worked in 4-ply on size 13 needles, making very fine and detailed configurations. The half diamond 'flag' pattern worked in solid purl is a very old pattern: it can be seen a lot on the North East coast of England around Whitby and Scarborough, where local knitters have adopted it as their own. At some time the Scottish fisher lassies will have passed the pattern on when visiting the port on their yearly visit following the herring migration. The Tree of Life pattern is one of many variations—it contains seven branches placed very tightly together. This pattern has come from the Fair Isle tradition in which the

Scottish fisher lassies packing herring on the south dene, Great Yarmouth.

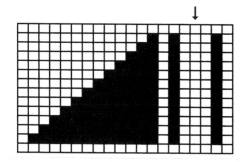

	K	P	K	P	K	P	K
Round 1		1	3	1	1	12	1
Round 2		1	3	1	1	11	2
Round 3		1	3	1	1	10	3
Round 4		1	3	1	1	9	4
Round 5		1	3	1	1	8	5
Round 6		1	3	1	1	7	6
Round 7		1	3	1	1	6	7
Round 8		1	3	1	1	5	8
Round 9		1	3	1	1	4	9
Round 10		1	3	1	1	3	10
Round 1		1	3	1	1	2	11
Round 2		1	3	1	1	1	12

Half flag, 12 sts and 12 rds; 3 st cable every 4th rd at arrow.

pattern is worked to mask the decreases on the shoulder shaping: the last stitch of the branch is judiciously placed where the decreasing occurs. The Anchor appears for the first time along this stretch of coast and there is an infinite variety of shapes, including this simple variation. The remaining patterns are a small open diamond and a 'heapy'.

The ladies explained their life as fisherwives. In the local industry, women played an essential part until the end of the last war. Their job was to gut and pack the fish for export, but for most of this work they received no pay, as they were considered partners to the fishermen. They worked in crews of three and followed the fishing fleets from Shetland and Outer Hebrides down to Lowestoft and Yarmouth, living in huts on the quayside on the islands and in lodgings on the mainland.

When they were paid, they each received 15s a week and 1s for each barrel packed. On a good day they would manage 20 barrels, working almost continuously from six in the morning until two the next morning, breaking off only when waiting for a batch of fish to be off loaded. This yearly tour began on the 28th May and lasted until 28th November. At the end of the season many weeks were spent mending the nets—work that was finished as quickly as possible, since each fisherman was responsible for his own net and during this time they received no income. The end result was that by the time the nets were finished, the income earned on the tour had all but disappeared. The general consensus in the village was that life was pretty easy nowadays.

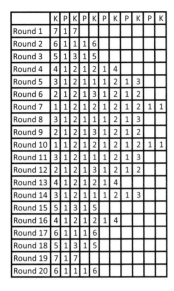

	K	P	K	P	K	P	K	P	K	P	K
Round 1	7	1	7								
Round 2	6	1	1	1	6						
Round 3	5	1	3	1	5						
Round 4	4	1	2	1	2	1	4				
Round 5	3	1	2	1	1	1	2	1	3		
Round 6	2	1	2	1	3	1	2	1	2		
Round 7	1	1	2	1	2	1	2	1	2	1	1
Round 8	3	1	2	1	1	1	2	1	3		
Round 9	2	1	2	1	3	1	2	1	2		
Round 10	1	1	2	1	2	1	2	1	2	1	1
Round 11	3	1	2	1	1	1	2	1	3		
Round 12	2	1	2	1	3	1	2	1	2		
Round 13	4	1	2	1	2	1	4				
Round 14	3	1	2	1	1	1	2	1	3		
Round 15	5	1	3	1	5						
Round 16	4	1	2	1	2	1	4				
Round 17	6	1	1	1	6						
Round 18	5	1	3	1	5						
Round 19	7	1	7								
Round 20	6	1	1	1	6						

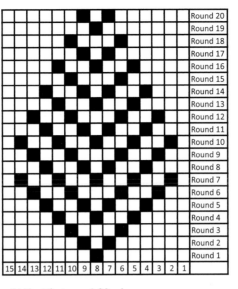

Tree of Life 15 sts and 20 rds.

	K	P	K	P	K	P	K	P
Round 1	7	1	7					
Round 2	6	3	6					
Round 3	5	5	5					
Round 4	4	1	5	1	4			
Round 5	3	1	3	1	3	1	3	
Round 6	2	1	9	1	2			
Round 7	1	4	2	1	2	4	1	
Round 8	2	2	7	2	2			
Round 9	7	1	7					
Round 10	15							
Round 11	7	1	7					
Round 12	15							
Round 13	7	1	7					
Round 14	15							
Round 15	7	1	7					
Round 16	3	9	3					
Round 17	3	9	3					
Round 18	7	1	7					
Round 19	6	1	1	6				
Round 20	15							

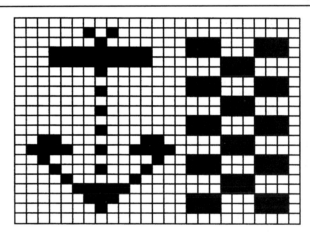

Anchor, 15 sts and 21 rds.

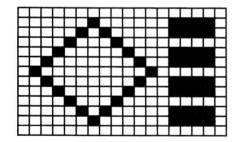

	K	P	K	P	K	P
Round 1	13					
Round 2	6	1	6			
Round 3	5	1	1	1	5	
Round 4	4	1	3	1	4	
Round 5	3	1	5	1	3	
Round 6	2	1	7	1	2	
Round 7	1	1	9	1	1	
Round 8	2	1	7	1	2	
Round 9	3	1	5	1	3	
Round 10	4	1	3	1	4	
Round 11	5	1	1	1	5	
Round 12	6	1	6			

Open diamond, 13 sts and 11 rds.

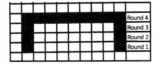

	p	k	p
Round 4	9		
Round 3	1	7	1
Round 2	1	7	1
Round 1	1	7	1

Ladder, 11 sts & 4 rds.

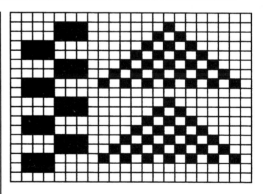

	K	P	K	P	K	P	K	P	K	P	K	P	K	P
Round 1	15													
Round 2	1	1	1	1	1	1	1	1	1	1	1	1	1	
Round 3	2	1	1	1	1	1	1	1	1	1	2			
Round 4	3	1	1	1	1	1	1	1	3					
Round 5	4	1	1	1	1	1	4							
Round 6	5	1	1	1	1	5								
Round 7	6	1	1	1	6									
Round 8	7	1	7											

Moss triangle heapy.

141

Wick.

WICK

In this fishing port close to the northern tip of Scotland, the industry relates more to the nearby nuclear power station and the oil industry than the more traditional crafts. There is a small fishing fleet, but the influence of the fishing is in deep decline. Although the fishing families continue to live in the area, it was difficult to find examples of knitting that were different in design and aspect from the others I have already documented. The local archive, however, revealed an amazing photograph of a local boat crew *(opposite)*. There was no information about the picture. One may presume, however, that the men had been presented with a cup for some significant activity—the biggest catch, perhaps, or a dramatic rescue. The men are wearing distinctive gansey patterns, all heavily worked. They are supreme examples, surpassed only by the patterns of the Hebrides. I have documented the major ones.

A Wick keel boat crew.

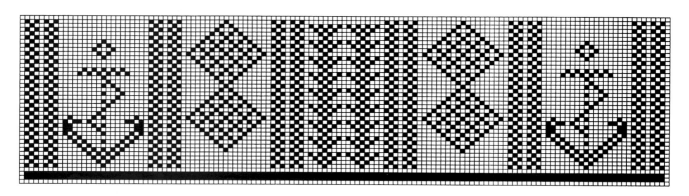

Wick crew, back left: Anchor, 19 sts and 32 rds; trellis diamond, 19 sts and 16 rds; heapy, 17 sts and 4 rds.

	K	P	K	P	K	P	K	P	K	P	K	P	K	P	K	P	K	P	K
Round 1	9	1	9																
Round 2	8	1	1	1	8														
Round 3	7	1	3	1	7														
Round 4	6	1	1	1	1	1	1	6											
Round 5	5	1	3	1	3	1	5												
Round 6	4	1	1	1	1	1	1	1	1	1	4								
Round 7	3	1	3	1	3	1	3	1	3										
Round 8	2	1	1	1	1	1	1	1	1	1	1	1	1	1	1	2			
Round 9	1	1	3	1	3	1	3	1	3	1	1								
Round 10	2	1	1	1	1	1	1	1	1	1	1	1	1	1	1	2			
Round 11	3	1	3	1	3	1	3	1	3										
Round 12	4	1	1	1	1	1	1	1	1	1	4								
Round 13	5	1	3	1	3	1	5												
Round 14	6	1	1	1	1	1	1	6											
Round 15	7	1	3	1	7														
Round 16	8	1	1	1	8														

Trellis diamond.

	K	P	K	P	K	P	K	P	K	P	K	P	K	P	K	P	K	P
Round 1	9	1	9															
Round 2	8	1	1	1	8													
Round 3	7	1	1	1	1	1	7											
Round 4	6	1	1	1	1	1	1	1	6									
Round 5	5	1	1	1	1	1	1	1	1	1	5							
Round 6	4	1	1	1	5	1	1	1	4									
Round 7	3	1	1	1	3	1	3	1	1	1	3							
Round 8	2	1	1	1	9	1	1	1	2									
Round 9	1	1	1	1	5	1	5	1	1	1	1							
Round 10	1	2	7	1	5	2	1											
Round 1	1	2	6	1	1	4	2	1										
Round 2	1	1	1	2	7	1	1	2	1	1	1							
Round 3	2	1	6	1	1	1	4	1	2									
Round 4	10	1	8															
Round 5	9	1																
Round 6	8	1																
Round 7	7	1	1	1														
Round 8	6	1																
Round 9	5	1	3	1														
Round 20	6	1																
Round 1	7	1	1	1														
Round 2	8	1																
Round 3	9	1																
Round 4	4	1	1	1	1	1	1	1	1	1	1	4						
Round 5	5	1	1	1	1	1	1	1	1	5								
Round 6	19																	
Round 7	19																	
Round 8	9	1	9															
Round 9	8	1	1	1	8													
Round 30	7	1	3	1	7													
Round 1	8	1	1	1	8													
Round 2	9	1	9															

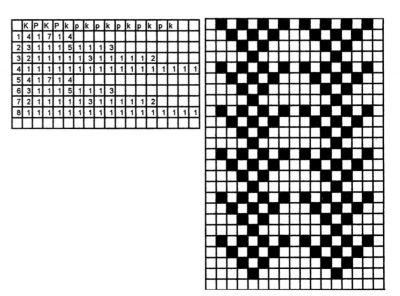

												Round 12
												Round 11
												Round 30
												Round 9
												Round 8
												Round 7
												Round 6
												Round 5
												Round 4
												Round 3
												Round 2
												Round 1
												round 20
												Round 9
												Round 8
												Round 7
												Round 6
												Round 5
												Round 4
												Round 3
												Round 2
												Round 1
												Round 10
												Round 9
												Round 8
												Round 7
												Round 6
												Round 5
												Round 4
												Round 3
												Round 2
												Round 1

9 8 7 6 5 4 3 2 1 10 9 8 7 6 5 4 3 2 1

Anchor.

	P	K	P	k	p	k
	1	3	1	1		
	1	1	1	1	1	1

	K	P	K	P	k	p	k	p	k	p	k	p	k
1	4	1	7	1	4								
2	3	1	1	1	5	1	1	1	3				
3	2	1	1	1	1	1	3	1	1	1	1	2	
4	1	1	1	1	1	1	1	1	1	1	1	1	1	1	1	1	1	1	1
5	4	1	7	1	4								
6	3	1	1	1	5	1	1	1	3				
7	2	1	1	1	1	1	3	1	1	1	1	2	
8	1	1	1	1	1	1	1	1	1	1	1	1	1	1	1	1	1	1	1

'Fives' seeding, 7 sts & 2 rds and heapy, 7 sts & 4 rds vertical combination.

144

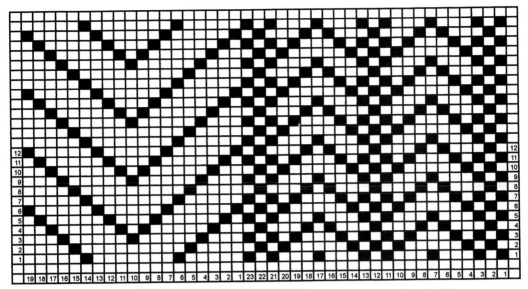

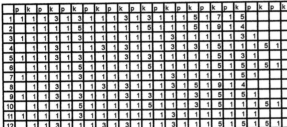

Wick crew, back right: Chevron variations set within 3 st seeding columns: variation 1: small chevrons, 23 sts & 8 rds; variation 2: 19 sts & 12 rds.

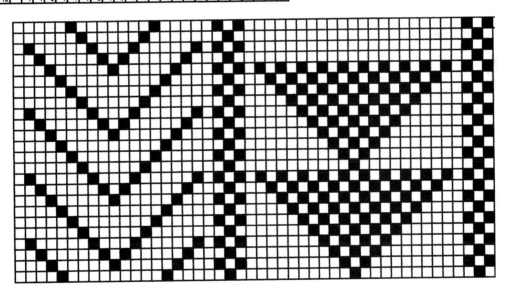

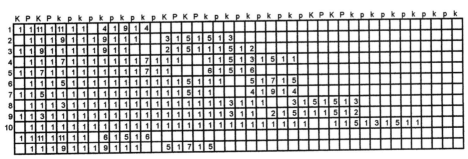

Wick crew, seated left and standing centre: chevron, 19 sts and 12 rds; reverse heapy, 21 sts and 10 rds separated by 'fives' seeding.

WICK PATTERN — MARRIAGE LINES

The size of the gansey if worked as indicated measures for a 40/42-inch (102/107 cm) chest.

Wool: 5-ply worsted wool.
Needles: One set of five No. 12 (2¾ mm) double-pointed pins.
7 stitches and 10 rows to 1 inch (2.5 cm); 28 sts and 40 rounds to 4 inches (10 cm).

Cast on thumb method 282 sts and distribute evenly over four needles using the wool double. K2, P2 for 4 inches (10 cm) keeping the wool double for the first five rounds. The pattern begins immediately. The sts shown as bold in the first round will form a 'seam' line which runs throughout the body and down the arms, and the points of division for the armholes. (Mark these sts with a length of contrast wool to remind you of their position exactly on the half round.)

Your first round will be:
P1, K1, P1, K1, (P1, K1, P1, K1, P1, K7, P3, K4, P1, K1, P1, K1, P1, K4, P3, K7) 3 times ending P1, K1, P1, K1, P1, K7, P3, K4, P1, K1, **P1, K1** to complete half round. **P1**, K1, P1, K1, (P1, K1, P1, K1, P1, K4, P3, K7, P1, K1, P1, K1, P1, K7, P3, K4) 3 times ending P1, K1, P1, K1, P1, K4, P3, K7, P1, K1, **P1, K1** to complete one round.

Refer to the chart and diagram below and continue the pattern until you are 3 inches (7.5 cm) below your underarm measurement. At this point you must make the increase under the arms to form the gusset. This is knitted in plain stitch throughout. **Locate sts marked in bold** and increase one st both sides of the centre st marked, on the next and every 4th round until the gusset is 19 sts wide. You are now ready to divide for the front and back, continuing in pattern over two needles, to your required height slip gusset sts and sts for back onto a holder and work up the front finishing on a complete section.

The shoulder

Make a 'rig and fur' shoulder pattern as follows. After reaching required height knit 2 rows in garter stitch and 2 rows in plain stocking stitch. Place centre 39 sts and sts for shoulder onto a holder and knit the other shoulder in 2 rows purl and 2 rows plain for 12 rows. Leave on holder. Repeat for the other shoulder, work the back as the front.

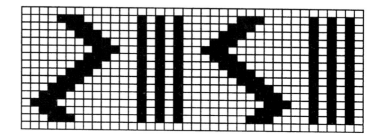

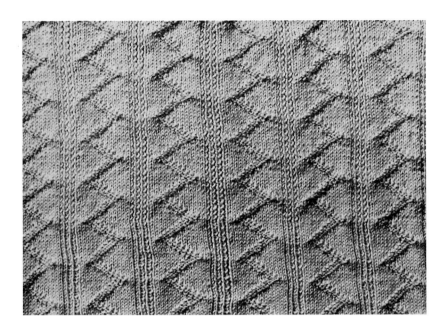

The sleeves

Pick up evenly around the armhole 140 sts (adjust to size) including gusset sts. Purl one st each side of gusset, picked up sts. Decrease one knit st either side of seam sts every 4th round until the gusset is worked out. Then decrease every 6th round until 96 sts, then every 4th until 60 sts (adjust width and length).

THE SLEEVE PATTERN: Place cable at centre of shoulder and work over pattern both sides of cable, ending on the column of plain and purl. Knit round the rest of the arm in plain knitting. This stops the arm becoming too bulky.

The cuff

K2, P2 for 3 inches (7.5 cm) casting off loosely ribwise.

The neck

Pick up evenly centre sts and the shoulder saddles 124/6 (adjust) K1, P1 rib working into the back of all rib sts for 5 inches (13 cm) or as preferred. Cast off loosely ribwise.

JOHN ROBERTSON   ANDREW GROAT   HENRY GROAT

Six of the crew of the Papa Westray boat
who gallantly rescued eight of the crew of
the S.S. Badger, wrecked on Bow Skerry,
Westray, 26th May 1906.

THE ORKNEYS

From Wick the journey for gansey patterns continued from the
Scottish mainland across the Pentland Firth to reach the Orkneys,
North and South Ronaldsay, Stronsay, Hoy and the mainland. Here
knitting continued, though two-colour work began to be more in
evidence than the plain ganseys. The indigenous sheep of these
islands produce fleece of many shades, which have been incorporated
in the Fair Isle designs *(p. 185).*

The photograph *(above)* of John Hourston's crew from Papa
Westray provides some clue to the patterns of this area. John's gansey
(back row, right) is made up of horizontal bands and ridges in garter
and single moss stitch. Each horizontal pattern is separated by three
bands of purl stitch knitted over two rounds, followed by four rounds
of plain knitting. The panels are moss stitch variations.

If one looks closely, one can see that he has had the bottom half of
his sleeves replaced—one of the many advantages of knitting from
the shoulder to the cuff. In modern patterns the technique is usually
to knit upwards from the cuff, which means that the sleeve is almost
impossible to repair other than by darning, which tends to look
unsightly.

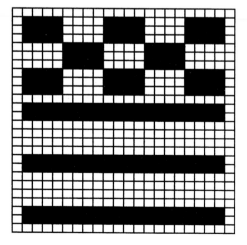

John Hourston.

SHETLAND AND THE HEBRIDES
FOULA

From the Orkneys it is a small step to the islands of Foula, Fair Isle and the Shetland Isles. Throughout these islands the major method of knitting is the multi-coloured technique, with the exception of Foula (population 40), and further west on the Hebrides where they still knit up what are called 'fisher froaks'. The inhabitants of Foula survived through self sufficiency in the style of the crofter. They had portions of land for crops, supplemented by fishing. Little money was earned, apart from the contract knitting.

It is not unusual to find that it is people coming from outside a community who are most interested in the traditions of the places they visit. When they settle in such places they tend to revive old customs which local people take for granted. Miss Vera Johnston and Miss Liz Booth are two such people. Both are 'outsiders'—and both have spent many years living on the islands.

Miss Johnston has earned her living in the classic 'cottage industry' style, contract knitting the Shetland and Fair Isles patterns. As a knitter and observer of life she has kept her eyes open, and over the years has collected hundreds of patterns. Her pattern for the Foula froak is from the house of Dyke on the south of the island. She explained that variations in the pattern occurred from family to family—through the use of plaits instead of cables and of every possible combination of the large centre diamond: moss, double moss, netting, diamond within diamond and central cross.

Miss Booth, a district nurse for the islands for a number of years, comes originally from Manchester. Between emergency visits by small boat from island to island, she knits avidly and was able to provide a pattern almost exactly the same as Miss Johnston's. This came from Mrs Janet Peterson of Sloag, who mentioned that it was

A fisher lassie of Foula about to fill her 'kishie' (basket) with peat, knitting while she walks.

Mrs. Peterson's pattern, 31 sts & 30 rds.

	K	P	K	P	K	P	K	P	K	P	K	P	K	P	K	P	K	P	K	P	K	P	K	P	
Round 1	15	1	15																						Round 1
Round 2	14	1	1	1	14																				Round 2
Round 3	13	1	3	1	13																				Round 3
Round 4	12	1	2	1	2	1	12																		Round 4
Round 5	11	1	2	1	2	1	2	1	11																Round 5
Round 6	10	1	7	1	3	1	2	1	10																Round 6
Round 7	9	1	2	1	2	1	2	1	2	1	9														Round 7
Round 8	8	1	2	1	2	1	1	1	2	1	2	1	8												Round 8
Round 9	7	1	2	1	2	1	3	1	2	1	2	1	7												Round 9
Round 10	6	1	2	1	2	1	2	1	2	1	2	1	6												Round 10
Round 1	5	1	2	1	2	1	2	1	1	1	2	1	2	1	2	1	5								Round 1
Round 2	4	1	2	1	2	1	2	1	1	1	2	1	2	1	2	1	4								Round 2
Round 3	3	1	2	1	2	1	2	1	1	1	1	1	1	1	2	1	2	1	2	1	3				Round 3
Round 4	2	1	2	1	2	1	2	1	1	1	1	1	1	1	1	1	2	1	2	1	2	1	2		Round 4
Round 5	1	1	2	1	2	1	2	1	1	1	1	1	2	1	1	1	2	1	2	1	2	1	1	1	Round 5
Round 6	2	1	2	1	2	1	2	1	1	1	1	1	1	1	1	1	2	1	2	1	2	1	2		Round 6
Round 7	3	1	2	1	2	1	2	1	1	1	1	1	2	1	2	1	2	1	3						Round 7
Round 8	4	1	2	1	2	1	2	1	1	1	2	1	2	1	2	1	4								Round 8
Round 9	5	1	2	1	2	1	2	1	1	1	2	1	2	1	5										Round 9
Round 20	6	1	2	1	2	1	2	1	2	1	2	1	6												Round 20
Round 1	7	1	2	1	2	1	3	1	2	1	2	1	7												Round 1
Round 2	8	1	2	1	2	1	1	1	2	1	2	1	8												Round 2
Round 3	9	1	2	1	2	1	2	1	9																Round 3
Round 4	10	1	2	1	3	1	2	1	10																Round 4
Round 5	11	1	2	1	1	1	2	1	11																Round 5
Round 6	12	1	2	1	2	1	12																		Round 6
Round 7	13	1	3	1	13																				Round 7
Round 8	14	1	1	1	14																				Round 8
Round 9	15	1	15																						Round 9
Round 30																									Round 30
Round 1																									Round 1

Chart (right):

Round labels (top to bottom): Round 1, Round 30, Round 9, Round 8, Round 7, Round 6, Round 5, Round 4, Round 3, Round 2, Round 1, Round 20, Round 9, Round 8, Round 7, Round 6, Round 5, Round 4, Round 3, Round 2, Round 1, Round 10, Round 9, Round 8, Round 7, Round 6, Round 5, Round 4, Round 3, Round 2, Round 1

Column numbers (bottom): 30 9 8 7 6 5 4 3 2 1 20 9 8 7 6 5 4 3 2 1 10 9 8 7 6 5 4 3 2 1

Mr and Mrs Cunwen of Foula, 1902. They probably belong to the main village community, since their house is substantial and slate-roofed, rather than in the classic croft style with a peat roof.

the practice to knit the froak over seven or eight glove wires to make the stitches extremely tight and waterproof.

Like most of the ganseys from the north, the first ten inches (25 cm) of the frock are knit plain and then the pattern is first worked in bands of purl stitch. A horizontal panel of moss stitch diamonds is then worked, edged again by bands of purl stitch. The vertical columns feature a large diamond pattern in the centre worked over 29 stitches, which is decorated by moss stitch and plain knitting to pick out three open diamonds surrounding a central closed diamond. The rest of the gansey is patterned with cables and ladder patterns.

FOULA PATTERN

The size of the gansey if worked as indicated measures for a 40/42 inch (102/107 cm) chest.
Wool: 5-ply worsted wool.
Needles: One set of five No. 12 (2¾ mm) double-pointed pins.
Tension: 7 stitches and 10 rows to 1 inch (2.5 cm).

Cast on 280 sts using thumb method evenly over four needles and knit 2 rounds plain—2 rounds purl. Repeat these four rounds six times. This forms the welt in this gansey. Continue in stocking stitch until work measures 12 inches (25 cm) keeping a seam line of P1, K1, K137, P1, K1, P1, K137, P1. The gusset increase now begins as well as the pattern.

On the first round of the pattern increase by 1st on centre knit st making 2 knit sts in centre with purl st each side. Increase 1st each side of the centre sts every 4th round until 20 stitches worked. The yoke pattern is as follows. * 2 rounds purl. 2 rounds plain * repeat once.

Round 1: K2, P2, repeat to end.
Round 2: Knit.
Round 3: P2, K2, repeat to end.
Round 4: Knit.
Repeat these four rounds five times for each panel.
One pattern is 28 rounds.

When gusset stitches are worked, you now divide for front and back by slipping gusset stitches including the purl stitches and stitches for back onto a stitch holder. Continue in pattern on two needles making the first and last 3 stitches in garter stitch. Work until there are 5 patterns. Knit first section of the sixth pattern.

Neck shaping (adjust to size)
Leave 87 sts for neck and shoulder on a holder. Knit 12 rows of 2 rows purl, 2 plain on other shoulder, finishing on a plain row, leave these sts on a stitch holder. Repeat for the corresponding shoulder leaving neck st on the holder. Repeat back as front. Cast off shoulders together on the right side forming a ridge.

The neck

Pick up 108 sts evenly around neck edge and K2, P2 for 3 inches (7.5 cm) finishing with 1 plain, 2 purl, 1 plain round. Cast off using wool double. (ribwise)

The sleeves

The sleeves are picked up evenly including the gusset (128 sts). The pattern for the arm is 2 rounds plain—2 rounds purl (keeping the gusset plain). Repeat these four rounds again. Work next 2 inches plain knitting, and the following pattern for 20 rounds.

ROUND 1: P2, K2 (repeat to end of round).
ROUND 2: Knit.
ROUND 3: K2, P2.
ROUND 4: Knit.

End the pattern with two rounds purl and continue for the rest of the sleeve in plain knitting. At the same time as working pattern decrease one stitch each side of the centre of the gusset every 4th row. Continue decreasing until 70 sts remain—knit straight to required length.

The cuff

K2, P1 for 3 inches (7.5 cm) casting off in rib using the wool double.

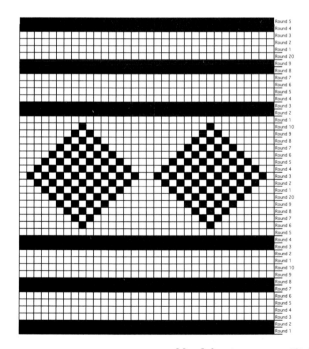

	K	P	K	P	K	P	K	P	K	P	K	P	K	P	K	P	K	P	K	P	K	P	K	P	K	P	K	P
Knit	1 round																											
Purl	1 round																											
Purl	1 round																											
Knit	4 rounds																											
Purl	1 round																											
Purl	1 roiund																											
Knit	4 rounds																											
Purl	1 round																											
Purl	1 round																											
Knit	1 round																											
Round 1	8		1	16	1	8																						
Round 2	7	1	1	1	14	1	1	7																				
Round 3	6	1	1	1	1	12	1	1	1	1	6																	
Round 4	5	1	1	1	1	1	10	1	1	1	1	1	5															
Round 5	4	1	1	1	1	1	1	8	1	1	1	1	1	1	4													
Round 6	3	1	1	1	1	1	1	1	6	1	1	1	1	1	1	1	3											
Round 7	2	1	1	1	1	1	1	1	1	4	1	1	1	1	1	1	1	1	2									
Round 8	1	1	1	1	1	1	1	1	1	1	2	1	1	1	1	1	1	1	1	1	1	1						
Round 9	2	1	1	1	1	1	1	1	1	4	1	1	1	1	1	1	1	1	2									
Round 10	3	1	1	1	1	1	1	1	6	1	1	1	1	1	1	1	3											
Round 11	4	1	1	1	1	1	1	8	1	1	1	1	1	1	4													
Round 12	5	1	1	1	1	1	10	1	1	1	1	1	5															
Round 13	6	1	1	1	1	12	1	1	1	1	6																	
Round 14	7	1	1	1	14	1	1	7																				
Round 15	8		1	16	1	8																						
Round 16																												
Round 17																												
Round 18																												
Round 19																												

Mrs Johnston, moss stitch diamond horizontal pattern.

ERISKAY

Hebridean gansey worn by
Mr McAllister, Eriskay.

The final part of my journey around the Scottish fishing communities was to the Hebrides and in particular to the island of Eriskay where they have had a long tradition of knitting unique patterns. You may know the island from its claim to fame—the sinking of the whisky ship the *SS Politician* and the ensuing film, *Whiskey Galore!* in which the parish priest is quoted as saying, 'I never regarded it as theft. It was an Act of God'. The *Politician,* minus its whisky, now lies off the coast, still serving the community as an oyster bed, and that day, 14 February 1941, is written into the island's folklore.

This tiny island, only 3 by 1½ miles, lies between Barra and South Uist. Most of it is uninhabitable and the population of 212 is concentrated around the shore line. Co. Chomunn Eirisgeidh is the islanders' community cooperative. In an effort to preserve and pursue services of benefit to the inhabitants, one of its projects has been to revive the unique Hebridean jersey. The cooperative now offers a service making up these patterns in the traditional manner.

I have taken particular trouble to concentrate on this area since in terms of economics it closely resembles the old cottage industry system that was so much a part of the life of fishing communities. In all the other areas of Britain, apart from Fair Isle and Aran, the continuation of the knitting tradition has been largely a personal one. Here in Eriskay a real attempt is being made to make the knitting contribute economically to the community.

The community revolves around the Coop shop and it was here that I went to speak to John McMillan and Ian MacInnes, secretary and manager of the cooperative scheme. They explained that the scheme was first set up in 1979 by the Highlands & Islands Development Board, using as a model the community schemes first begun in Ireland. The idea was that instead of bringing in people from outside to organise work, the people themselves could create and provide it. The Board required a minimum of three projects so that the community could be titled a 'multi-functional' Coop and thus be eligible for grants.

The first desperate need was for a shop, since the nearest was in South Uist, a boat journey away. The knitting of Eriskay jerseys

Eriskay—the ferry landing,
buildings and church.

already existed on an ad hoc basis. These two inputs, together with fishing—the main activity on the island—became the basis for the scheme. It has four years to become self-sufficient and the signs are very encouraging.

The knitting is looked upon as a social activity, rather than a crucial element in the scheme of things, since by its nature it is time-consuming and the returns do not as yet reflect the true value of the women's craftsmanship. There are bright spots occasionally—export to the USA and to The Scottish Merchant, a shop in London, has done much to help—and a rise in individual orders, enabling them to supply direct, will increase the revenue enormously.

To gain this extra income, all the womenfolk on the island knit in their spare moments between looking after their homes and their crofting, while the men work on the boats fishing for prawns and whitefish. Before discussing their patterns, however, I would like to note a little of their history, since it gives an insight into their lifestyle.

Historically, Eriskay is a new community—the island has been inhabited only since the early 1800s. Once simply part of the Boycdale 'Tack' (estate), it was occupied as a result of the evictions from the crofts of Barra and Uist. I talked to Donald McDonald, the retired headmaster and local bard, who told me that the evictions were still thought of with distaste throughout Scotland, particularly in the Western Isles. The laird allowed the population to develop the land for their sheep and cattle, then, as soon as the scrub had been turned to pasture, they were evicted and their stock replaced with his own. Mr McDonald explained that his neighbour's great-grandfather was evicted seven times before he and his family finally found refuge on Eriskay.

The island was considered uneconomic and the new population was allowed to stay. At first the islanders continued with their farming, but this proved insufficient to support them. Through necessity, they had to turn to fishing. They learnt their new trade by joining the great fishing fleets based at Aberdeen, Peterhead and as far afield as the Shetlands and Orkneys. Then they obtained their own boats and developed the industry from Eriskay itself.

Lugging manure by Shetland pony to the 'lazy beds' for potato cropping on Eriskay, looking over the sound towards South Uist.

Eriskay knitting group.

But they were still prey to the more organised and ruthless merchants, from whom they had to borrow the money for their boats and who owned the shops. Mr McDonald explained: 'The summer fishing was important, starting at the beginning of May and ending late August. They were not paid for the fish they landed during that time, but at the end of the season they made a settlement. During this period the wives just took the goods from the merchants' shops on credit and then when the settlement came, what usually happened was that all the money went to the merchant and they were left with nothing. Then when the winter came they fished the lochs on the mainland until Christmas time and I remember quite well as boys going up to the hilltop and watching the fleet come in. We were always anxious as to whether they would get back in time for Midnight Mass. Usually this was the season that they had money in their pockets because they dealt with the buyers direct. My father was always full of praise for the Loch Nevis buyers'.

With the formation of the cooperative, these old days of exploitation are finally fading. 'There is no great prosperity but we do reasonably well enough and things have improved a great deal since my time as a youngster. We used to go to school barefoot and many was the time I'd go home for dinner and there would be nothing to eat. Our fathers had it even worse—they had a bad time of it and they were exploited by the merchants, there's no question of that'. The islanders' lassitude—the debilitating legacy of the evictions—has taken a long time to get over.

Now we come to the patterns and—as the photographs reveal—the configurations are truly unique to this island. Since everyone knits it is unfair to concentrate on anyone in particular, but unfortunately lack of space means that I must. In a meeting with some of the ladies of the cooperative I discussed this problem and we came to the conclusion that if I were to pick anyone it should be the oldest knitter on the island, Mrs Cath McMillan.

When I visited Mrs McMillan, she had as usual a gansey on the go and, over tea, I asked her who had taught her to knit. She explained that it was her aunt, when she went to the east coast with all the girls in gutting crews: 'We went up as far as the Shetlands and Fair Isle in those days'. Her aunt must have been an extraordinary knitter since, according to Mrs McMillan, she was the first to begin the distinctive yoke pattern configuration. As far as she could remember, they had always knit just one pattern, very much like the rest of Scotland. The patterns she showed me were very beautiful; she explained that she always liked to include every pattern she knew. Her collection is a small representation of the character of the knitting from all the islanders.

The photographs show six of her ganseys, which I have notated on pages 157 to 169. You will observe that the method for constructing patterns places emphasis on the yoke where many of the pattern orientations are only ever constructed on two needles. All the configurations follow the major combination of two sets of patterns arranged vertically, separated at the yoke by a horizontal net mesh

Mrs Cath McMillan knitting outside her home.

picked out in garter, or more popularly a slipover stitch. The larger vertical panels above the yoke are set into square blocks, each containing a pattern. These blocks are picked out in slipover or moss stitch, set vertically. The centre panel is sometimes featured by being flanked with cables and an open horseshoe. The shoulders are worked as a flap and cast off on the inside at the back on one shoulder and the front on the other shoulder. They are usually decorated with slipover stitches, or occasionally with a small pattern taken from the body or the trellis.

I think you will agree that Cath McMillan's ganseys are a unique collection of pattern combinations that radiate the essence of what informs the Eriskay Gansey; and yet among the remaining knitters of the cooperative they showed me even more spectacular patterns: statements revolving around the Tree of Life, the Anchor and the diamond. I have included their notations on pages 170 and 171. In conclusion I note that these ganseys have been looked upon as having no equal. I would agree, excepting that my heart will forever leap at the sight of plait cables, Hen's Claw, the Crown, the Anchor, the Tree of Life, the underarm gusset, garter stitch panels and knitting in the round.

CATH McMILLAN GANSEY NO. 1

This first pattern combination begins with a K2, P2 welt where the wool has been knitted double over the first 5 rounds. The welt is completed by 3 rows of garter and the trunk pattern sequence begins in the form of a vertical column repeat moss and purl diamond pattern (#6). Each vertical column is separated by a 6 stitch seeding column of P2, K2, P2, slipping the centre knit stitches every 8 rounds (#28). The columns are repeated seven times over the entire trunk to the start of a horizontal trellis sequence (#8) that forms the beginning of the yoke pattern sequences.

The yoke now begins a nine column sequence; three columns of alternate double moss open diamonds (#4) and Tree of Life (#18) are the major columns centred midway; each pattern is framed horizontally by garter slip stitch flanked by columns of Starfish and diamond (#1), cable (#34) and multi-five seeding columns at each edge of the yoke. Each of the nine columns is separated by a 2 purl stitch seeding column.

The yoke is completed by placement of three garter rounds (#22) and the shoulders completed as a trellis.

The sleeves are worked from the top in three columns—a closed double moss (#3) and purl diamond (#20) sequence , flanked by a double moss zigzag (#5), each column separated by a 6 stitch seeding column, slipping the centre knit stitches every 8 rounds for the length of the sleeve.

The neck is worked in K2, P2, and finished with two garter panels on the left to accommodate three buttonholes and their buttons—a device to maintain a tight fit and yet have sufficient elasticity to fit over the wearer's head.

157

This second pattern combination begins with K1, P1 fishermen's rib, with the trunk sequence beginning with 2 rounds of the garter slip stitch tightly worked throughout each round. This slip manipulation is indeed worked throughout the gansey as a 2 round/row combination that borders all vertical pattern sequences and horizontally frames the majority of pattern elements on the trunk, the yoke and the arms.

The trunk pattern sequence begins in the form of seven vertical column repeats beginning with a double moss closed diamond (#3). The diamond vertical columns are repeated three times centred at the neck and flanked by a double moss diagonal bar (#13) and double moss zigzag (#5) over the entire trunk to the start of a wide horizontal trellis (#9) that forms the beginning of the yoke pattern

sequences. This second pattern sequence on the yoke features extensive use of openwork centred at the neck with an openwork diamond (#16) and double purl crossover (#12) flanked by cable and openwork horseshoe columns (#15) which are in turn flanked by double moss Tree of Life (#18) vertical columns. The centre one of three in each column is open worked (#17) The pattern elements are completed on the yoke with a stepladder sequence (#32). The shoulder pattern element repeats the trellis.

The arms, worked from the top, are knitted plain except for the front edge worked in double moss closed diamond edged by 3 columns of slip seeding finishing with a double round of the slip sequence at the cuff finished in fishermens' rib which is echoed at the neck.

This third pattern combination begins with a K2, P2 welt where the wool has been knitted double over the first 5 rounds. The welt is completed by 3 rows of garter and the trunk pattern sequence begins in the form of 2 vertical column repeats: a moss and purl diamond pattern repeat (#6) and a double moss diagonal bar (#13). The columns are repeated seven times, with the diamond vertical set at the centre flanked by the double moss diagonal, thus making three repeats of the diamond column and four repeats of the bar. Each vertical column is separated by a 3 stitch seeding column of P1, K1, P1 noted as 'fives' seedings. A horizontal trellis (#8) forms the beginning of the yoke pattern sequences. The yoke features a large double purl crossover (#12) and a double moss open diamond

combination (#4) set as a column, centred at the neck. This central column is flanked by a plain diamond and moss diamond pattern combination set vertically, which in turn is flanked by a large solid purl diamond (#20) and double moss Tree of Life (#18), each pattern framed by the slip stitch sequence. Each edge of the yoke is completed by chevron columns (#11) and the stitches picked up for sleeves—where a large open double moss diamond and solid purl diamond is worked over the top half of the sleeve for the whole length, each element framed by the slip stitch sequence. This whole column at the centre of the arm is flanked by diagonal columns separated by 2 purl seed columns, echoing the structure of the pattern elements which decorate the yoke.

The fourth pattern combination begins with K1, P1 fishermen's rib, with the trunk sequence beginning with 2 garter, 2 plain rounds to set the pattern sequence of seven columns; the centre column as a wide double moss zigzag (#5) flanked by a double moss open (#3) and double moss closed diamond (#4) arranged vertically. This sequence is repeated four times on the trunk edged by two Starfish diamond columns (#1). All the columns are separated vertically with the slip seeding sequence (#24) and each design element is framed by three garter rounds. The trunk is completed with a garter ridge which is repeated to begin a horizontal trellis (#9) which ends with two garter rows. The yoke sets three large columns—the centre of the three displays a 4 cornered Starfish (#7), and Anchor (#18) and moss stitch diamond

(#36) at the neck. The remaining two dominant columns both have a large Tree of Life (#18), a large open diamond (#3) and a solid purl diamond (#19). These columns are set within wide seeding borders which take on almost equal prominence to the pattern elements which they border. The centre column is bordered by cables and openwork horseshoes (#15). All columns are worked to the shoulder and neck edge—the shoulders brought together with the slip stitch seeding sequence and the neck stitches worked in K1, P1. The sleeves are worked to the cuff with three columns patterned at the shoulder edge, with the remaining sleeve stitches knit plain. The pattern element centres open and closed double moss diamond, flanked with the zigzag, echoing the centre trunk column.

CATH McMILLAN GANSEY NO. 5

The fifth pattern combination begins with K1, P1 fishermen's rib, with the trunk sequence beginning with 2 rounds of the slip stitch manipulation tightly worked throughout each round. This slip manipulation is worked throughout the gansey as a 2 round/row combination that horizontally frames the majority of pattern elements on the trunk, the yoke and the arms. The vertical seeding separating the pattern elements arranged vertically are in two similar forms; within the trunk the seeding is a 6 st moss panel and on the yoke the seeding is 3sts seeding known as 'fives'.

The trunk is set out in seven columns where the first, the third, the fifth and the seventh columns feature a large open (#4) and closed diamond (#3) sequence. The fourth pattern column is a Starfish diamond arranged vertically (#1). The second and sixth column pattern is a double purl diagonal (#13). All columns are completed with two rows in the slip seeding combination followed by a wide trellis configuration (#9) finished with two rows of seeding. The yoke displays nine columns, with three major columns. The second and eighth feature a Tree of Life (#18), double crossover (#12) and purl diamond(#19)—each element framed by the slip stitch seeding. The fifth column centred at the neck features a 4 cornered Starfish (#7), small Anchor (#14) and moss diamond (#30). This centred column is flanked by cables (columns 4 and 6) which in turn are flanked by openwork horseshoes (#15) (columns 3 and 7). The first and last columns are simple ladder patterns which are worked to the shoulder. The centre panel and adjacent rope columns provide the neck stitches which form a tightly worked fishermens' rib separated at the right side with 2 garter stitch panels to accommodate buttonholes and their buttons. The shoulders are worked as flaps in multiple rows of the garter slip sequence. The sleeves, worked from the shoulder to the cuff, display a double moss open and closed diamond column; each element framed by the garter slip sequence at the centre of the sleeve. This central column is flanked on both sides by 6 stitch seeding and the double moss bar pattern. All patterns are worked to the cuff which is completed in fishermen's rib.

The sixth pattern combination begins with a K1, P1 welt and is completed with 2 rounds of garter slip sequence (#26, #27) before the trunk combination begins with a 7 column repeat—the centre column being a closed (#3) and open (#4) double moss diamond framed horizontally by 2 rounds of the garter slip sequence. This central column is flanked by a double purl diagonal repetition (#13) and the edges of the trunk are completed by two stepladder sequences (#32, #33) featuring a purl, knit, purl framing. All columns are seeded by the garter slip sequence including the horizontal elements of each pattern.

The trunk is completed by 2 rows of the garter slip sequence to introduce a horizontal net trellis (#8) which ends with a repeat of the garter slip sequence. The yoke has seven columns—unlike the body these columns are of unequal width. Columns 2, 4 and 6 are nearly twice as wide as columns 1, 3, 5 and 7, made up of a large double moss closed dia-

mond (#3) and a double moss crossover pattern element (#12), each pattern presented in alternate sequence; the centre panel is flanked by a single Starfish repeat (#10).The first and last columns are a double purl diagonal repeat; all columns are separated by the garter slip sequence. At the completion of the yoke the shoulders are worked in garter slip sequence to create a flap which picks up the shoulder stitches on the opposite side. The neck stitches are worked straight off the yoke sequence in K1, P1 with a garter panel worked at the right side to accommodate buttonholes and buttons. The sleeves are knit to the cuff in plain knitting except for the top of the sleeve which is worked in a double moss open and closed diamond sequence, each element framed horizontally by two rows of garter slip; the column as a whole framed by the 'fives' seeding. The sleeve ends with two rounds of the garter slip sequence and the cuff worked in K1, P1 and cast off in rib.

162

Cath McMillan's pattern combinations over 6 Eriskay ganseys.

1. Starfish with diamond
2. Starfish variation
3. Double moss closed diamond. 15x30
4. Double moss open diamond 15x30
5. Large double moss zigzag
6. Purl & moss diamond vertical
7. 4 Cornered Starfish
8. Small trellis
9. Large trellis
10. Single Starfish
11. Flying Geese(Chevron)
12. Double moss crossover
13. Double purl diagonal
14. Anchor
15. Openwork Horseshoe
16. Openwork diamond
17. Openwork Tree of Life
18. Tree of Life
19. Plain purl diamond
20. Large plain purl diamond
21. Garter ridge A
22. Garter ridge B
23. Garter ridge C
24. Vertical slip stitch in the round
25. Vertical slip stitch over two needles
26. Horizontal slip stitch in the round
27. Horizontal slip stitch over two needles
28. Slip stitch cable every 7 in the round
29. Slip stitch cable every 7 over two needles
30. Slip stitch cable every 5 in the round
31. Slip stitch cable every 5 over two needles
32. Stepladder sequence on two needles
33. Stepladder sequence in the round
34. Cable
35. Moss stitch seeding
36. Moss & purl closed diamond

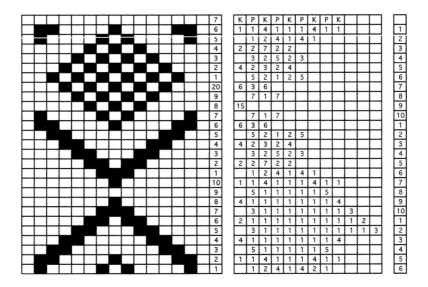

Design 1 Starfish with diamond, 13 sts & 26 rds
with instructions for knitting in the round and on 2 needles.

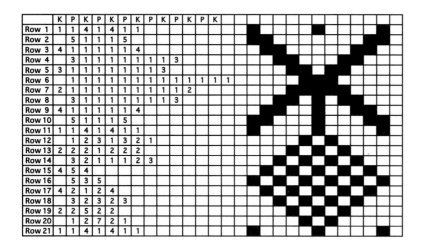

Design 2 chart (11 + 2 sts and 20 rows):

	K	P	K	P	K	P	K	P	K	P	K	P	K
Row 1	1	1	4	1	4	1	1						
Row 2		5	1	1	1	5							
Row 3	4	1	1	1	1	1	4						
Row 4		3	1	1	1	1	1	1	3				
Row 5	3	1	1	1	1	1	1	3					
Row 6	1	1	1	1	1	1	1	1	1	1	1	1	1
Row 7	2	1	1	1	1	1	1	1	1	1	2		
Row 8		3	1	1	1	1	1	1	3				
Row 9	4	1	1	1	1	1	4						
Row 10		5	1	1	1	5							
Row 11	1	1	4	1	4	1	1						
Row 12	1	2	3	1	3	2	1						
Row 13	2	2	2	1	2	2	2						
Row 14		3	2	1	1	1	2	3					
Row 15	4	5	4										
Row 16		5	3	5									
Row 17	4	2	1	2	4								
Row 18		3	2	3	2	3							
Row 19	2	2	5	2	2								
Row 20		1	2	7	2	1							
Row 21	1	1	4	1	4	1	1						

Design 2 Starfish variation, 11 + 2 sts and 20 rows
with instructions for knitting over 2 needles and in the round.

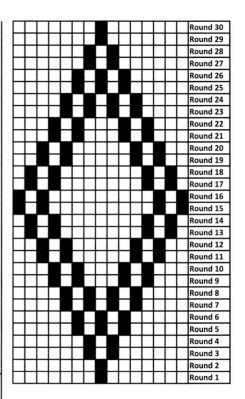

Design 3 chart (15 sts & 30 rds):

	K	P	K	P	K	P	K	P	K	P	K	P	K	P	K	P
Row 1	7	1	7													
Row 2		7	1	7												
Row 3	6	1	1	6												
Row 4		6	1	1	6											
Row 5	5	1	1	1	5											
Row 6		5	1	1	1	1	5									
Row 7	4	1	1	1	1	1	4									
Row 8		4	1	1	1	1	1	1	4							
Row 9	3	1	1	1	1	1	1	1	3							
Row 10		3	1	1	1	1	1	1	1	3						
Row 11	2	1	1	1	1	1	1	1	1	1	2					
Row 12		2	1	1	1	1	1	1	1	1	1	2				
Row 13	1	1	1	1	1	1	1	1	1	1	1	1	1			
Row 14		1	1	1	1	1	1	1	1	1	1	1	1	1		
Row 15		1	1	1	1	1	1	1	1	1	1	1	1	1	1	
Row 16		1	1	1	1	1	1	1	1	1	1	1	1	1	1	
Row 17		1	1	1	1	1	1	1	1	1	1	1	1	1	1	
Row 18	1	1	1	1	1	1	1	1	1	1	1	1	1			
Row 19		2	1	1	1	1	1	1	1	1	1	2				
Row 20	2	1	1	1	1	1	1	1	1	1	2					
Row 21		3	1	1	1	1	1	1	1	3						
Row 22	3	1	1	1	1	1	1	1	3							
Row 23		4	1	1	1	1	1	1	4							
Row 24	4	1	1	1	1	1	4									
Row 25		5	1	1	1	1	5									
Row 26	5	1	1	1	1	5										
Row 27		6	1	1	1	6										
Row 28	6	1	1	1	6											
Row 29		7	1	7												
Row 30	7	1	7													

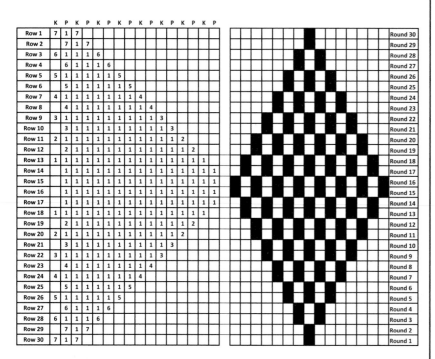

Design 3 Double moss closed diamond, 15 sts & 30 rds.
Instructions for 2 needle knitting and knitting in the round.

Design 4 chart (15 + 2 sts & 30 rds):

	K	P	K	P	K	P	K	P	K	P
Row 1	7	1	7							
Row 2		7	1	7						
Row 3	6	1	1	6						
Row 4		6	1	1	6					
Row 5	5	1	1	1	1	5				
Row 6		5	1	1	1	1	5			
Row 7	4	1	1	1	1	1	1	4		
Row 8		4	1	1	1	1	1	1	4	
Row 9	3	1	1	1	3	1	1	3		
Row 10		3	1	1	1	3	1	1	1	3
Row 11	2	1	1	1	5	1	1	2		
Row 12		2	1	1	1	5	1	1	1	2
Row 13	1	1	1	1	7	1	1	1		
Row 14		1	1	1	1	7	1	1	1	1
Row 15	1	1	1	9	1	1	1			
Row 16		1	1	1	9	1	1	1		
Row 17	1	1	1	1	7	1	1	1		
Row 18		1	1	1	1	7	1	1	1	1
Row 19	2	1	1	1	5	1	1	2		
Row 20		2	1	1	1	5	1	1	1	2
Row 21	3	1	1	1	3	1	1	3		
Row 22		3	1	1	1	3	1	1	1	3
Row 23	4	1	1	1	1	1	1	4		
Row 24		4	1	1	1	1	1	1	4	
Row 25	5	1	1	1	1	5				
Row 26		5	1	1	1	1	5			
Row 27	6	1	1	6						
Row 28		6	1	1	6					
Row 29	7	1	7							
Row 30		7	1	7						

Design 4 Double moss open
diamond, 15 + 2 sts & 30 rds.
Instructions for knitting in the
round and over 2 needles.

Design 5 table (K P K P K P):

	K	P	K	P	K	P
Row 1	1	1	1	1	1	11
Row 2	1	1	1	1	1	11
Row 3	2	1	1	1	1	10
Row 4	2	1	1	1	1	10
Row 5	3	1	1	1	1	9
Row 6	3	1	1	1	1	9
Row 7	4	1	1	1	1	8
Row 8	4	1	1	1	1	8
Row 9	5	1	1	1	1	7
Row 10	5	1	1	1	1	7
Row 11	6	1	1	1	1	6
Row 12	6	1	1	1	1	6
Row 13	7	1	1	1	1	5
Row 14	7	1	1	1	1	5
Row 15	8	1	1	1	1	4
Row 16	8	1	1	1	1	4
Row 17	9	1	1	1	1	3
Row 18	9	1	1	1	1	3
Row 19	10	1	1	1	1	2
Row 20	10	1	1	1	1	2
Row 21	11	1	1	1	1	1
Row 22	11	1	1	1	1	1
Row 23	10	1	1	1	1	2
Row 24	10	1	1	1	1	2
Row 25	9	1	1	1	1	3
Row 26	9	1	1	1	1	3
Row 27	8	1	1	1	1	4
Row 28	8	1	1	1	1	4
Row 29	7	1	1	1	1	5
Row 30	7	1	1	1	1	5
Row 31	6	1	1	1	1	6
Row 32	6	1	1	1	1	6
Row 33	5	1	1	1	1	7
Row 34	5	1	1	1	1	7
Row 35	4	1	1	1	1	8
Row 36	4	1	1	1	1	8
Row 37	3	1	1	1	1	9
Row 38	3	1	1	1	1	9
Row 39	2	1	1	1	1	10
Row 40	2	1	1	1	1	10
Row 41	1	1	1	1	1	11
Row 42	1	1	1	1	1	11

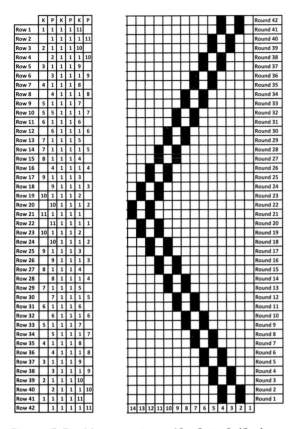

Grid rounds: Round 42 (top) down to Round 1 (bottom). Bottom column numbers: 14 13 12 11 10 9 8 7 6 5 4 3 2 1.

Design 5 Double moss zigzag, 13 + 2 sts & 42 rds.
Instructions for knitting in the round and on 2 needles.

Design 7 table (K P K P K P):

	K	P	K	P	K	P
Row 1		5	1	7	1	5
Row 2	5	2	5	2	5	
Row 3		5	3	3	3	5
Row 4	6	3	1	3	6	
Row 5		7	2	1	2	7
Row 6	8	1	1	1	8	
Row 7		19				
Row 8	1	4	9	4	1	
Row 9		2	4	9	4	2
Row 10	3	4	5	4	3	
Row 1		4	4	4	3	4
Row 2	5	4	1	4	5	
Row 3		4	4	3	4	4
Row 4	3	4	5	4	3	
Row 5		2	4	7	4	2
Row 6	1	4	9	4	1	
Row 7		19				
Row 8	8	1	1	1	8	
Row 9		7	2	1	2	7
Row 20	6	3	1	3	6	
Row 1		5	3	3	3	5
Row 2	5	2	5	2	5	
Row 3		5	1	7	1	5
Row 4						
	K	P	K	P	K	P

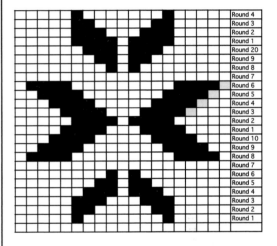

Design 7 4 Cornered Starfish (Snowflake), 17 sts & 24 rds.
Instructions for knitting over 2 needles and in the round.

Design 6 table:

	K	P	K	P	K	P	K	P	K	P	K	P
Row 1	5	1	5									
Row 2	4	3	4									
Row 3	3	5	3									
Row 4	2	7	2									
Row 5	1	9	1									
Row 6	11											
Row 7	1	9	1									
Row 8	2	7	2									
Row 9	3	5	3									
Row 10	4	3	4									
Row 11	5	1	5									
Row 12	5	1	5									
Row 13	5	1	5									
Row 14	4	1	1	1	4							
Row 15	3	1	1	1	1	1	3					
Row 16	2	1	1	1	1	1	1	1	2			
Row 17	1	1	1	1	1	1	1	1	1	1	1	
Row 18	1	1	1	1	1	1	1	1	1	1	1	
Row 19	1	1	1	1	1	1	1	1	1	1	1	
Row 20	2	1	1	1	1	1	1	1	2			
Row 21	3	1	1	1	1	1	3					
Row 22	4	1	1	1	4							
Row 23	5	1	5									

Grid rounds: Round 24 (top) down to Round 1 (bottom). Bottom numbers: 11 10 9 8 7 6 5 4 3 2 1.

Design 6 Purl and moss diamond vertical, 11 sts & 24 rds.
Instructions for knitting in the round and on 2 needles

Design 8 table (P K P K P K P):

	P	K	P	K	P	K	P
Row 1	1	7					
Row 2		1	1	5	1		
Row 3	2	1	3	1	1		
Row 4		3	1	1	1	2	
Row 5	4	1	3				
Row 6		3	1	1	1	2	
Row 7	2	1	3	1	1		
Row 8		1	1	5	1		
Row 9	1	7					

Grid rounds: Round 9 (top) down to Round 1 (bottom). Bottom numbers: 8 7 6 5 4 3 2 1.

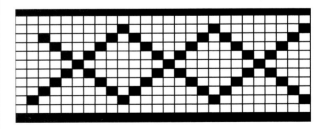

Design 8 Narrow trellis, 8 sts & 9 rds.
Instructions for knitting over 2 needles and in the round.

	k	p	k	p	k	p	k
Round 1	5	1	4				
Round 2		4	1	1	1	3	
Round 3	3	1	3	1	2		
Round 4		2	1	5	1	1	
Round 5	1	1	7	1			
Round 6		1	9				
Round 7	1	1	7	1			
Round 8		2	1	5	1	1	
Round 9	3	1	3	1	2		
Round 10		4	1	1	1	3	
Round 11	5	1	4				
Round 12		4	1	1	1	3	
Round 13	3	1	3	1	2		
Round 14		2	1	5	1	1	
Round 15	1	1	7	1			
Round 16		1	9				

(chart rows labeled Round 16 down to Round 1; bottom scale: 10 9 8 7 6 5 4 3 2 1)

Design 9 Wide trellis, 10 sts & 16 rds.
Instructions for knitting over 2 needles and in the round.

	p	k	p	k	p	k	p	k
Row 1	1	5	1	5	1			
Row 2		1	1	#	1	1		
Row 3	2	1	3	1	3	1	2	
Row 4		3	1	5	1	3		
Row 5	4	1	1	1	1	1	4	
Row 6		5	1	1	1	5		
Row 7	6	1	6					

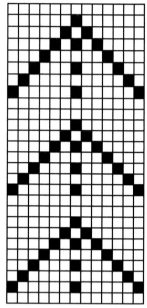

Design 11 Flying Geese,
(chevron), 13 sts & 7 rds.
Instructions for knitting
yoke and in the round.

	K	P	K	P	K	P
Row 1	15					
Row 2		6	1	1	1	6
Row 3	5	2	1	2	5	
Row 4		4	2	3	2	4
Row 5	3	2	5	2	3	
Row 6		2	2	7	2	2
Row 7	1	2	9	2	1	
Row 8		15				
Row 9	1	2	9	2	1	
Row 10		2	2	7	2	2
Row 11	3	2	5	2	3	
Row 12		4	2	3	2	4
Row 13	5	2	1	2	5	
Row 14		6	1	1	1	6

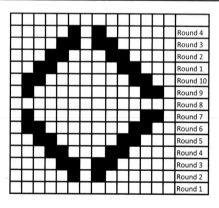

(chart rows labeled Round 4, Round 3, Round 2, Round 1, Round 10, Round 9, Round 8, Round 7, Round 6, Round 5, Round 4, Round 3, Round 2, Round 1)

Design 10 Single Starfish, 15 sts & 14 rds.
Instructions for knitting in the round and on 2 needles.

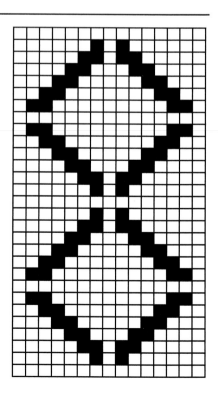

Design 12 chart (top-left number table):

	p	k	p	k	p	k	p	k	p	k
1		1	1	1	1	9	1	1	1	1
2			1	1	1	1	9	1	1	1	1
3		2	1	1	1	7	1	1	1	2
4			2	1	1	1	7	1	1	1	2
5		3	1	1	1	5	1	1	1	3
6			3	1	1	1	5	1	1	1	3
7		4	1	1	1	3	1	1	1	4
8			4	1	1	1	3	1	1	1	4
9		5	1	1	1	1	1	1	1	5
10			5	1	1	1	1	1	1	1	5
11		6	1	1	1	1	1	6
12			6	1	1	1	1	1	6
13		7	1	1	1	7
14			7	1	1	1	7
15		7	1	1	1	7
16			6	1	1	1	1	1	6
17		6	1	1	1	1	1	6
18			5	1	1	1	1	1	1	1	5
19		5	1	1	1	1	1	1	1	5
20			4	1	1	1	3	1	1	1	4
21		4	1	1	1	3	1	1	1	4
22			3	1	1	1	5	1	1	1	3
23		3	1	1	1	5	1	1	1	3
24			2	1	1	1	7	1	1	1	2
25		2	1	1	1	7	1	1	1	2
26			1	1	1	1	9	1	1	1	1

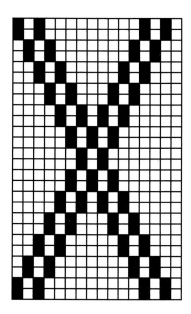

Design 12 Double moss crossover,
15 + 2 sts & 26 rds.
Instructions for knitting over 2
needles and in the round.

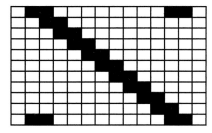

	k	p	k	p	k	p
Row 1		1	2	8	2	1
Row 2	2	2	10			
Row 3		3	2	9		
Row 4	4	2	8			
Row 5		5	2	7		
Row 6	6	2	6			
Row 7		7	2	5		
Row 8	8	2	4	1		
Row 9		9	2	3		
Row 10	10	2	2			
Row 11		1	2	11		

Design 13 Double purl diagonal, 14 sts & 10 rds.
Instructions for knitting in the round and on 2 needles

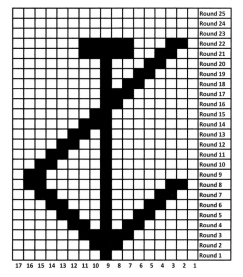

Round 25
Round 24
Round 23
Round 22
Round 21
Round 20
Round 19
Round 18
Round 17
Round 16
Round 15
Round 14
Round 13
Round 12
Round 11
Round 10
Round 9
Round 8
Round 7
Round 6
Round 5
Round 4
Round 3
Round 2
Round 1

17 16 15 14 13 12 11 10 9 8 7 6 5 4 3 2 1

2 needle:

	K	P	K	P	K	P	K	P
Row 1	8	1	8					
Row 2	7	3	7					
Row 3	6	5	6					
Row 4	5	2	1	1	1	2	5	
Row 5	4	2	2	1	2	2	4	
Row 6	3	2	3	1	3	2	3	
Row 7	2	2	4	1	4	2	2	
Row 8	1	2	5	1	5	2	1	
Row 9	8	1	5	2	1			
Row 10	8	1	4	2	2			
Row 11	8	1	3	2	3			
Row 12	8	1	2	2	4			
Row 13	8	1	1	2	5			
Row 14	8	3	6					
Row 15	8	2	7					
Row 16	7	2	8					
Row 17	6	3	8					
Row 18	5	2	1	1	8			
Row 19	4	2	2	1	8			
Row 20	3	2	3	1	8			
Row 21	2	2	2	5	6			
Row 22	1	2	3	5	6			
Row 23	2	3	5	7				

Design 14 Anchor, 17 sts & 23 rds.
Instructions for knitting over 2 needles and in the round.

	K	P	K	P	K	P	K	P	K	P	K
row 1		6	2	1	2	6					
row 2	5	2	3	2	5						
row 3		4	2	5	2	4					
row 4	3	2	2	1	1	2	2	3			
row 5		2	2	2	2	1	2	2	2	2	
row 6	1	2	2	2	3	2	2	2	1		
row 7		2	2	2	5	2	2	2			
row 8	1	2	2	2	1	1	1	2	2	2	1
row 9		2	2	2	2	1	2	2	2	2	
row 10	1	2	2	2	3	2	2	2	1		
row 11		1	1	2	2	5	2	2	1	1	
row 12	3	2	2	1	1	1	2	2	3		
row 13		2	2	2	2	1	2	2	2	2	
row 14	2	1	2	2	3	2	2	1	2		
row 15		4	2	5	2	4					
row 16	3	2	2	1	1	1	2	2	3		
row 17		3	1	2	2	1	2	2	1	3	
row 18	5	2	3	2	5						
row 19		4	2	5	2	4					
row 20	4	1	2	1	1	1	2	1	4		
row 21		6	2	1	2	6					
row 22	5	2	3	2	5						
row 23		5	1	5	1	5					
row 24	7	1	1	1	7						
row 25		6	2	1	2	6					
row 26	6	1	3	1	6						
row 27		17									
row 28	7	1	1	1	7						
row 29		7	1	1	1	1	7				

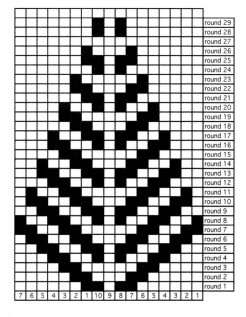

round 29
round 28
round 27
round 26
round 25
round 24
round 23
round 22
round 21
round 20
round 19
round 18
round 17
round 16
round 15
round 14
round 13
round 12
round 11
round 10
round 9
round 8
round 7
round 6
round 5
round 4
round 3
round 2
round 1

7 6 5 4 3 2 1 10 9 8 7 6 5 4 3 2 1

Design 18 Tree of Life, 17 sts & 29 rds.
Instructions for knitting over 2 needles and in the round.

Design 15 Openwork Horseshoe
13 sts & 11 rows
Pattern instructions for yoke.
Row 1: K2, *yfwd, K3, sl1, K2tog, psso, K3, psso, yfwd, K1, repeat from *, end K1.
Row 2 and all other even numbered rows: Purl.
Row 3: K2, *K1, yfwd, K2, sl1, K2tog, psso, K2, repeat from *, end K1.
Row 5: K2, *K2, yfwd, K1, sl1, K2tog, psso, K1, yfwd, K3, repeat from *, end K1.
Row 7: K2, *K3, yfwd, sl1, K2tog, psso, yfwd, K4, repeat from *, end K1.
Row 8: Purl.
Repeat rows 1 to 8.

Design 16 Openwork diamond
19 sts & 30 rows
Pattern instructions for yoke.
Row 1: K7, K2tog, yfwd, K1, yfwd, sl1, K1, psso, K7.
Row 2 and all even numbered rows to Row 26: Purl.
Row 3: K6, K2tog, yfwd, K3, yfwd, sl1, K1, psso, K6.
Row 5: K5, (K2tog, yfwd) twice, K1, (yfwd, sl1, K1, psso) twice, K5.
Row 7: K4, (K2tog, yfwd) twice, K3, (yfwd, sl1, K1, psso) twice, K4.
Row 9: K3, (K2tog, yfwd) twice, K5, (yfwd, sl1, K1, psso) twice, k3.
Row 11: K2, (K2tog, yfwd) twice, K7, (yfwd, sl1, K1, psso) twice, K2.
Row 13: K1, (K2tog, yfwd) twice, K9, (yfwd, sl1, K1, psso) twice, K1.
Row 15: K3, (yfwd, sl1, K1, psso) twice, K5, (K2tog, yfwd) twice, K3.
Row 17: K4, (yfwd, sl1, K1, psso) twice, K3, (K2tog, yfwd) twice, K4.
Row 19: K5, (yfwd, sl1, K1, psso) twice, K1, (K2tog, yfwd) twice, K5.
Row 21: K6, yfwd, sl1, K1, psso, yfwd, sl1, K2tog, psso, yfwd, K2tog, yfwd, K6.
Row 23: K7, yfwd, sl1, K1, psso, K1, K2tog, yfwd, K7.
Row 25: K8, yfwd, sl1, K2tog, psso, yfwd, K8.
Row 26: Purl.
Rows 27 to Row 30: Knit.

Design 17 Openwork Tree of Life
19 sts & 30 rows
Row 1: K8, K2tog, yfwd, K1, yfwd, sl1, K1, psso, K8.
Row 2 and all even numbered rows to Row 26: Purl.
Row 3: K7, K2tog, yfwd, K3, yfwd, sl1, K1, psso, K7
Row 5: K6, (K2tog, yfwd) twice, K1, (yfwd, sl1, K1, psso) twice, K6.
Row 7: K5, (K2tog, yfwd) twice, K3, (yfwd, sl1, K1, psso) twice, K5.
Row 9: K4, (K2tog, yfwd) three times, K1, (yfwd, sl1, K1, psso) three times, K4.
Row 11: K3, (K2tog, yfwd) three times, K3, (yfwd, sl1, K1, psso) three times, K3.
Row 13: K2, (K2tog, yfwd) four times, K1, (yfwd, sl1, K1, psso) four times, K2.
Row 15: As Row 11.
Row 17: As Row 9
Row 19: As Row 7.
Row 21: As Row 5.
Row 23: As Row 3.
Row 15: As Row 1.
Row 27 to Row 30: Knit.

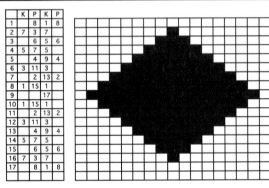

	K	P	K	P
1		8	1	8
2	7	3	7	
3		6	5	6
4	5	7	5	
5		4	9	4
6	3	11	3	
7		2	13	2
8	1	15	1	
9			17	
10	1	15	1	
11		2	13	2
12	3	11	3	
13		4	9	4
14	5	7	5	
15		6	5	6
16	7	3	7	
17		8	1	8

Design 19 Plain purl diamond, 17 sts & 17 rds.
Instructions for knitting over 2 needles and in the round.

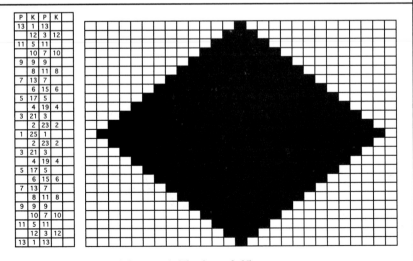

P	K	P	K
13	1	13	
	12	3	12
11	5	11	
	10	7	10
9	9	9	
	8	11	8
7	13	7	
	6	15	6
5	17	5	
	4	19	4
3	21	3	
	2	23	2
1	25	1	
	2	23	2
3	21	3	
	4	19	4
5	17	5	
	6	15	6
7	13	7	
	8	11	8
9	9	9	
	10	7	10
11	5	11	
	12	3	12
13	1	13	

Design 20 Plain purl diamond, 25 + 2 sts & 25 rows.
Instructions for knitting over 2 needles and in the round.

Cath's Horizontal Garter ridge patterns separate major structural elements from each other (the trunk/yoke divide for example.)
They have the following variations:

Design 21 Garter ridge A
Major pattern ends
Knit 1 round
Purl 1 round
Knit 1 round
Purl 1 round
Knit 1 round
New pattern begins

Design 22 Garter ridge B
Pattern ends
Knit 1 round
Purl 1 round
Purl 1 round
Purl 1 round
Knit 1 round
New pattern begins

Design 23 Garter ridge C
Pattern ends
Knit 1 round
Purl 1 round
Purl 1 round
Knit 1 round
Purl 1 round
Purl 1 round
Knit 1 round
New pattern begins

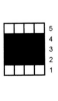

The slip stitch seeding begins as follows:

Design 24 Vertical slip stitch (in the round)
Round 1: Purl 2, wool forward to make a stitch, knit 2, now pass new stitch over the 2 knit stitches just completed, purl 2.
Round 2: Purl 2, knit 2, purl 2.
    In abbreviation:
Rd 1: P2, yarn fwd to M1, K2, psso, P2.
Rd 2: P2, K2, P2.

Design 25 Vertical slip stitch (on two needles)
Row 1: Purl 2, wool forward to make a stitch, knit 2, pass new stitch over the two knit stitches, purl 2.
Row 2: Knit 2, purl 2, knit 2.
Repeat the previous 2 rows.
    In abbreviation:
Row 1: P2, yarn fwd to M1, K2, psso, P2.
Row 2: K2, P2, K2.

Design 26 Horizontal slip stitch (in the round)
Round 1 *(Wool forward to M1),* K2, (pass M1 over K2),* repeat * to * to end of pattern width.
Round 2: Knit to end of pattern width.

Design 27 Horizontal slip stitch (2 needles)
Row 1: *(Wool forward to M1), K2, pass M1 over K2 just knitted,* repeat * to * to end of pattern width.
Row 2: Purl to end of pattern width.

Design 28 slip cable 1 (7 rounds) in the round

	P	K	P
Round 1	2	2	2
Round 2	2	2	2
Round 3	2	2	2
Round 4	2	2	2
Round 5	2	2	2
Round 6	2	2	2

Round 7 P2, wool forward to M1, K2, pass M1 over K2, P2.

Design 29 slip cable 1 (7 rounds) over 2 needles

	P	K	P	K
Round 1	2	2	2	
Round 2		2	2	2
Round 3	2	2	2	
Round 4		2	2	2
Round 5	2	2	2	
Round 6		2	2	2

Round 7 P2, wool forward to M1, K2, pass M1 over K2, P2.

Design 30 slip cable 1 (5 rounds)

	P	K	P
Round 1	2	2	2
Round 2	2	2	2
Round 3	2	2	2
Round 4	2	2	2

Round 5 P2, wool forward to M1, K2, pass M1 over K2, P2.

Design 31 slip cable 1 (7 rounds) over 2 needles

	P	K	P	K
Round 1	2	2	2	
Round 2		2	2	2
Round 3	2	2	2	
Round 4		2	2	2

Round 5 P2, wool forward to M1, K2, pass M1 over K2, P2.

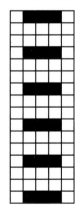

	P	K	P	K	P	K
Round 1		1	3	1		
Round 2			5			
Round 3		5				
Round 4			1	3	1	

Design 32 Stepladder sequence on 2 needles.
Design 33 Stepladder sequence in the round.

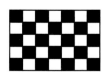

Design 35 Moss stitch seeding: varies in number according to pattern combination.

Round 1	7	1	7												
Round 2	6	1	1	1	6										
Round 3	5	1	1	1	1	1	5								
Round 4	4	1	1	1	1	1	1	1	4						
Round 5	3	1	1	1	1	1	1	1	1	1	3				
Round 6	2	1	1	1	1	1	1	1	1	1	1	1	2		
Round 7	1	1	1	1	1	1	1	1	1	1	1	1	1	1	1
Round 8	2	1	1	1	1	1	1	1	1	1	1	1	2		
Round 9	3	1	1	1	1	1	1	1	1	1	3				
Round 10	4	1	1	1	1	1	1	1	4						
Round 1	5	1	1	1	1	1	5								
Round 2	6	1	1	1	6										
Round 3	7	1	7												
Round 4															

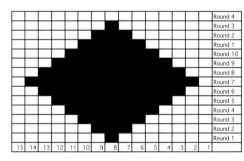

	K	P	K	P
Round 1	7	1	7	
Round 2	6	3	6	
Round 3	5	5	5	
Round 4	4	7	4	
Round 5	3	9	3	
Round 6	2	11	2	
Round 7	1	13	1	
Round 8	2	11	2	
Round 9	3	9	3	
Round 10	4	7	4	
Round 1	5	5	5	
Round 2	6	3	6	
Round 3	7	1	7	
Round 4				

Design 36 Moss diamond and purl, 15 sts & 13 rds.
Instructions for knitting over 2 needles and in the round.

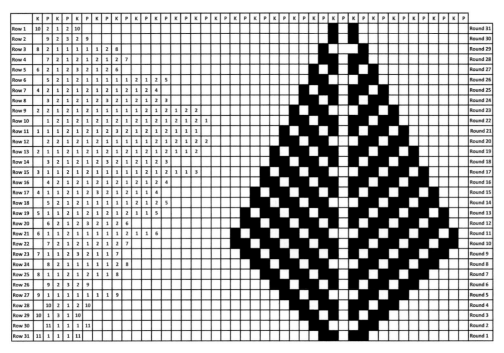

Eriskay collective Large Tree of Life, 23 sts + 2 & 31 rds.
Instructions for knitting over 2 needles and in the round.

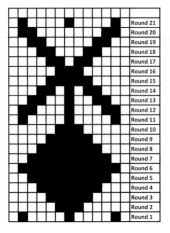

Eriskay collective Starfish variation, 11 sts + 2 & 20 rows.
Instructions for knitting over 2
needles and in the round.

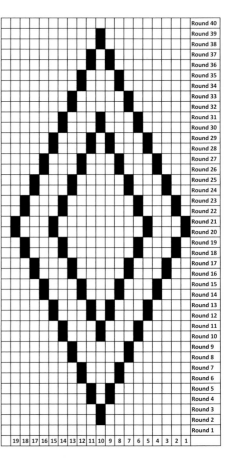

Eriskay collective Large open diamond, 19 sts & 40 rds.
Instructions for knitting in the round and over 2 needles

170

	K	P	K	P	K	P	K	P	K	P	K	P	K	P	K	P
Round 1		1	2	1	9	1	2	1								
Round 2			1	1	2	1	7	1	2	1	1					
Round 3		1	4	1	5	1	4	1								
Round 4	1	1	4	1	3	1	4	1	1							
Round 5		1	6	1	1	1	6	1								
Round 6	1	1	6	1	6	1	1									
Round 7		1	7	1	7	1										
Round 8	1	1	5	1	1	1	5	1	1							
Round 9		1	6	1	1	1	6	1								
Round 10	1	1	5	1	1	1	1	1	5	1	1					
Round 1		1	5	1	1	1	1	1	5	1						
Round 2	1	1	3	1	1	1	1	1	1	3	1	1				
Round 3		1	4	1	1	1	1	1	1	4	1					
Round 4	1	1	2	1	1	1	1	1	1	1	1	2	1	1		
Round 5		1	3	1	1	1	1	1	1	1	1	3	1			
Round 6	1	1	1	1	1	1	1	1	1	1	1	1	1			
Round 7		1	2	1	1	1	1	1	1	1	1	1	1	1	1	
Round 8	1	1	2	1	1	1	1	1	1	1	1	1	1	1	1	
Round 9		1	3	1	1	1	1	1	1	1	3	1				
Round 20	1	1	3	1	1	1	1	1	1	3	1	1				
Round 1		1	4	1	1	1	1	1	1	4	1					
Round 2	1	1	4	1	1	1	1	4	1	1						
Round 3		1	5	1	1	1	1	5	1							
Round 4	1	1	5	1	1	1	5	1	1							
Round 5		1	6	1	1	1	6	1								
Round 6	1	1	6	1	6	1	1									
Round 7		1	7	1	7	1										
Round 8	1	1	5	1	1	1	5	1	1							
Round 9		1	5	1	3	1	5	1								
Round 30	1	1	3	1	5	1	3	1	1							
Round 1		1	3	1	5	1	3	1								

Eriskay collective Double Diamond, 17 sts & 21 rows.
Instructions for 2 needles and in the round.

	K	P	K	P	K	P	K	P	K	P
Row 1	25									
Row 2		12	1	12						
Row 3	11	3	11							
Row 4		10	5	10						
Row 5	9	2	1	1	1	2	9			
Row 6		8	2	2	1	2	2	8		
Row 7	7	2	3	1	3	2	7			
Row 8		6	2	4	1	4	2	6		
Row 9	5	2	5	1	5	2	5			
Row 10		4	2	6	1	6	2	4		
Row 1	3	2	7	1	7	2	3			
Row 2		2	2	8	1	8	2	2		
Row 3	1	2	9	1	9	2	1			
Row 4		12	1	8	2	2				
Row 5	12	1	7	2	3					
Row 6		12	1	6	2	4				
Row 7	12	1	5	2	5					
Row 8		12	1	4	2	6				
Row 9	12	1	3	2	7					
Row 20		12	1	2	2	8				
Row 1	12	1	1	2	9					
Row 2		12	3	10						
Row 3	12	2	11							
Row 4		11	2	12						
Row 5	10	3	12							
Row 6		9	2	1	1	12				
Row 7	8	2	2	1	12					
Row 8		7	2	3	1	12				
Row 9	6	2	4	1	12					
Row 30		5	2	5	1	12				
Row 1	4	2	6	1	12					
Row 2		3	2	7	1	12				
Row 3	2	2	8	1	12					
Row 4		1	2	9	1	12				
Row 5	8	9	8							
Row 6		8	9	8						
Row 7	12	1	12							
Row 8		10	5	10						
Row 9	10	5	10							
Row 40		25								
	K	P	K	P	K	P	K	P	K	P

Eriskay collective Large Anchor, 25 sts & 41 rds.
Instructions for 2 needles and in the round.

The Knitting of Shetland and Fair Isle

A Shetland view.

A Short History and Description of Island Life

Before discussing Fair Isle and Shetland knitting, let me give you a taste of island life because I believe in its telling it will begin to reveal that life on these islands has influenced and moulded the inhabitants and the character of their creativity.

For most of us, the Shetland Islands are tucked away in a little box on the edge of the map of Britain, and have only lately been brought into prominence with the discovery of oil.

The map reproduced here puts the islands in the centre to give you an idea of their relationship with their surroundings. Placed as illustrated the map clearly corrects the perception that these islands are connected to the British Isles. They lie to the north east of Britain and are in fact closer to Norway than mainland Scotland. They consist of two major groupings: the four larger islands of Unst, Fetlar, Yell and Mainland, which are surrounded by the smaller islands of Out Skerries, Whalsay, Papa Stour, Foula and Fair Isle. The inhabitants owe their heritage to the Norsemen who settled in the 8th and 9th centuries, living under the patronage of Norway for over 500 years before the influx of Scottish mainlanders in the 13th century. Norse influence then began to fade and ended with the sale of the islands in 1469 by Norway to the Scottish Crown.

From this date right through to the present day the history of the inhabitants has been one of ruthless exploitation—by the Stuart family until 1615 and then from splitting up the islands into estates run by rich

172

immigrant Churchmen and landowners, who took over the locals' crofts and forced the people into fishing. Later, the pastures were turned over to sheep and the majority of the population evicted from the land which they had cultivated continuously for centuries. By the 1700s most Shetlanders had ceased to be small landowners supporting themselves on their farms, and had become mere tenants cultivating patches of land for which they paid rent to the newcomers.

Today they still earn their living at someone else's behest—this time that of the oil companies. One can understand their bitterness and their insistence that they should get something out of it for themselves. These unique islanders of mixed Nordic and Scottish blood had for centuries practised a way of life that, although hard, was an example of harmonious cooperation with the land, the sea and their community. All they have ever wanted was to continue to do so.

The heart of this way of life was the croft—a dwelling surrounded by a few acres of land set in the narrow strip of ground between the hills and the sea. By working the land and fishing the sea a modest living was possible. The system was worked on a loose cooperative basis—a few crofts would group together, enclosed by hill dykes that separated the arable land from the hillside. These dykes ran down to the shoreline giving the township or 'room' access to the sea with its valuable resources of shellfish, seaweed, flotsam, jetsum and winter grazing.

Within the dykes, a system called the 'rigga rendal' operated—the land was split into strips or 'rigs', the size of which was dependent upon their productive quality. These 'rigs' were worked in rotation by the crofters so that they all had equal opportunity to use the best and the worst.

The Miss Garricks collecting peat for burning. At hand is their prize Shetland Ram — a source of reasonable income.

Around each croft was a personal piece of land called the 'toon-mail' where the crofter had his yard and kept his milking cattle. Outside the dykes, on the hillsides, the animals grazed for most of the year on what they called the 'scattalds'.

Each town had its own designated area bounded by an imaginary line, the 'hagra', picked out occasionally by stones or landmarks. The whole system was based on cooperation, whether it was spinning, cultivating or fishing; where each individual was subject to the wellbeing of the community.

The outcome of this lifestyle was self-sufficiency, and according to the observations of contemporary ethnographers the crofters who lived this life possessed remarkable versatility within and beyond life's duties around the croft. In 1844 a visitor to the island wrote that a great number of women and girls occupied themselves with knitting, and that during the past few years had made elaborate shawls, scarves and designs of their own invention. And of course crofters had to acknowledge their allegiance to Norway through a payment of land tax in the form of a woven coarse cloth called 'wadmail'. Its production finally disappeared in the 18th century and was replaced by 'claith', ropes and 'taatit' rugs, mostly for home use.

The wool for these was homegrown from a Nordic breed of sheep, which, over the centuries was developed to produce a wool of surprising softness. At this time, the development of the Shetland breed was haphazard and the wool produced was coarser. It was made up into stockings and traded with the Dutch and Hansiatic fleets who fished the immensely rich grounds off the islands. Nowadays the Shetlanders themselves fish these grounds and the economy of the islands has veered away from the croft to fishing.

This is how William Peace of Kirkwall in Orkney saw the tiny island of Fair Isle in the 1870s:

> 'This island lies midway between Orkney and Shetland. It is inhabited by about three hundred people whose chief employment is fishing . . . they are excellent boatmen and manage their little skiffs with great dexterity. Several boats and crews of four or five men board almost every passing vessel and are at all times prepared to sell fresh fish and native hosiery or, possibly what in former times used to pay them better, barter their goods for tobacco or gin which at convenient seasons they again smuggle into the towns of Kirkwall and Lerwick.

Shetland fishing boats.

'While the male portion of the islands prosecute the fishing the females employ themselves in knitting hosiery, gloves, caps, stockings and vests with curious patterns and variegated colours each combined with the fine softness of texture making the articles so much sought after that they are kept for sale by most of the merchants both in Kirkwall and Lerwick'.

In 1895,Dr James Bridon comments in a newspaper article:

'They make their own turning lathes, looms, spinning wheels, cloth, clothes, boots, clogs, furniture of all sorts, boats, spades, mills, wheelbarrows, in fact everything they need. The islands had few resources, yet what they had was utilised in a surprising number of ways. Stone was a universal building material—soap stone was carved into fishing weights, whirls for spindles, and weights for looms. What the island lacked in home-grown timber, the beaches made up for in driftwood. Deal from passing ships and even timbers of wrecked ships were sawn up and fashioned into chairs, dressers and household items ... nothing produced in the croft was wasted'.

Shetland and Fair Isle Knitting: Its History and Development as an Industry on the Islands

Two-colour knitting has been practised almost since knitting began, although in the past the technique was different from that used today. For details of current technique see page 13.

The earliest samples of a fabric resembling knitting are the sandal socks of the Coptic Christians of pre-Islamic Egypt (4th century) and the turbans and shawls of the Paracus and Nazca periods in Peru (3 BC to 3 AD). These were made in 'cross knit looping'—a method whereby a single needle with an eye takes a loop around the crossing of the loop in the previous row. It is not until the 12th century that we find evidence of two-colour knitting practised in the faster method we know today. This technique was developed by the Arabs, whose knitting became a source of inspiration to Europe.

Under the auspices of the guild system, knitting craft reached its height by the turn of the 16th century in Germany, Spain, Holland, France, Denmark, Italy and England. The male fashion of the courts, with their proclivity for knit-hose, diffused throughout the general population. A gradual change from fine two-colour knitting in silk to single-colour

A very fine Shetland lace shawl knitted in 1898.

A Shetland Lace Knitter taking advantage of daylight to work the intricacies of lace.

knitting in wool heralded the start of the cottage industry system which has played so great a part in the lives of the rural and coastal populations of our islands.

For anyone fascinated to discover the history of world knitting you will find that Richard Rutt has synthesised the majority of historical records in his 1987 publication *The History of Knitting*, published by Batsford.

Shetland and Fair Isle were not immune to large scale hand knitting enterprise and at first, knitting was concentrated upon coarse hose, as elsewhere in Britain. Nor were the islands immune to the influence of the Industrial revolution.

When the Hawick frame knitters took over plain hosiery from the hand knitters, the latter responded by producing lace shawls because plain knitting was much faster than two-colour knitting and it was possible to make decorative patterns in a single colour by the simple employment of the purl stitch and the slip stitch.

The application of this skill led to Shetland being famous for its very fine lace knitting (a subject of study in its own right and beyond the scope of this book*).

A market for lace shawls developed and it is recorded that most islanders concentrated on knitting lace.

In 1837, Queen Victoria was presented with some fine lace knitting as a way of stimulating trade. But the end of the 19th century saw the

* For further information see Sarah Don, *Lace Knitting*, 1979.

176

A Shetland jersey stretched out to dry, Lerwick.

collapse of this industry, due to the mechanisation of the craft, notably in Nottingham which then provoked the reintroduction throughout the whole of the Shetlands of two-colour knitting which, until then, had been exclusive to the tiny island of Fair Isle. More and more of the Fair Isle knitting was being made by the mainlanders of Shetland.

Lace knitting by hand continued in a small way on the island of Unst.

Demand was so great that the major wool brokers began to spin and dye the wool in bulk. Needless to say, the inhabitants of Fair Isle were a little upset that their 'Fair Isle patterns were becoming diluted; never more so than when the Shetland mainlanders had a label woven reading 'Fair Isle garment made in Shetland' in blatant breach of copyright law—a law in its infancy. The Fair Isle knitting industry countered by producing their own label, 'Fair Isle garment made in Fair Isle'… and very many since—labels such as 'The Shetland Knitters' Association', 'The Shetland Trader' and 'Shetlands from Shetland'. No doubt in future they will become valuable collectors' items. .

By the 1920s the industry had begun to decline and, to give it a boost, the Prince of Wales accepted gifts of a Fair Isle V-necked pullover for himself and a Fair Isle outfit for the Princess Mary. They wore them publicly—the Prince at St Andrews in 1921 when, as Captain of the Royal and Ancient Golf Club, he drove off at the first tee *(see pages 214–217)*. He gave the garment 'society' approval and

The Prince of Wales painted by Sir Henry Lander.

it again became fashionable to wear Fair Isles for sporting activities. The Xmas edition of *Vogue* magazine for 30th December 1922 featured Shetland knitwear prominently, with photographs of old ladies spinning the wool and Shetland girls knitting whilst carrying peat on their backs, all accompanied by a tentative description of the origin of the patterns. It makes strange reading compared with the rest of the magazine, with advertisements for furs and motor-cars, its gossip columns and society adventures.

The demand for Fair Isle fashion garments continued throughout the 1930s, and after the second world war many of the men who had been stationed on Shetland took scarves, gloves and jerseys back home as presents. In this way, the Fair Isle knitting technique became known throughout Britain. The depth of demand stretched Shetlanders in terms of authenticity. They bowed to the wishes of fashion buyers by creating new patterns and changing their traditional colour combinations.

Many hundreds of patterns were published attempting to retain elements of Fair Isle and yet, as the two patterns below illustrate (from many hundreds), they missed the essential characteristics of Fair Isle knitting— colour harmony, the conscious search for rythmn and depth within the range of their chosen yarn colours and the application of this colour range within the sets of pattern chosen.

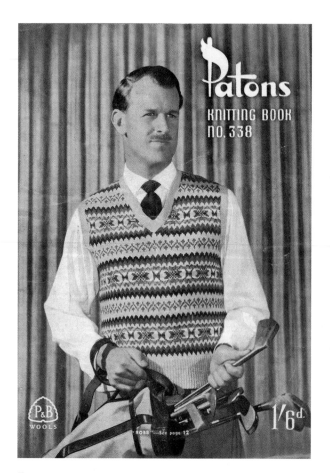

Fair Isle Knitting patterns by Paton and Baldwin.

Sadly in circumstances where the elements of this tradition were crudely maintained, the inevitable arrival of knitting machines developed for home use exacerbated the decline to the point where it was possible to purchase the collar already knitted where the knitter had only to complete the garment in plain stocking stitch with her Empisal or Passap. By the late 1960s, traditional Fair Isle knitting had become to all intent and purpose defunct on the Islands of Shetland.

Shetland and Fair Isle Knitting—A Reawakening

Having spent many years becoming familiar with single colour knitting I had to readily admit my lack of knowledge of pattern and colour. I therefore needed help in interpreting artefacts, in sourcing the knitters and their knowledge. It was my good fortune to have been trading ganseys to the Scottish Merchant in Covent Garden, who introduced me to one their suppliers of Fair Isle knitwear—Margaret Stuart. Margaret looks after some two hundred knitters who now reproduce the traditional patterns found on shawls and scarves knitted on Fair Isle before the first world war.

She was instrumental in giving me access to her knitters and over some hospitable Scottish evening conversations I became familiar with pattern developments from the mid 1800's to today. Most important of all I was to learn that Margaret and her contemporaries were responsible for the resurgence of traditional Shetland and Fair Isle knitting.

Margaret described the situation on returning to Shetland in the late 1960's to find the collapse of Shetland knitting cooperatives. She explained her shock to find that the majority of the knitting was done on machines using pastel colours and designs that were Norwegian in origin, the old patterns having disappeared. She vowed that she would revive the old patterns using the original colour combinations,

Buy a Yoke — an industry knit collar sold with wool to knit your own jumper.

Margaret Stuart collecting Fair Isle jerseys from her knitters.

Three Fair Isles stretch drying on frames to ensure no shrinkage.

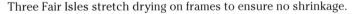

using as inspiration an old allover scarf her mother used to wear, knitted on Fair Isle around 1910 using hand spun and hand dyed wool.

'This is the sort of Fair Isle we had always grown up with,' she said, 'A very vibrant alive Fair Isle'. Margaret observed. 'It was always having seen Fair Isle like this that made me so depressed seeing the Norwegian allover patterns, and of course those horrible yokes—plain pullovers with patterned borders round the neck. We looked everywhere and I went into Jamiesons and I asked them what had happened—they didn't even have the right colours then. . . Well, it just started from that'.

Toward Recognising the Essential Characteristics of Shetland and Fair Isle Knitters and Knitting

As I have already noted, it was generally recognised that two-colour knitting became the domain skill of the Shetlands as a consequence of industrialisation. Shetland had to develop a product that would become synonymous with the technique and the Islands. It makes a fascinating story.

Two-colour knitting requires two major elements. The first element is to use different coloured yarn to knit the second element—patterns within the fabric of the garment.

Where did these patterns originate? How did Shetlanders create colours for dyeing their yarn?

Examining the dyeing technique of these islanders is to witness a wonderful example of their resource ability. Before the advent of Fairy dyes, colours were obtained from a variety of sources. Indigo and madder

Fair Isle Scarves knitted by Margeret Dennis.1900–1920
Scarves on the edge of photograph knitted around 1900.
Centre scarf knitted in 1920—the major patterns from the base up have become known as "Meeting Hearts", the "Armada Cross", "The Wheel" and the "Flight of Birds".

dyes were imported, first from Hansiatic traders in the 17th century, and later from the Dutch herring fleets. Golds, yellows and greens were probably imported as well, although there is plenty of evidence to suggest that local dyes were also used. A purple dye was made from 'lichen tartereus', known locally as 'korkelit', obtained by scraping it off the rocks after rain, then reducing it to a powder and soaking it in household 'lay' (part urine, part water). Similarly, 'lichen saxitlis' ('old man's beard') produced a yellowish brown or red, 'lichen parietinus' known locally as 'scroita', an orange, and 'lichen omphaloides' a brownish purple. Yellows came from 'doken' leaves and grass, black from 'yuleburse' and 'meadowsweet' or from peat impregnated with bog iron. Further variations of shades were gained from the natural wool colours of the indigenous sheep: from 'moorit' (dark brown), through shades of purple browns, greys and creams to Shetland white which was obtained by bleaching the wool over sulphur on peat.

The year 1840 was a significant one for Shetland knitters as this was the year Fairy Dyes began to market chemical based dyes, and it was also the year that two-colour knitting began its next wave of popularity. Imagine the excitement of knitters as they feasted their eyes on these bright chemical colours. Looking back at early examples the bright and vibrant combinations of the 1850s come across as almost violent in comparison to the subtle colour variations that decorate contemporary Fair Isles

As to the second element of two-colour knitting, searching for pattern origins has generated stories of mythical proportion.

In reality patterns are mostly derived from other techniques of working strands of yarn, such as weaving and embroidery. One would, of course, like to be able to say that a certain pattern comes from a particular source on such and such a date. This is, however, an impossibility. Indeed, it is even difficult to determine when and where two-colour knitting was first practised.

When Fair Isle became widely known earlier this century, British knitters assumed that Fair Isle was the place where two-colour knitting was invented because Spanish sailors from the Armada ships sunk off the coast in the 16th century were responsible for teaching the islanders. The truth, of course, was that the islanders were far too concerned with surviving on their meagre resources to sit down and take knitting lessons. Some of the sailors' clothes might have been patterned, and one or two knitters might have copied them. To do so, of course, the technique of two-colour knitting would have had to be already known. In any case, there really is no doubt that the technique has been practised for as long as there have been people on the islands.

A more important question is: how did the knitters come to create particular patterns?

If one looks at the patterns produced in other countries, two trends emerge: one towards geometrics and one towards representation. There are, of course, crossover points between these two approaches where representation is geometricised, but this has more to do with solving the problems of realistic representation that arise from the technique.

In the knitting of Italy, Spain and Peru the tradition is representational. In the Scandinavian countries, including Shetland, it is geometrical. In the former countries, the decoration on the garments was a celebration, more often than not a religious one. The patterns were designed before the knitting was started. In Shetland it was a celebration of the knitting itself and of the creative pleasure of discovering new patterns and colour combinations as the work progressed. The patterns thus produced closely related to the technique of maintaining, adding or subtracting a colour round by round. The results of this are columns, triangles, diamonds and bands. Combinations of these form crosses, lozenges and the like.

A central factor of knitting technique must also be taken into account when when determining the creation of patterns. This is the 'floating' of the yarn not in use, behind the colour in the pattern. This stranded technique of knitting means that if your second colour comes a long way along the round on the pattern you fancy, the result would be a large loop at the back which would tend to pull the garment out of shape. The way round this was to introduce a pattern within a pattern. The best examples are seen in the lozenge shapes—columns, crosses and diamonds introduced to cut down the stranding at the back of the work.

Every knitter would have a collection such as this, built up over the years
along with graph notations and details of colour combinations..

Tam o'Shanter and 'Haf' caps,
knitted 1860.

In the hands of a truly creative knitter, the work would be a series of
bands and colour juxtapositions without a single repeat, the harmony
being created in the work as a whole. Any new pattern discovered would
be notated on graph paper for future use and development. For the less
creative, the source of inspiration might be other geometric shapes in
everyday life—lace patterns, weaving, other people's knitting, even the
lino on the floor.

Early examples of colour knitting concentrate on the lozenge shape
with a later introduction of the cross: alternating the two makes the
familiar 'oxo' combination. They are almost always worked in horizontal
bands, similar to the purl stitch designs of the single-colour ganseys of
Foula and the Western Isles.

In some, the horizontal bands are separated by small rounds of colour
like the garter stitching on a gansey, with only a rudimentary attempt
at patterning *(see tasselled scarf)*. A later development was to present
the patterns alternately *(see fringed scarf)*; by the time the whole of

Early Fair Isle 1880 Fringed scarf (centre)
Tasselled scarf (outer)

A modern V-neck pullover photographed in situ, hinting at a seaside inspiration for its pattern source. The reality of extending existing lozenge patterns creates a natural diamond tessellation. You will find excellent graph samples on pages 133–135 of Sheila McGregor's *Traditional Fair Isle Knitting*, 1981, B T Batsford, reprinted by Dover Publications.

Shetland was knitting Fair Isle, the border patterns between the 'oxo' bands had disappeared entirely, leaving the lozenges to merge together in an allover tessellation

I must add here that this creative development was not universal and border panels continue to this day. There is, however, a tendency now to go for the complete allover pattern as it lends itself to machine production. Despite this tendency the development of border patterns continued, particularly the use of "peaks"—diamond shapes, that interlaced three or four times before the start of major repeats. Within a pattern sequence, made up from natural variations of colour, each diamond would be graded from dark to light and then reversed from light to dark. In the centre of this would be placed a contrasting pattern sequence echoing this illusion of depth.

Fair Isle pattern sequence detailing the use of 'peaks' to create depth and rythmn

The natural colours of Shetland wool.

This pattern is notated in the natural colours of the Shetland sheep, ranging from the darkest brown (Shetland black) which forms the majority of the darkest background contrast, and ranges through to Shetland white (achieved by sulphurizing). The pattern itself is a sequence of banded widths on top of which-is placed a pattern in contrast. You will note that each pattern is, in turn, bordered by 2 'peerie' (small) bands of similar rows derived from the same pattern. This whole sequence is then divided from its repeat by a similar band width that supports a different pattern on each repeat.

Colour sequencing follows a general convention—the most obvious being the reversal of the colour relationships within the major pattern areas. The centre banding on one pattern becoming the borders for the next major sequence: a simple and pleasing design harmonic. It was the general tendency for the backgrounds to employ the darkest and lightest colours—with the pattern work formed from the mid ranges. The resulting tonal relationship creates the illusion of depth—one major pattern appearing to come forward from the edge to the centre—the next receding from the outside to the middle. The introduction of a greater range of colour created a challenge for convention, which eventually gave rise to the following colour relationships.

1. All Gold and Yellow shades are worked as a contrast to Shetland Black.
2. Shetland White is worked as a contrast to Madder Red.
3. Bands of Black and White are contrasted with Black on White and Gold on White.
4. All major bands of colour and peerie bands alternate the colour relationships, where the ultimate aim is the creation of depth and rhythm.

A swatch collection noting welt details and pattern combinations for future reference.

In this collection of pattern swatches it is timely to observe how the welt of jerseys have been made up of out of the darkest and lightest colour. At first sight this may seem a rather bold inclusion, but a little thought about the normal alternative: a band of plain colour that would be included around the base, the neck and the cuff, would render the richness of the body fabric out of place. And what colour would you choose? Whatever decision, it would serve only to make the jersey and its wearer look as though they were playing with hula hoops. Granted, the purl and plaining of the welt does not make for the most efficient of bases (indeed in time there is a tendency for it to curl) but this design decision is much the most preferable particularly when it must be remembered that the garment was largely decorative and the welt therefore consequential.

There is an alternative and that was to repeat the colour bands as they occur on the jersey in a 1 round repeat of K1, P1. The final effect was to mirror the tonal relationships of the main body. But here lies an important consideration which determined that this method was a sure sign that the knitter had made the garment in like form on some previous occasion, not as personal expression, more likely this knitting was for payment

This consideration and observation lies central to the point I have been making—that ordinary knitters of these Scottish and Scandinavian traditions required their work to be a creative challenge. There is ample historical evidence to note that most of these knitters considered their knitting much like a painter does their canvas—a vehicle for creative problem solving. The problem: how to use whatever wool they had at hand (especially if left over from a knitting contract to some local entrepreneur!), how to put it together as harmoniously as possible (the bottom line being the possibility of a specific colour running out before the completion of the garment) and yet still retain the harmonics of the pattern and colour sequencing. Knitting in horizontal banding in the manner I have already described makes the possibility of a near match of colour not so obvious, especially when worked in order to create the illusion of movement. Secondly, and much more importantly the knitters of these garments understood by experience that colour values are totally dependant on their relationship with other colours. They discovered that it is impossible to be really sure whether colours work together within a knitted pattern fabric unless it is actually knitted.

A true Fair Isle knitter would have no idea what relationship they would end up with (apart from a popular use of the Shetland Black as background or they were knitting up a Gold and Madder Red traditional piece). Their knitting would begin with the darkest and lightest for the welt and the fabric would be trial and error as they went up the body. It was not uncommon for the first real repeat to begin under the arm. This continual knitting and re- knitting would often serve to create the most harmonious blend of seeming disparate colours.

This experimentation of course follows two major rules which is absolutely central to this tradition. (This applies to highly traditional colour combinations as well as personal expression.)

Never work more than two colours in a round. There is no exception to this rule except when working the centre round of a major pattern. Equally importantly only ever change one colour in any round, ie making changes to the colours either on the background or the contrast.

Put simply, following these rules will maximise the very nature of the knitted stitch—its shape lends itself to the merging of colours—a blue background changing to a red background over two rounds optically blends to a purple transition, particularly if this changeover has a red or blue tinge to the contrast working over the top. This manipulation of contrast and background is the great challenge to Shetland knitters particularly if the wool they are using is leftovers. There is only one way to find out if it works—and that is to do it.

A cozy Shetland fireside.

An old man in his
'allover' Fair Isle, 1920.

KNITTING PATTERN INSTRUCTIONS FOR AN ALLOVER FAIR ISLE

The graph system I have used throughout this section to denote the Fair Isle patterns relies on the fact that no more than two colours are ever worked in one round (hence the name 'two-colour' knitting). In each round, the white squares represent background stitches and the black squares stitches worked in a contrasting colour. Both of these colours will change regularly. The recommended colour combinations are indicated for you round by round, although you may, of course, substitute your own if you prefer.

The pattern fully written out here is an old Fair Isle one made around the turn of the century in the old Fair Isle colours. You will note that the colour configurations for this pattern and the samples I have constructed to illustrate structure, etc., are consistent throughout. There is no alternation of colours within the major bands and no evidence of white on blue within the peerie band. I propose, therefore, that this pattern is an example of Fair Isle knitting immediately before what I would term 'Classic Fair Isle'. Within this pattern are all the features expected. The 'oxo' (lozenge and cross) configuration is the main feature, separated by numerous 'peerie' (small) patterns. The 'oxo' bands take up 13 rounds, with 24 sts to each pattern; the peeries are 7 rounds deep, with pattern repeats of 4, 5, 6 or 7 sts.

Like all traditional knitting the garment is worked in the round. Its construction and knitting technique are similar to those of the fisher ganseys: the body is knit in a tube and each sleeve is knit down from the shoulder to the cuff, incorporating an underarm gusset. Where it differs from a gansey is that instead of putting the work on a holder after the gussets and then knitting the pattern up the front and back with two needles, the Fair Isle knitter bridges the sleeve opening so that she can continue to work up the yokes in the round. There are two ways of doing this: either cast on and work an extra 8 to 10 stitches or wrap all wool in use 10 or 12 times around the needle where the armholes are to be divided, and repeat the procedure on every round. Whichever method is used, when the sleeves are finished, the extra stitches or lengths of wool are cut and sewn into the back of the work.

Instructions for construction of a Fair Isle Classic can be found on page 194, titled 'Miss Flora Campbell's Classic Fair Isle Cardigan'.

The pattern instructions begin:

Size: to fit 38–40 inch (96–102 cm) chest.

Wool: about 24 oz Shetland Heritage yarn *(see page 248)* as follows:
   Main yarn (Peat) 8 oz;
   Secondary colours (Madder Red, Snaa White, Auld Gold) 5 oz each.
A brighter combination would include: Main yarn (Coll Black) 8 oz; 5 oz each Auld Gold, Snaa White Madder Red.
Needles: set each of No. 12 (2¾ mm) and No. 11 (3 mm) double-pointed needles; set each of circular twin pins.
Tension: 9 stitches and 7 rows to 1 inch (2.5 cm) over patterned stocking stitch using No. 11 (3 mm) needles.

The body
With No. 12 (2¾ mm) needles cast on 320 sts in Peat and work 3 rounds of K1, P1 rib. Change to Madder Red and work 3 more rounds, followed by 3 rounds each of Gold, White, Gold, Red and Peat, 27 rounds of rib altogether. Change to No. 11 (3 mm) needles and, still with Peat, work 2 rounds in plain stocking stitch, increasing evenly until you have 360 sts. Mark the half rounds with a contrast colour for the seam lines. The pattern now begins.

Pattern sequence
Work the patterns shown on the next two pages in the following order on the body of the garment (the peerie bands are numbered and the major patterns are lettered):

MAJOR PATTERNS

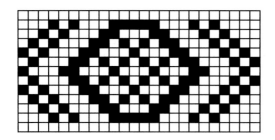

A	B	C	B	C	B	C	B	C	B	C	B	C	B	C	B	C	B	C	B
Round 1	24																		
Round 2	4	1	1	1	3	5	3	1	1	1	3								
Round 3	3	1	1	1	3	2	3	2	3	1	1	1	2						
Round 4	2	1	1	1	3	2	1	1	1	1	1	2	3	1	1	1	1		
Round 5	1	1	1	1	3	2	3	1	3	2	3	1	1	1					
Round 6		1	1	1	3	2	1	1	1	1	1	1	1	2	3	1	1		
Round 7	1	1	3	2	3	1	3	1	3	2	3	1							
Round 8		1	1	1	3	2	1	1	1	1	1	1	1	2	3	1	1		
Round 9	1	1	1	1	3	2	3	1	3	2	3	1	1	1					
Round 10	2	1	1	1	3	2	1	1	1	1	1	2	3	1	1	1	1		
Round 11	3	1	1	1	3	2	3	2	3	1	1	1	2						
Round 12	4	1	1	1	3	5	3	1	1	1	3								
Round 13	24																		

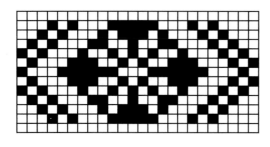

B	B	C	B	C	B	C	B	C	B	C	B	C	B	C	B	C	B	C
Round 1	24																	
Round 2	4	1	1	1	3	5	3	1	1	1	3							
Round 3	3	1	1	1	3	1	1	3	1	1	3	1	1	1	2			
Round 4	2	1	1	1	3	2	2	1	2	2	3	1	1	1	1			
Round 5	1	1	1	1	3	1	2	1	1	1	1	2	1	3	1	1	1
Round 6		1	1	1	3	3	2	1	1	1	2	3	3	1	1			
Round 7	1	1	3	6	3	6	3	1										
Round 8		1	1	1	3	3	2	1	1	1	2	3	3	1	1			
Round 9	1	1	1	1	3	1	2	1	1	1	1	2	1	3	1	1	1
Round 10	2	1	1	1	3	2	2	1	2	2	3	1	1	1	1			
Round 11	3	1	1	1	3	1	1	3	1	1	3	1	1	1	2			
Round 12	4	1	1	1	3	5	3	1	1	1	3							
Round 13	24																	

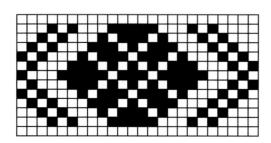

C	B	C	B	C	B	C	B	C	B	C	B	C	B	C	B	C
Round 1	24															
Round 2	4	1	1	1	3	5	3	1	1	1	3					
Round 3	3	1	1	1	3	1	1	3	1	1	3	1	1	1	2	
Round 4	2	1	1	1	3	3	1	1	1	3	3	1	1	1	1	
Round 5	1	1	1	1	3	1	1	3	1	3	1	1	3	1	1	1
Round 6		1	1	1	3	3	1	1	1	1	1	1	3	3	1	1
Round 7	1	1	3	5	1	3	1	5	3	1						
Round 8		1	1	1	3	3	1	1	1	1	1	1	3	3	1	1
Round 9	1	1	1	1	3	1	1	3	1	3	1	1	3	1	1	1
Round 10	2	1	1	1	3	3	1	1	1	3	3	1	1	1	1	
Round 11	3	1	1	1	3	1	1	3	1	1	3	1	1	1	2	
Round 12	4	1	1	1	3	5	3	1	1	1	3					
Round 13	24															

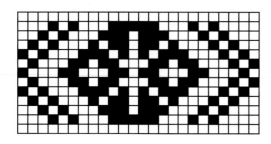

D	B	C	B	C	B	C	B	C	B	C	B	C	B	C	B	C
Round 1	24															
Round 2	4	1	1	1	3	5	3	1	1	1	3					
Round 3	3	1	1	1	3	1	1	1	1	1	3	1	1	1	2	
Round 4	2	1	1	1	3	1	1	1	1	1	1	1	3	1	1	1
Round 5	1	1	1	1	3	3	1	1	1	1	3	3	1	1	1	
Round 6		1	1	1	3	2	1	2	3	2	1	2	3	1	1	
Round 7	1	1	3	2	3	2	1	2	3	2	3	1				
Round 8		1	1	1	3	2	1	2	3	2	1	2	3	1	1	
Round 9	1	1	1	1	3	3	1	1	1	1	3	3	1	1	1	
Round 10	2	1	1	1	3	1	1	2	1	2	1	1	3	1	1	1
Round 11	3	1	1	1	3	3	1	3	3	1	1	1	2			
Round 12	4	1	1	1	3	5	3	1	1	1	3					
Round 13	24															

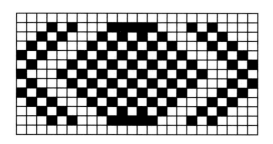

E	B	C	B	C	B	C	B	C	B	C	B	C	B	C	B	C	B
Round 1	24																
Round 2	4	1	1	1	3	5	3	1	1	1	3						
Round 3	3	1	1	1	3	1	1	1	1	1	1	3	1	1	1	3	
Round 4	2	1	1	1	3	1	1	1	1	1	1	1	1	3	1	1	1
Round 5	1	1	1	1	3	1	1	1	1	1	1	1	1	1	3	1	1
Round 6		1	1	1	3	1	1	1	1	1	1	1	1	1	1	3	1
Round 7	1	1	3	1	1	1	1	1	1	1	1	1	1	1	1	3	1
Round 8		1	1	1	3	1	1	1	1	1	1	1	1	1	1	3	1
Round 9	1	1	1	1	3	1	1	1	1	1	1	1	1	1	3	1	1
Round 10	2	1	1	1	3	1	1	1	1	1	1	1	1	3	1	1	1
Round 11	3	1	1	1	3	1	1	1	1	1	1	3	1	1	1	3	
Round 12	4	1	1	1	3	5	3	1	1	1	3						
Round 13	24																

No.1

5x7	B	C	B	C	B
Round 1	5				
Round 2	1	1	1	1	1
Round 3	1	3	1		
Round 4	1	3	1		
Round 5	1	3	1		
Round 6	1	1	1	1	1
Round 7	5				

Peerie No.1
single repeat
5sts and 7 rds

No.2

6x7	B	C	B	C	B
Round 1	6				
Round 2	2	3	1		
Round 3	1	1	3	1	
Round 4		1	2	1	2
Round 5	1	1	3	1	
Round 6	2	3	1		
Round 7	6				

Peerie No.2
single repeat
6sts and 7 rds

No.3

7x7	B	C	B	C	B	C
Round 1	7					
Round 2	3	1	3			
Round 3	2	3	2			
Round 4	1	2	1	2	1	
Round 5	2	3	2			
Round 6	3	1	3			
Round 7	7					

Peerie No.3
single repeat
7sts and 7 rds

No.4

6x7	B	C	B	C	B
Round 1	6				
Round 2		1	2	1	2
Round 3		2	3	1	
Round 4	1	2	1	2	
Round 5	2	3	1		
Round 6		1	2	1	2
Round 7	6				

Peerie No.4
single repeat
6sts and 7 rds

No.5

5x7	B	C	B	C	B
Round 1	5				
Round 2		1	3	1	
Round 3	3	2			
Round 4	2	2	1		
Round 5	1	2	2		
Round 6		2	3		
Round 7	5				

Peerie No.5
single repeat
5sts and 7rds

No 6

8x7	B	C	B	C	B
Round 1	8				
Round 2	1	2	3	2	
Round 3		2	5	1	
Round 4		1	3	1	3
Round 5	3	3	2		
Round 6	2	2	1	2	1
Round 7	8				

Peerie No.6
single repeat
8sts and 7rds

No 7

4x7	B	C	B	C	B
Round 1	4				
Round 2	2	2			
Round 3		1	2	1	
Round 4		4			
Round 5		1	2	1	
Round 6	2	2			
Round 7	4				

Peerie No.7
single
repeat
4sts x 7rds

The old man in his Fair Isle pullover has the following sequence:
    1, A, 1, 2, 1, B, 1, 3, 1, C, 1, 4, 1, D, 1, 5, 1, E, 1, 6, 1
The arm sequence is:
    1, 4, 1, C, 1, 3, 1, B, 1, 2, 1, A, 1, 7, 1
The extra peerie (7) may also be worked for extra length on the sleeve or as needed.

The pattern sample I wear is as follows:
    1, A, 1, 2, 1, B, 1, 3, 1, C, 1, 4, 1, D, 1, 5, 1, E, 1, 6, 1
Note the arm sequence is from the top, where it is traditional to omit the last pattern sequence on the body (E) in order to 'match' the arm sequence with the body:
    Thus: 1, 5, 1, D, 1, 4, 1, C, 1, 3, 1, B, 1, 2, 1, A

The colour combinations are notated as follows:
B = background; C = contrast)

The colours of the 'peerie' patterns:
No. 1: B = Madder Red; C = Snaa White
Nos. 2, 3, 4, 5, 6, 7: B = Peat; C = Snaa White

The colours of all major patterns: A, B, C, D, E
1st rd: peat

2nd, 3rd and 4th rds:	B = Peat; C= Gold
5th rd:	B = Peat; C= White
6th, 7th and 8th rds:	B = Red; C = White
9th rd:	B = Peat; C = White
10th, 11th and 12th rds:	B = Peat; C = Gold
13th rd:	Peat

The gussets

Work in pattern until you come to 3 inches (7.5 cm) below your underarm height. Increase 1 st on each side of the seam line which you have marked on the next and every following 4th round. Working in pattern but leaving the gusset stitches plain, continue in this way until you reach the underarm. Place the gusset stitches on holders.

The yokes

Cast on 10 sts at each side where the gusset stitches were, and continue in the round up the front and back yokes, keeping the extra stitches plain. When you have reached the required shoulder height, finishing at the end of a major pattern, cast off the plain extra stitches you made across the armholes.

The shoulder panels

Place the centre 60 sts at front and back on holders for the neck. With two needles, work one more major pattern on the front right shoulder. Place these stitches on a holder. Repeat for the other front shoulder (leave the back shoulder stitches unworked). Now graft these two shoulder panels onto the back shoulder stitches by putting the right sides together and casting off the stitches simultaneously.

The sleeves

Pick up stitches for the sleeve evenly around the shoulder panels, knitting into the edge of the plain section where the pattern ends and picking up the gusset stitches from the holder. Before starting to work the sleeve, beginning with the pattern used on the body just above the armhole cut down the centre of the plain knitting that bridges the armhole.

Start to work the sleeve, beginning with the pattern used on the body just above the armhole. Keeping the gusset plain and decreasing 1 st on each side on the next and every following 4th round until the gusset is worked out, continue the sleeve, working the patterns in reverse order from that used on the body so that when completed the sleeve and body patterns will more or less match across the garment.

Once the gusset is worked out, the decreasing on the remainder of the sleeve depends largely on its length. 1 st on each side of the seam line every 7th round should suffice, until 90 sts remain. Continue without further decreasing until you reach the required length, allowing about 2½ inches (6.5 cm) for the cuff. Change to No. 12 (2¾ mm) needles and red. Work 4 rounds knitwise, then 4 rounds in K3, P3 rib. Then work 20 rounds in K3, P3 rib, using white for the knit stitches and red for the purl stitches. Work 2 rounds knitwise using red only and cast off ribwise.

Work the other sleeve to match.

Michael Pearson wearing a Fair Isle classic, 1982.

The neck

Using red and No. 12 (2¾ mm) needles, pick up stitches evenly for the neck from the holders and around the shoulder panels. Work 1 round in K3, P3 rib. Then work 10 rounds in K3, P3 rib, using white for the knit stitches and red for the purl stitches. Work 1 round knitwise in red only and cast off ribwise.

Finishing

Turn the garment inside out. Sew the edges of the plain bridging sections that were cut for the armholes gently into the armholes to a depth of about 1 inch (2.5 cm). Cut off any excess. Gather the neck edge lightly with string to stop any stretching and then wash the garment gently in tepid water and pure soap flakes. Rinse it thoroughly and dry it flat—do not force the drying by tumbling. The classic method of drying in Shetland is to board the garments. The wool, stretched when damp, is pulled into shape as it dries, preventing shrinkage.

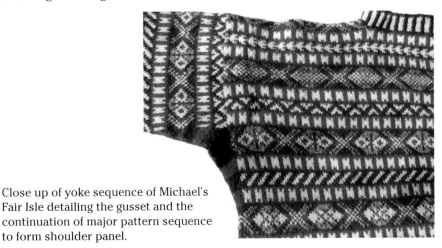

Close up of yoke sequence of Michael's Fair Isle detailing the gusset and the continuation of major pattern sequence to form shoulder panel.

MISS FLORA CAMPBELL'S CLASSIC FAIR ISLE CARDIGAN PATTERN

The next stage in understanding Fair Isle is to include a pattern that implements developments in the conventions of the tradition. Miss Flora Campbell's cardigan pattern is a Classic—the traditional colour sequence has a contrasting blue added—a chemical-based blue from the Fairy Dye Company. In addition Miss Flora Campbell introduces a fully worked pattern that applies the traditional internal colour sequencing within the major pattern elements; and in the tradition of 'never sewing when you can knit' Flora has structured the making of the jersey to include 'steeking' the cardigan centre front, which entails knitting a plain knitted panel at the quarter round which is then cut down the middle to make the opening of the cardigan. Further, she has, in the sleeve shaping and construction, made for a soft line where the pattern runs over the shoulder in a continuing sequence. The main patterns are all equal in size, each taking up 11 rounds and 20 stitches. The peeries vary between 6 and 8 rounds and 4 and 20 stitches. The sleeves are picked up from shaped armholes and there are no underarm gussets.

Size: to fit 36–38 inch (91–96 cm) bust or chest.
Wool: about 22 oz (624 g) Jamieson & Smith Shetland Heritage yarn as follows:

   Main colour (Peat): 6 oz (170 g);
   Secondary colours (Indigo, Madder Red, Auld Gold and Snaa White): 4 oz (114 g) each.
Needles: set each of No. 12 (2¾ mm) and No. 11 (3 mm) double-pointed needles; *or* set each circular twin pins.
Tension: 9 stitches and 7 rows to 1 inch (2.5 cm) over patterned stocking stitch using No. 11 (3 mm) needles.

The body

With No. 12 (2¾ mm) needles cast on 320 sts in Peat. Work in K1, P1 rib for 75 sts, K10 for the steek, then K1, P1 rib for a further 75 sts to complete the half round. Work the remaining 160 sts in rib to complete the full round. Repeat for the second round. Keeping the steek in plain knitting and Peat, continue in K1, P1 rib, introducing the secondary colours, one per round, over the knit stitches only, in the following order: Red, White, Indigo, Gold, Indigo, White. Repeat this colour combination four times (24 rounds). Then finish the welt with 2 rounds in Peat (28 rounds of rib altogether).

Change to No. 11 (3 mm) needles. In Peat, work 2 plain rounds, increasing evenly (except over the steek) to 360 sts. Mark the half rounds with contrast wool. The pattern now begins. Work in the sequence indicated *(see pages 197–199)*, remembering to knit the 10 sts plain for the steek on every round as follows: pattern 80 sts *(i.e.* four full major patterns), K10 sts in one of the two colours in use, pick up the pattern again for 10 sts *(i.e.* the second half of the 5th major pattern), then continue in complete patterns for the next 80 sts (to make the half round) and the remaining 180 sts (to make the full round). There will be nine full major patterns across the back, and eight and a half across the front, together with the 10 sts of the steek.

Flora Campbell's cardigan.

The back yoke

Continue in pattern until you reach the required height to the underarm. Divide the work for front and back by working one half round for the front (180 sts) and placing these stitches on a holder. Working on the back 180 sts with two needles only, decrease 1 st at each end of the next 6 rows, then 1 st at each end of every alternate row for the next 12 rows, then 1 st at each end of the following 3rd row (154 sts).

Continue without further shaping until you reach the required shoulder height, ending on a wrong-side (purl) row. Work 42 sts for the right shoulder; leave them on a holder. Work 70 sts for the back neck; leave them on a holder. Work the remaining 42 sts for the left shoulder; leave them on a holder.

The front yoke

Right front: with correct side of the work facing, rejoin yarn at right edge and, with two needles and working over the first 80 sts only, decrease 1 st at armhole edge for the next 6 rows, then every 3rd row for the next 12 rows (70 sts).

Continue without further shaping until you are 3 inches (7.5 cm) below the required shoulder height. Now decrease 1 st at the neck edge every row for the next 28 rows (42 sts). Continue until you reach the required shoulder height. Leave the stitches on a holder.

Left front: rejoin yarn at right edge of left front, leaving stitches for the steek on a holder. Work the left front to match the right.

Graft the shoulder seams, putting the right sides together.

The sleeves

With No. 12 (2¾ mm) needles and Peat, pick up 160 sts evenly around the armhole. Knit 2 rounds. Change to No. 11 (3 mm) needles and continue in pattern, remembering to work the patterns in reverse order from that on the body. Decrease 1 st each side of the seam line at the underarm every 6th round, or as necessary depending on the sleeve length, until you have 90 sts.

Continue without further shaping until you reach the required length, allowing 3 inches (7.5 cm) for the cuff welt, finishing on a peerie pattern band. Change to No. 12 (2¾ mm) needles and knit 2 rounds in Peat. Then work 28 rounds of K1, P1 rib to match the welt on the body. Cast off ribwise.

Work the other sleeve to match.

Cardigan opening

Cut the steek down the centre. With No. 12 (2¾ mm) needles and Peatj, pick up sts from the left steek edge where it meets the pattern evenly from neck to base. Work 2 inches (5 cm) in moss stitch and cast off in moss stitch, not too tightly. Work the right band to match, dividing the length into equal parts and making small buttonholes at equal intervals, here there are eight.

The neckband

With No. 12 (2¾ mm) needles and Peat, pick up stitches evenly around the neck and work 1½ inches (4 cm) in moss stitch. Cast off in moss stitch, not too tightly.

Finishing

Turn the garment inside out and sew the steek edges neatly into the back of the opening bands. Sew buttons on the left band. Wash, rinse and dry the garment as indicated on p. 199.

MAJOR PATTERNS

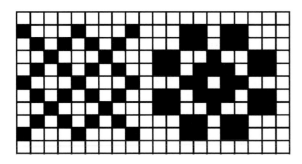

	B	C	B	C	B	C	B	C	B	C	B	C	B	C	B	C	B	C	B
Round 1	20																		
Round 2	3	2	1	2	3	1	3	1	3	1									
Round 3	3	2	1	2	4	1	1	1	1	1	1	1							
Round 4	1	2	2	1	2	2	3	1	3	1	2								
Round 5	1	2	1	3	1	2	2	1	1	1	1	1	1	1	1				
Round 6	3	2	1	2	3	1	3	1	3	1									
Round 7	1	2	1	3	1	2	2	1	1	1	1	1	1	1					
Round 8	1	2	2	1	2	2	3	1	3	1	2								
Round 9	3	2	1	2	4	1	1	1	1	1	1	1							
Round 10	3	2	1	2	3	1	3	1	3	1									
Round 11	20																		

A

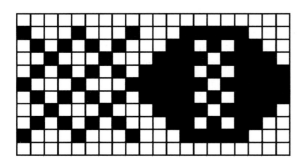

	B	C	B	C	B	C	B	C	B	C	B	C	B	C	B	C	B	C	B
Round 1	20																		
Round 2	3	5	3	1	3	1	3	1											
Round 3	2	2	1	1	1	2	3	1	1	1	1	1	1	1					
Round 4	1	4	1	4	3	1	3	1	2										
Round 5		4	1	1	1	4	1	1	1	1	1	1	1	1	1				
Round 6		5	1	6	3	1	3	1											
Round 7		4	1	1	1	1	4	1	1	1	1	1	1	1	1				
Round 8	1	4	1	4	3	1	3	1	2										
Round 9	2	2	1	1	1	2	3	1	1	1	1	1	1	1					
Round 10	3	5	3	1	3	1	3	1											
Round 11	20																		

B

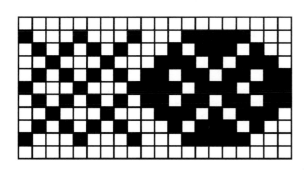

	B	C	B	C	B	C	B	C	B	C	B	C	B	C	B	C	B	C	B
Round 1	20																		
Round 2	3	5	3	1	3	1	3	1											
Round 3	2	1	1	3	1	1	3	1	1	1	1	1	1	1					
Round 4	1	3	1	1	1	3	3	1	3	1	2								
Round 5		2	1	2	1	2	1	2	1	1	1	1	1	1	1	1	1		
Round 6		3	1	3	1	4	3	1	3	1									
Round 7		2	1	2	1	2	1	2	1	1	1	1	1	1	1	1	1		
Round 8	1	3	1	1	1	3	3	1	3	1	2								
Round 9	2	1	1	3	1	1	3	1	1	1	1	1	1	1					
Round 10	3	5	3	1	3	1	3	1											
Round 11	20																		

C

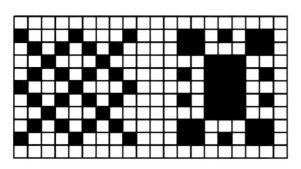

	B	C	B	C	B	C	B	C	B	C	B	C	B	C	B	C	B	C	B
Round 1	20																		
Round 2	1	2	1	1	1	2	3	1	3	1	3	1							
Round 3	1	2	3	2	4	1	1	1	1	1	1	1							
Round 4	3	3	7	1	3	1	2												
Round 5	1	1	1	3	1	1	4	1	1	1	1	1	1	1	1				
Round 6	3	3	5	1	3	1	3	1											
Round 7	1	1	1	3	1	1	4	1	1	1	1	1	1	1	1				
Round 8	3	3	7	1	3	1	2												
Round 9	1	2	3	2	4	1	1	1	1	1	1	1							
Round 10	1	2	1	1	1	2	3	1	3	1	3	1							
Round 11	20																		

D

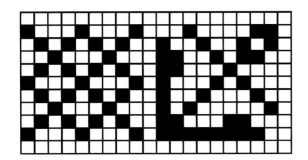

	B	C	B	C	B	C	B	C	B	C	B	C	B	C	B	C	B	C	B	C	B
Round 1	20																				
Round 2	2	8	1	1	3	1	3	1													
Round 3	3	2	3	2	2	1	1	1	1	1	1	1	1								
Round 4	1	1	5	1	1	1	3	1	3	1	2										
Round 5	2	1	3	1	2	1	2	1	1	1	1	1	1	1	1						
Round 6	3	1	1	1	3	1	1	3	1	3	1										
Round 7	4	1	3	2	2	1	1	1	1	1	1										
Round 8	2	2	1	1	2	2	3	1	3	1	2										
Round 9	1	1	1	1	2	1	2	1	2	1	1	1	1	1	1	1					
Round 10	1	2	4	1	3	1	3	1	3	1											
Round 11	20																				

E

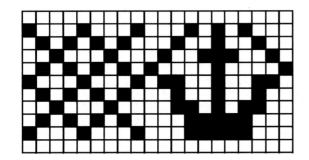

	B	C	B	C	B	C	B	C	B	C	B	C	B	C	B	C
Round 1	20															
Round 2	3	5	3	1	3	1	3	1								
Round 3	3	5	4	1	1	1	1	1	1	1	1					
Round 4	2	2	1	1	1	2	4	1	3	1	2					
Round 5	2	1	2	1	2	1	3	1	1	1	1	1	1	1	1	
Round 6	1	2	2	1	2	2	1	1	3	1	3	1				
Round 7		1	4	1	4	1	1	1	1	1	1	1	1	1	1	1
Round 8	1	1	2	3	2	1	3	1	3	1	2					
Round 9	2	1	2	1	2	1	3	1	1	1	1	1	1	1	1	
Round 10	3	1	1	1	1	1	3	1	3	1	3	1				
Round 11	20															

F

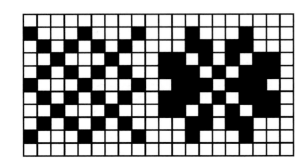

	B	C	B	C	B	C	B	C	B	C	B	C	B	C	B	C
Round 1	20															
Round 2	3	1	3	1	3	1	3	1	3	1						
Round 3	3	2	1	1	4	1	1	1	1	1	1	1	1			
Round 4	1	2	1	1	1	1	1	2	3	1	3	1	2			
Round 5	1	3	1	1	1	3	2	1	1	1	1	1	1	1	1	
Round 6	2	3	1	3	2	1	3	1	3	1						
Round 7	1	3	1	1	1	3	2	1	1	1	1	1	1	1	1	
Round 8	1	2	1	1	1	1	1	2	3	1	3	1	2			
Round 9	3	2	1	1	4	1	1	1	1	1	1	1	1			
Round 10	3	1	3	1	3	1	3	1	3	1						
Round 11	20															

G

All Peeries

B blue: C white

Major Patterns A, C, E, G

1st rd:	Madder Red
2nd, 3rd and 4th rds:	B Madder Red; C Snaa White
5th, 6th and 7th rds:	B Peat; C Auld Gold
8th, 9th and 10th rds:	B Madder Red; C Snaa White
11th rd:	Madder Red

Major Patterns B, D, F

1st rd:	Peat
2nd, 3rd and 4th rds:	B Peat; C Auld Gold
5th, 6th and 7th rds:	B Madder Red; C Snaa White
8th, 9th and 10th rds:	B Peat; C Auld Gold
11th rd:	Peat

8x7	B	C	B	C	B
Round 1	8				
Round 2	2	2	1	2	1
Round 3	2	2	1	2	1
Round 4		1	3	1	3
Round 5	2	2	1	2	1
Round 6	2	2	1	2	1
Round 7					

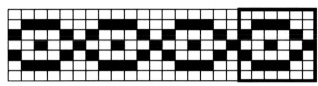

Peerie No. 1 repetition

6x7	B	C	B	C	B
Round 1	6				
Round 2	2	3	1		
Round 3	1	1	3	1	
Round 4		1	2	1	2
Round 5	1	1	3	1	
Round 6	2	3	1		
Round 7	6				

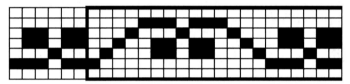

Peerie No. 2 repetition

20x7	B	C	B	C	B	C	B	C	B	C		
Round 1	20											
Round 2	3	3	13									
Round 3	3	1	3	1	3	2	1	2	3	1		
Round 4	1	2	1	2	2	1	2	2	1	2	2	1	1
Round 5	1	2	1	2	3	1	3	1	3	1	2	
Round 6	10	3	1	3	3							
Round 7	20											

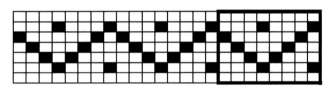

Peerie No. 3 repetition

8x7	B	C	B	C	B
Round 1	8				
Round 2		1	3	1	3
Round 3	3	1	1	1	2
Round 4	2	1	3	1	1
Round 5	1	1	5	1	
Round 6		1	3	1	3
Round 7	8				

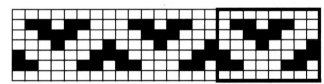

Peerie No. 4 repetition

5x7	B	C	B	C	B
Round 1	8				
Round 2	1	2	3	2	
Round 3		2	5	1	
Round 4		1	3	1	3
Round 5	3	3	2		
Round 6	2	2	1	2	1
Round 7	8				

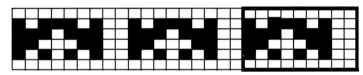

Peerie No. 5 repetition

9x6	B	C	B	C	B	C	B
Round 1	9						
Round 2	2	1	1	1	1	1	1
Round 3	2	2	3	2			
Round 4	2	3	1	3			
Round 5	2	1	1	3	1	1	
Round 6	9						

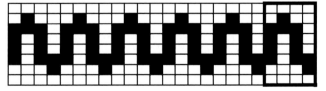

Peerie No. 6 repetition

4x8	B	C	B	C	B
Round 1	4				
Round 2		1	3		
Round 3		2	1	1	
Round 4	1	1	1	1	
Round 5	1	1	1	1	
Round 6	1	3			
Round 7	2	1	1		
Round 8	4				

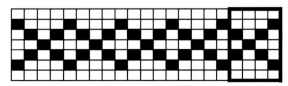

Peerie No. 7 repetition

4x7	B	C	B	C	B
Round 1	4				
Round 2		1	3		
Round 3	1	1	1	1	
Round 4	2	1	1		
Round 5	1	1	1		
Round 6		1	3		
Round 7	4				

Peerie No. 8 repetition

199

Mainland of Shetland.

FAIR ISLE AND SHETLAND MAINLAND

As we shall see in the patterns I have documented, their creative expression—within the limited confines of the tradition—reveals an extremely sophisticated sense of colour and balance. Space dictates that I cannot include everyone I met, so I have concentrated on those people who either knitted beautiful patterns for themselves and their families or who in some way reflected best the atmosphere of the island's tradition.

Visiting these knitters is a major undertaking. The distances are not so much great, as tortuous—winding over hills, round endless inlets and bays and hopping from island to island by boat. It was no wonder that visitors in the 18th and 19th centuries observed in some detail that there was more communication with the international fishing fleets than there was between island neighbours. There were no proper roads between communities at that time and all communication was by boat, illustrated by the many derelict trading posts and chapels that we passed, conveniently situated on the shoreline.

As I travelled around I learned that even today some of the islanders have never been off the island, their only communication with relatives and friends who have moved being by letter and telephone. The Miss Garricks (whose patterns we will see later) were typical; by way of saying thank you for permission to photograph them, I took them to Papa Stour to see some of their relatives. This made their day: it was the first time in twenty years.

Because of the difficulty in travelling, Margaret cannot manage to visit all the knitters and she relies on local organisers. The system is quite simple. One knitter is paid extra for collecting and distributing the work and determining the quality. Margaret has only to visit her and give instructions and colour combinations for the next batch.

Whalsay harbour.

Mr Polson and his sons.

WHALSAY

The first island we visited was Whalsay and here I met the Polson family. John Polson and his sons are all fishermen working on the massive seine netters that fish out of this island. Unfortunately they are out of work as the fishing is in decline; at best they work only six months of the year. Extra income from knitting is therefore of great importance. Their spare time is spent building fast sailing dinghies, based on ancient Norwegian lines, for the yearly Shetland Regatta. Every fishing family participates in the regatta as a matter of course, and social prestige within the community is not judged on material wealth, or titles inherited, but on the winning of the race.

MRS POLSON'S PATTERN

The island's knitting also is unique within the tradition as, over the years, tessellated patterns have taken over from the more traditional bands. I asked Mrs Polson to show me her masterpiece. It was knitted for her husband many years ago and is worn here by their youngest son. It is made up in dark blue Shetland wool and silk, using the Shetland Star and Maltese Cross. To make it, you will need about 7 oz (200 g) of wool in the main colour, here dark navy blue, 2 oz (56 g) each of Light Natural, Gold, Shetland Pink and Shetland Blue and 1 oz (28 g) of Madder Red, all in Ecru silk. The single pattern takes up 26 rounds and 26 stitches.

The garment is made as usual in the round as far as the armholes. For a 38–40 inch (96–102 cm) chest, cast on 320 stitches for the rib (K1, P1 for 4 inches or 10 cm), then increase evenly over 4 stocking stitch rounds to 364 stitches—this will give you exactly 14 pattern repeats over the full round. The top of the garment, with a deep V-neck, is worked as follows:

Armhole division

Work 11 sts and place on a holder. Work 182 sts, placing the last 22 on a holder. Work 160 sts, then place the remaining 11 sts on the first holder.

The back yoke

Working over the back 160 sts with two needles, shape the armholes as for the cardigan on p. 194 (134 sts). Continue to shoulder height then divide the stitches onto separate holders: 32 for each shoulder and 70 for the neck.

The front yoke

To shape the front armholes as for the cardigan on p. 194, divide for the neck on the second row by knitting as far as the centre stitch and placing it on a safety pin. Working on the right front only (73 sts), continue up the yoke, making the armhole shaping and, at the same time, decreasing 1 st at the neck edge every other row until there are 42 sts, then every 3rd row until you have 32 sts. Continue without further shaping until the work measures the same as the back. Leave the stitches on a holder. Work the left front to match. Graft the shoulder seams together.

The armbands

Work 22 sts from the holder under one arm and pick up stitches evenly around the armhole (about 230 sts altogether). Work 10 rounds of rib in navy and cast off ribwise. Work the other armband to match.

The neckband

Work the 70 sts from the holder at the back of the neck and pick up 101 sts evenly down the right neck edge to the pin. Knit the stitch from the pin and pick up a further 101 sts up the left neck edge (273 sts altogether). Work 10 rounds of rib in navy, purling 2 sts together on each side of the centre front stitch on every round. The centre front stitch is always worked knitwise. Cast off in rib.

The colour combinations are as follows with the background in Spindrift 730 Dark Navy throughout.

1st rd.	C Scarlet 500
2nd & 3rd rds.	C Scholmit 119
4th rd	C Gold 289
5th & 6th rd.	C Rose 550
7th & 8th rds.	C Royal 700
9th &10th rds.	C Rose 550
11th rd.	C Gold 289
12th & 13th rds.	C Scholmit 119
14th rd.	C Scarlet 500
15th & 16th rds.	C Scholmit 119
17th rd.	C Gold 289
18th & 19th rds.	C Rose 550
20th & 21st rds.	C Royal 700
22nd & 23rd rds.	C Rose 550
24th rd	C Gold 289
25th & 26th rds.	C Scholmit 119

26x26	b	c	b	c	b	c	b	c	b	c	b	c	b	c	b	c	b
Rnd 1	1	3	8	1	8	3	1	1									
Rnd 2		1	1	3	4	1	1	1	1	1	1	1	1	4	3	1	1
Rnd 3	1	1	1	3	3	2	3	2	3	3	1	1	1	1			
Rnd 4	1	1	1	6	3	1	3	6	1	1	1	1					
Rnd 5		2	1	1	2	1	1	1	7	1	1	1	2	1	1	3	
Rnd 6		2	4	2	9	2	4	2	1								
Rnd 7	1	1	4	3	7	3	4	1	2								
Rnd 8	3	3	4	1	3	1	4	3	4								
Rnd 9	4	2	4	2	1	2	4	2	5								
Rnd 10	3	1	1	1	2	1	1	5	1	1	2	1	1	1	4		
Rnd 11	3	6	1	1	3	1	1	6	3	1							
Rnd 12	1	2	3	3	1	1	1	1	1	1	1	3	3	2	2		
Rnd 13		1	1	1	4	3	1	1	1	1	1	3	4	1	1	1	1
Rnd 14	8	3	1	1	1	3	8	1									
Rnd 15		1	1	1	4	3	1	1	1	1	1	3	4	1	1	1	1
Rnd 16	1	2	3	3	1	1	1	1	1	1	1	3	3	2	2		
Rnd 17		3	6	1	1	3	1	1	6	3	1						
Rnd 18	3	1	1	1	2	1	1	5	1	1	2	1	1	1	4		
Rnd 19	4	2	4	2	1	2	4	2	5								
Rnd 20	3	3	4	1	3	1	4	3	4								
Rnd 21	1	1	4	3	7	3	4	1	2								
Rnd 22		2	4	2	9	2	4	2	1								
Rnd 23		2	1	2	1	1	1	7	1	1	1	2	1	1	3		
Rnd 24		1	1	1	6	3	1	3	6	1	1	2					
Rnd 25	1	1	1	3	3	2	3	2	3	3	1	1	1	1			
Rnd 26		1	1	3	4	1	1	1	1	1	1	1	1	4	3	1	1

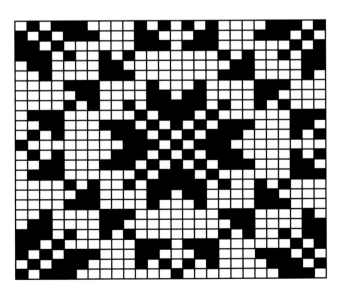

SHETLAND MAINLAND—LERWICK HARBOUR

MRS DALZILL'S PATTERN

Back on the mainland at Lerwick Harbour I met Mrs Dalzill, whose beautiful tessellated pattern I have included here. She has worked out the combinations for herself, using configurations and colours taken from her own collection of swatches and graph notations, which every Fair Isle knitter keeps as source material. In addition, she has worked a pattern repeat into the welt to very great effect.

To make it for a 38–40 inch (96–102 cm) chest, you will need 7 oz (200 g) of the main colour, Shetland Black, and 2 oz (56 g) each of the contrast colours, Tangerine, Purple/Blue, Green, Ice Blue, Very Light Brown, Yellow and Shetland White. The pattern is worked over 30 rounds and 30 stitches. The construction of the pullover is similar to Mrs Polson's of Whalsay *(p. 202)*, but after the welt the stitches are increased to 360 for the pattern repeats to fit in exactly. The ribbings on the welt, armbands and neck have all the contrast colours in, and the welt itself features a repeated flower cross worked in plain stitches. The distinctive features are described here for you to follow.

Lerwick waterfront.

Mrs Dalzill's pattern.

	b	c	b	c	b	c	b	c	b	c	b	c	b	c	b	c	b	c
Round 1	2	2	2	3	1	4	1	1	1	4	1	3	2	2	1			
Round 2	1	2	2	3	3	2	1	1	1	1	1	2	3	3	2	2		
Round 3		2	2	3	6	1	1	1	1	1	6	3	2	1				
Round 4		1	3	2	6	1	1	3	1	1	6	2	3					
Round 5	2	2	7	1	2	3	2	1	7	2	1							
Round 6	1	3	3	4	4	1	4	4	3	3								
Round 7		3	7	1	9	1	7	2										
Round 8		2	3	4	1	1	1	4	1	4	1	1	4	3				
Round 9		1	7	1	1	1	3	3	3	1	1	1	7					
Round 10	3	4	1	1	4	5	4	1	1	4	2							
Round 11		1	4	2	1	1	3	3	1	3	3	1	1	2	4			
Round 12		2	2	1	1	5	2	3	2	5	1	1	1	2	1			
Round 13		2	1	1	2	1	3	2	3	1	3	2	3	1	2	1	1	1
Round 14		1	1	1	6	3	2	3	2	3	6	1	1					
Round 15		1	1	1	2	3	3	2	2	1	2	2	3	3	2	1	1	
Round 16		1	1	4	1	3	2	2	3	2	2	3	1	4	1			
Round 17		1	1	1	2	3	3	2	2	1	2	2	3	3	2	1	1	
Round 18		1	1	1	6	3	2	3	2	3	6	1	1					
Round 19		2	1	1	6	2	3	1	3	2	6	1	1	1				
Round 20		2	2	1	7	2	3	2	7	1	2	1						
Round 21		1	4	4	3	3	1	3	3	4	4							
Round 22	5	1	7	5	5	7	1	4										
Round 23		1	4	1	1	4	3	3	3	4	1	1	4					
Round 24		2	3	1	1	7	1	7	1	1	1	3	1					
Round 25		3	4	1	1	4	5	4	1	1	4	2						
Round 26	1	3	3	1	1	2	4	1	4	2	1	1	3	3				
Round 27	2	2	5	1	1	1	2	3	2	1	1	1	5	2	1			
Round 28		1	3	2	3	1	2	1	1	3	1	1	2	1	3	2	3	
Round 29		2	2	3	6	1	1	1	1	1	6	3	2	1				
Round 30	1	2	3	3	2	1	1	1	1	1	1	2	3	3	2	2	2	

The welt

Cast on 320 sts in Black and work 2 rounds in K1 P1 rib. The colours are then introduced, 2 rounds of each in the same order as for the main pattern but starting with Purple/Blue, except for Tangerine, which is worked over 1 round only. As for the Allover Fair Isle Pullover written out in full on pp. 188–93, the contrast colours on the welt are worked on the knit stitches only, the purl stitches remaining in the base colour. After the Tangerine round, work back through the colours in reverse order (27 rounds altogether).

At the same time, work the flower pattern at regular intervals as shown on the graph. The pattern panels, including the encircling background, are all worked in knit stitches, not rib.

Armhole division

When you reach the correct height for the armholes, divide the work for front and back as follows: work 10 sts and place on a holder; work 180 sts, placing the last 20 on a holder; work 160 sts, then place the remaining 10 sts on the first holder.

The armbands and neckband

Work in K1, P1 rib, with contrast colours on knit stitches only, in the same order as for the welt, 1 round of each only. Finish with 2 rounds of Black and cast off ribwise.

Welt pattern with flower.

SHETLAND MAINLAND

THE MISS GARRICKS' PATTERNS

In Shetland, as everywhere else I visited, the wealth of information is too great to contain within these pages and I have had to concentrate on a few people who best reflect the spirit of the tradition. I have chosen the Miss Garricks.

They were pleased that I intended to include them in my collection but anxious that their privacy should not be disturbed, so I promised that their whereabouts would remain unknown. It is sufficient to mention that they live in exactly the manner I described earlier when outlining the crofting system. Both are now over eighty and still working the land in a way that would tax the strength of the best of us. They put down their health to hard work, fresh air and their own supply of sweet-tasting water.

In conversation over tea they revealed their lifestyle to me and showed me their oldest pieces of knitting and the jerseys they were wearing. I asked them the question I first asked everyone I met which was whether they had ever knitted up any navy blue ganseys—I could not bring myself to believe that the two traditions existed in isolation. In Dentdale, both two-colour knitting and fisher ganseys were made—evidence enough that the traditions were not mutually exclusive in specific areas; and I had found evidence that ganseys were knitted in Foula.

Early Fair Isle gloves. The one on the right belonged to the Miss Garricks' mother; the long glove on the left was knitted c.1910. Both are made from hand spun wool.

The Miss Garricks of Shetland outside their croft.

	b	c	b	c	b	c	b	c	b	c	b	c	b	c	b	c	b
Round 1	16																
Round 2		2	3	2	3	2	3	1									
Round 3	1	2	1	1	1	2	1	1	1	2	1	1	1				
Round 4	2	2	3	2	3	2	2										
Round 5	16																
Round 6	1	1	1	1	1	1	1	1	1	1	1	1	1	1	1	1	1
Round 7	16																
Round 8		1	4	1	5	1	4											
Round 9		2	3	2	3	2	3	1										
Round 10		1	4	3	1	3	4											
Round 11	2	3	1	2	1	2	1	3	1								
Round 12	3	3	1	1	1	1	1	3	2								
Round 13		1	3	3	1	1	1	3	3								
Round 14		2	5	3	5	1												
Round 15		1	3	3	1	1	1	3	3								
Round 16	3	3	1	1	1	1	1	3	2								
Round 17	2	3	1	2	1	2	1	3	1								
Round 18		1	4	3	1	3	4											
Round 19		2	3	2	3	2	3	1										
Round 20		1	4	1	5	1	4											
Round 21	16																	
Round 22	1	1	1	1	1	1	1	1	1	1	1	1	1	1	1	1	1
Round 23	16																	
Round 24	2	2	3	2	3	2	2											
Round 25	1	1	1	2	1	1	1	2	1	1	1	2	1				
Round 26		1	3	2	3	2	3	2										
Round 27	16																	
Round 28	16																	
Round 29	3	1	3	1	3	1	3	1									
Round 30		1	1	1	1	1	1	1	1	1	1	1	1	1	1	1	1
Round 31	1	1	3	1	3	1	3	1	2								
Round 32	16																	

The colour combinations are as follows
(B = background; C = contrast):

1st rd:	Russet
2nd, 3rd and 4th rds:	B Russet; C Gold
5th rd:	Russet
6th rd:	B Russet; C Black
7th rd:	Black
8th, 9th and 10th rds:	B Black: C Gold
11th and 12th rds:	B Blue: C Light Brown
13th rd:	B Red; C White
14th rd:	B Red; C Yellow
15th rd:	B Red; C White
16th and 17th rds:	B Blue; C Light Brown
18th, 19th and 20th rds	B Black; C Gold
21st rd:	Black
22nd rd:	B Russet: C Black
23rd rd:	Russet
24th, 25th and 26th rds:	B Russet; C Gold
27th rd:	Russet
28th rd:	Mid-Brown
29th, 30th and 31st rds:	B Mid-Brown; C Yellow
32nd rd:	Mid-Brown

Shetland Star, 15 rds. x 16 sts.
with Border, 16 rds x 16 sts.

At first the Miss Garricks were vague, but the more we talked the more they remembered. They had knitted fisher ganseys but not for over fifty years. I asked if they could remember the patterns and they explained that they were 'knit with the stitch inside out'—a graphic description of the purl stitch. With a little prompting they soon revealed that they used to knit garments for their family, patterned with purl diamonds set horizontally and separated by garter panels—in other words, exactly like the Foula patterns documented on pages 150–151.

They illustrated the diamond by producing an old glove pattern knitted in colours from hand spun and undyed wool that their mother had made over a hundred years ago *(see photograph, page 207)*. It reminded me very much of the block patterns of Eriskay. They explained that in the beginning these were the only patterns they knitted; it was not until they were teenagers that they began knitting Fair Isle patterns on jerseys. Like most Shetland crofters, they did not only learn knitting. A lot of time was spent weaving 'claith' in the same way as the islanders of Lewis now produce Harris Tweed, and while the men were away they were responsible for looking after the croft.

I asked them about making up the 'taatit' rugs from old pieces of cloth, and they were quick to point out to me, 'Oh, we didn't have time for that—we were much too busy. The men used to make those in the evenings'. Their father, like most Shetlanders, was a man of many talents. He was the Laird's stonemason, the local cobbler and was also widely regarded in the community as the local doctor, practising the medical knowledge he had gained as a young man when he sailed on the whalers and merchant vessels that plied their trade with South America.

Turning to the knitting, I asked them how they came to choose the patterns and colours they used. They explained that it depended simply on what bits of wool they had lying around. They got the patterns from their graphs or from something they liked—such as embroidery or curtains—which they then worked out in graph form. Then, using the largest amount of wool they had as the main colour, they started without further ado: no swatches, no checks—they simply knitted up the patterns in colours they liked over the first few rounds after the welt. If they didn't fancy it, they pulled it back to a combination they did like and tried something else, until they 'felt it looked right'. They prefer a good dark colour as the background—particularly Shetland Black as it gives good contrast.

The round-necked jersey is a delightfully simple, yet very effective pattern, made up from a Shetland Star worked over 15 rounds and 16 stitches, and a border panel 16 rounds deep. The ribbing is all worked in just the base colour. To make the jersey, you will need about 6 oz (170 g) of Russet, 4 oz (114 g) of Shetland Black, 3 oz (85 g) of Light Brown, 2 oz (56 g) each of Mid-Brown and Madder Red, and 1 oz (28 g) each of Yellow, Gold, Bright Blue and Shetland White. Cast on 300 sts for size 36 inch (90 cm) bust or chest and increase after the welt to 320 sts, which will give you twenty full pattern repeats. But the technique departs from the classic tradition in the way the sleeves are set into the armholes. The ladies have worked some shaping into the shoulders to make the pattern sequence on the body of the garment pass over the shoulder in a pleasing and eye-catching continuation.

Armhole division

Divide the work equally for front and back, 160 sts each.

The front yoke

Working over the front 160 sts with two needles, decrease 1 st at each end of the next 6 rows; then 1st at each end of every other row for 6 rows; then 1st at each end of the following 3rd row (140 sts). Continue without further shaping until the work measures 6½-7 inches (16-17 cm) from the beginning of the armhole, ending on a purl row.

Front neck shaping

Place central 34 sts on a holder for the neck. Working on the right-hand 53 sts, decrease 1st at the neck edge on the next 4 rows and then on every other row until you have 45 sts. Continue without further shaping until the work measures 8½ inches (21 cm) from the beginning of the armhole and leave these sts on a holder. Work the left front to match.

The back yoke

Working over the back 160 sts with two needles, decrease to match the front yoke, then continue without shaping until the work measures 8 inches (20 cm) from the beginning of the armhole, ending on a purl row.

Back neck shaping

Place central 34 sts on a holder for the neck. Working on the left-hand 53 sts, decrease 1st at the neck edge on the next 8 rows (45 sts). Continue until the work is equal to the front and leave the stitches on a holder. Work the right back to match. Graft the shoulder seams together.

The neckband

Pick up stitches evenly around the neck and work 10 rounds of rib, casting off ribwise.

The sleeves

So that the sleeves can be set into the shaped armholes, they must be worked in the modern manner upwards from the cuff. Cast on the desired number of stitches and work to match the body, increasing gradually after the welt (every 6th or 8th row) so that at the armhole you will have 144 sts (9 complete pattern repeats).

Start the shaping for the armholes at the same stage in the pattern as on the body. Decrease 1 st at each end of every row until you have 16 sts left. Cast off.

Finishing

Sew the sleeves into the armholes so that the patterns match as exactly as possible.

The Miss Garricks' Polo Neck Jersey No. 1

	b	c	b	c	b	c	b	c	b	c	b	c	b	c	b	c	b	c	b
Round 1	18																		
Round 2	3	1	3	1	3	1	3	1	2										
Round 3		1	1	1	1	1	1	1	1	1	1	1	1	1	1	1	1	1	1
Round 4	1	1	3	1	3	1	3	1	4										
Round 5	18																		
Round 6	18																		
Round 7	1	2	1	2	3	3	1	3	2										
Round 8	1	2	1	2	2	1	3	1	3	1	1								
Round 9	3	1	3	1	2	2	1	2	2	1									
Round 10		3	1	3	3	2	1	2	3										
Round 11	18																		
Round 12	18																		
Round 13		1	4	3	3	3	4												
Round 14		2	2	2	2	1	1	1	2	2	2	1							
Round 15		1	3	2	1	2	1	2	1	2	3								
Round 16	2	2	1	2	5	2	1	2	1										
Round 17	1	4	1	2	3	2	1	4											
Round 18	1	1	2	2	1	2	1	2	1	2	2	1							
Round 19	1	1	1	1	1	2	1	3	1	2	1	1	1	1					
Round 20	2	2	2	2	1	1	2	2	2	1									
Round 21		1	6	2	1	2	6												
Round 22	2	2	2	2	1	1	1	2	2	2	1								
Round 23	1	1	1	1	1	2	1	3	1	2	1	1	1	1					
Round 24	1	1	2	2	1	2	1	2	2	1									
Round 25	1	4	1	2	3	2	1	4											
Round 26	2	2	1	2	5	2	1	2	1										
Round 27		1	3	2	1	2	1	2	1	2	3								
Round 28		2	2	2	2	1	1	1	2	2	2	1							
Round 29		1	4	3	3	3	4												
Round 30	18																		

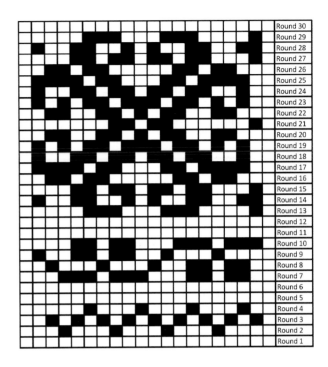

The Miss Garricks' Polo Neck Jersey No. 2

	b	c	b	c	b	c	b	c	b	c	b	c	b	c
Round 1	18													
Round 2	4	2	4	2	4	2								
Round 3		1	2	1	2	1	2	1	2	1	2	1	2	
Round 4	1	1	2	1	2	1	2	1	2	1	2	1	1	
Round 5		3	3	3	3	3	3							
Round 6		4	1	5	1	5	1	1						
Round 7	18													
Round 8		1	2	1	2	1	2	1	2	1	2	1	2	
Round 9	2	1	2	1	2	3	2	1	2	1	1			
Round 10	1	1	2	1	2	1	1	1	1	1	2	1	2	1
Round 11		1	2	1	2	3	1	3	2	1	2			
Round 12	2	1	2	1	1	2	1	2	1	1	2	1	1	
Round 13	1	1	2	3	1	1	1	1	3	2	1			
Round 14		1	2	1	1	2	2	1	2	2	1	1	2	
Round 15	2	3	3	3	3	3	1							
Round 16		1	2	1	1	2	2	1	2	2	1	1	2	
Round 17	1	1	2	3	1	1	1	1	1	3	2	1		
Round 18	2	1	2	1	1	2	1	2	1	1	2	1	1	
Round 19		1	2	1	2	3	1	3	2	1	2			
Round 20	1	1	2	1	2	1	1	1	1	1	2	1	2	1
Round 21	2	1	2	1	2	3	2	1	2	1	1			
Round 22		1	2	1	2	1	2	1	2	1	2	1	2	
Round 23	18													
Round 24		4	1	5	1	5	1	1						
Round 25		3	3	3	3	3	3							
Round 26	1	1	2	1	2	1	2	1	2	1	2	1	1	
Round 27		1	2	1	2	1	2	1	2	1	2	1	2	
Round 28	4	2	4	2	4	2								
Round 29	18													
Round 30		2	3	2	3	2	3	2	1					
Round 31	1	2	1	1	1	2	1	1	1	2	1	1	2	
Round 32	2	2	3	2	3	2	3	1						

211

THE MISS GARRICK'S CREATIVE CLASSIC FAIR ISLES

In describing these two beautiful jerseys as creative and classic is to make clear the distinction between a traditional and a creative knitter. This distinction, is clearly illustrated when examining the pattern; to learn that the configurations patterned on the two jerseys have been created by the knitters themselves, and that the yarn colour interactions follow the rules of traditional Shetland knitting to indicate that these artifacts are indeed master-pieces

Both patterns are worked over 18 stitch repeats. If you want to knit them up, I suggest that you use the Allover Fair Isle pullover pattern

written out on pp. 188–193 for a man and the Classic Fair Isle Cardigan on pp. 194–199 for a woman. You will need 18 pattern repeats for a 34 inch (87 cm) size; 20 for a 38 inch (95 cm); and 22 for a 42 inch (106 cm).

After spending so much time with the Miss Garricks I was sad to say goodbye—they are two wonderful old ladies at peace and in harmony with the land they live on. Their patterns signal the end of my trip to the Shetlands where this beautiful technique of knitting is practised as a major economic force. It is hoped that it will continue and will not be too adversely affected by the growing use of machines.

The Prince of Wales, 1921, painted by Sir Henry Lander.

THE PRINCE OF WALES' V-NECK JERSEY PATTERN

The final pattern I would like to leave you with is that of the V-necked jersey given to the Prince of Wales in 1921. It is a little difficult to decipher as Sir Henry Lander, who painted the portrait, was of course more concerned that our attention should focus on the face rather than the Fair Isle. The pattern I have come up with should resemble it as closely as possible. The main configurations are worked over 11 rounds and 24 stitches, and the zigzags over 8 stitches.

The construction is the same as for the Allover Fair Isle Pullover on pp. 188–93, with underarm gussets and dropped shoulders, but is, as expected, worked over two needles for the yoke to accommodate the V-neck. The colours are Light Ochre, Dark Orange, Blue, Dark Brown, Dark Yellow, Madder Red and Green.

For a 38–40 inch (96–102 cm) chest, cast on 320 sts and work 2 rounds of K2, P2 rib in Light Ochre. Then continue in rib for 24 more rounds, using Blue as the contrast colour over the knit stitches only. Increase evenly over two plain rounds to 360 sts, which will give you 15 full pattern repeats in a round. When you come to the underarm measurement, divide the work for front and back, placing the gusset stitches at each arm on holders, and continue on two needles.

The Prince of Wales' Jersey
Main Pattern, 24 sts and 11 rds.
Rectangle peerie, 8 sts and 3 rds.
Zizzag peerie, 8 sts and 5 rds.

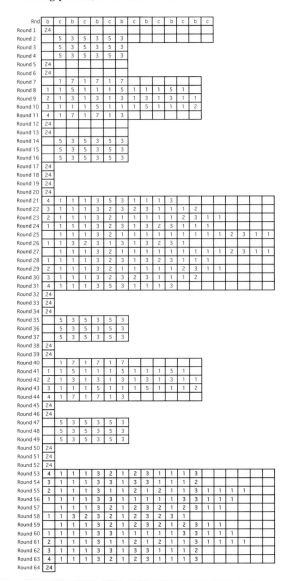

Rnd	b	c	b	c	b	c	b	c	b	c	b	c	b	c	b	c
Round 1	24															
Round 2		5	3	5	3	5	3									
Round 3		5	3	5	3	5	3									
Round 4		5	3	5	3	5	3									
Round 5	24															
Round 6	24															
Round 7		1	7	1	7	1	7									
Round 8	1	1	5	1	1	1	1	5	1	1	1	5	1			
Round 9	2	1	3	1	3	1	3	1	3	1	3	1	1			
Round 10	3	1	1	1	5	1	1	1	5	1	1	1	2			
Round 11	4	1	7	1	7	1	3									
Round 12	24															
Round 13	24															
Round 14		5	3	5	3	5	3									
Round 15		5	3	5	3	5	3									
Round 16		5	3	5	3	5	3									
Round 17	24															
Round 18	24															
Round 19	24															
Round 20	24															
Round 21	4	1	1	1	3	5	3	1	1	1	3					
Round 22	3	1	1	1	3	2	3	2	3	1	1	1	2			
Round 23	2	1	1	1	3	2	1	1	1	1	1	2	3	1	1	
Round 24	1	1	1	1	3	2	3	1	3	2	3	1	1	1		
Round 25		1	1	1	3	2	1	1	1	1	1	1	1	2	3	1 1
Round 26	1	1	3	2	3	1	1	1	3	2	3	1				
Round 27		1	1	1	3	2	1	1	1	1	1	1	1	2	3	1 1
Round 28	1	1	1	1	3	2	3	1	3	2	3	1	1	1		
Round 29	2	1	1	1	3	2	1	1	1	1	1	2	3	1	1	
Round 30	3	1	1	1	3	2	3	2	3	1	1	1	2			
Round 31	4	1	1	1	3	5	3	1	1	1	3					
Round 32	24															
Round 33	24															
Round 34	24															
Round 35		5	3	5	3	5	3									
Round 36		5	3	5	3	5	3									
Round 37		5	3	5	3	5	3									
Round 38	24															
Round 39	24															
Round 40		1	7	1	7	1	7									
Round 41	1	1	5	1	1	1	1	5	1	1	1	5	1			
Round 42	2	1	3	1	3	1	3	1	3	1	3	1	1			
Round 43	3	1	1	1	5	1	1	1	5	1	1	1	2			
Round 44	4	1	7	1	7	1	3									
Round 45	24															
Round 46	24															
Round 47		5	3	5	3	5	3									
Round 48		5	3	5	3	5	3									
Round 49		5	3	5	3	5	3									
Round 50	24															
Round 51	24															
Round 52	24															
Round 53	4	1	1	1	3	2	1	2	3	1	1	1	3			
Round 54	3	1	1	1	3	3	1	3	3	1	1	1	2			
Round 55	2	1	1	1	3	1	1	2	1	2	1	1	3	1	1	1 1
Round 56	1	1	1	1	3	3	1	1	1	1	3	3	1	1	1	
Round 57		1	1	1	3	2	1	1	1	1	2	3	1	1		
Round 58	1	1	3	2	3	2	1	2	3	2	3	1				
Round 59		1	1	1	3	2	1	2	3	2	1	2	3	1	1	
Round 60		1	1	1	3	3	1	1	1	1	3	3	1	1	1	
Round 61	2	1	1	1	3	1	1	2	1	2	1	1	3	1	1	1 1
Round 62	3	1	1	1	3	3	1	3	3	1	1	1	2			
Round 63	4	1	1	1	3	2	1	2	3	1	1	1	3			
Round 64	24															

The colour combinations are as follows:
(B = background; C = contrast)

Peeries
Background in Light Ochre throughout.
Block patterns worked in Dark Orange;
zigzags worked in Blue.

Major Patterns (each is 11 rounds deep)
1st, 2nd and 3rd rds:
  B Dark Brown; C Dark Yellow
4th and 5th rds:
  B Green; C Dark Yellow
6th rd:
  B Red; C Dark Yellow
7th and 8th rds:
  B Green: C Dark Yellow
9th, 10th and 11th rds:
  B Dark brown: C Dark Yellow

The back yoke

Continue without shaping on the 180 sts for the back until the work measures the required shoulder height, ending with a purl row half way through a major pattern. Divide for the neckband and shoulders as follows: 70 sts for the back neck and 55 sts for each shoulder. Leave these sts on separate holders.

The front yoke

Work 6 rows of the front 180 sts over two needles, then divide for the neck: K2 tog., K88, place next st on safety pin, turn, purl to the end (89 sts). Continuing on these sts only, work the neck edge as follows: decrease 1 st at neck edge only on every following 3rd row until you have 58 sts. Continue without further shaping until the work measures the same as the back. Leave sts on a holder. Work the left front to match. Graft the shoulder seams together.

The sleeves

Work the sleeves as usual, remembering to put the patterns in reverse order from that of the body. Work the cuffs to match the welt on the body.

The neck band

Work 10 rounds in rib to match the cuffs and welt, remembering to decrease at centre front by purling 2 sts together on each side of the centre st which is to be knitted on every round.

The Book of Kells, *f. 130R*

The Knitting of Aran

My tour of traditional knitting around Britain ends with what is, perhaps, the best known of all folk knitting: that of the islands of Aran. Most good knitters will at some time have ventured into and enjoyed the complex organic designs practised by the peoples of these tiny islands off the west coast of Ireland. In the past fifty years their unique image has graced most of the wool spinners' knitting catalogues; for many, therefore, the patterns notated in this section will be familiar.

Before we look at these patterns in detail, it is worth describing the atmosphere and lifestyle of the tiny islands where they originated. Like the Hebrides and the Shetlands, the islands of Inishmaan, Inishmore and Inisheer are unique to themselves, even within Ireland as a whole.

When one visits nowadays, from the air, one is presented with a jigsaw puzzle of fields all dry-stone-walled, of which many, much to one's surprise, seem to be without any visible means of entry. (I learnt later that it was quite normal to take down the wall on entry and build it up when you left.) Ancient Celtic forts and workings are in ample supply and the islanders' Celtic heritage is met at every turn.

Aran woman knitting.

The massive stone fort of Dun Conor. Ring forts of this kind, either of stone or earthen banks, are the commonest ancient monuments to be seen from the air and were the fortified homesteads of early Irish farmers.

I had thought that the remoteness of the islands was the reason for so much evidence of religious settlement. It was soon pointed out to me, however, that the Aran islands were once at the very centre of communication since most of Ireland was heavily wooded with vast tracts of undrained bogland, making travel and agriculture difficult. Travel was easier by boat and around the islands this mode of transport was the *curragh*—the direct descendant of the skin-covered craft of pre-history. These remarkable boats were traditionally crewed by three skilful oarsmen and could tackle the largest of seas, which were mighty indeed, as Aran is the first landfall from the Atlantic and the 'reach' of the ocean is so great that the 'storm beaches' on Inishmaan in particular are over 170 feet above sea level.

Like the islanders of the Hebrides and Shetland the people of Aran fished the sea and farmed the sparse soil of the land. It was not until after the Easter rising of 1916 and the subsequent formation of the Irish Free State that the islanders' standard of living improved and their old traditions began to disappear, particularly after the second world war. In his *Topographical Dictionary* of 1837, Samuel Lewis succinctly described them:

> The surface of all the islands is barren rock, interspersed with numerous verdant and fertile spots. There are many springs and rivulets, but these afford in dry weather a very inadequate supply of water. . . . The prevailing crops are potatoes, rye, and a small kind of black oats; the inhabitants raise also small quantities of barley and wheat . . . but the produce of their harvests seldom exceeds what is required for their own consumption. The pasture land is appropriated to sheep and goats, and a few cows and horses, for which they also reserve some meadow: the mutton is of fine flavour and superior quality; but the most profitable stock is their breed of calves, which are reputed to be the best in Ireland. . . . The grasses are intermingled with a variety of

The landscape of the Aran Islands.

medicinal and sweet herbs . . . there is a plant which gives a fine blue dye and is used in colouring the woollen cloth which the inhabitants manufacture for their own wear.

The fisheries are a great source of profit, and in the whole employ about 120 boats; of these 30 or 40 have sails and are from five to ten tons burden; the rest are small row-boats and canoes or corachs. The spring and beginning of summer are the season for the spillard fishery; immense quantities of cod, ling, haddock, turbot, gurnet, mackerel, glassin, bream and herring are taken here; and lobsters, crabs, cockles and mussels are also found in abundance. The inhabitants rely chiefly on the herring fishery, which is very productive; and in April and May, many of them are employed in spearing the sun fish or basking shark for the liver, from which they extract considerable quantities of oil. . . .

In one of the islands a very fine stratum of dove coloured and black marble has been discovered; and from the various natural resources of this apparently barren district, the inhabitants are enabled to pay a rental of from £2,000 to £3,000 per annum to the proprietor.

Seventy years later, J. M. Synge's *The Aran Islands* (1907) was the first book of any real note that brought the islanders to the attention of the general public. In the 1930s, Richard Flaherty immortalised them in his film *Man of Aran*, recreating their lifestyle of a hundred years earlier; for all its romanticism and inaccuracies, the film is a worthy document of a way of life that has disappeared forever.

You now no longer see what was once a common sight: the womenfolk in their bright red skirts and brown shawls and the men in homespun tweeds (*bawneen*), Tam o'Shanters and rawhide shoes (pampouties).

Young Aran girl on Inishmore (*left*) and making *criosanna* belts on the Aran Islands.

221

The Patterns of Aran

For all their popularity, the history of the patterns of Aran and the way they have diffused into almost every knitter's stitch vocabulary remains uncertain. What is certain is that there have been vigorous champions of the tradition, Mary Thomas, Heinz Edgar Kiewe and Gladys Thompson in particular. Their research has been crucial in bringing to light the tradition, which was then taken up by the knitting manufacturers who saw the potential of Aran's unusually thick wool yarn which is very quickly made up into the finished garment.

In his book *Sacred History of Knitting* (1971), Heinz Kiewe wrote that he first came across Aran patterns in the early 1930s. 'To us it looked at that time too odd for words, being hard as a board, shapeless as a Coptic priest's shirt and with an atmosphere of Stonehenge all around it'. He recalls how he showed it to Mary Thomas, at that time fashion editor of *The Morning Post*, who became very excited about it. She later published an Aran pattern in her *Book of Knitting Patterns* (1938 and 1955), describing it as a 'magnificent example of "cross-over motifs" arranged in pattern; it is a classical choice, every pattern being of the same cross-over family. The knitting is intricate but traditional of Aran and worn by the fishermen of that island'. For Mr Kiewe this was to be the start of a long relationship with the patterns of Aran which he collected for the next thirty years, having them made up as garments by outworkers in the Outer Hebrides. By the 1950s these patterns had disseminated to the general public and were soon featured as *haute couture*, just like the Fair Isle patterns thirty years earlier.

It is worth pondering at this point whether the change in style of the Hebridean gansey from the allover pattern to the multiple motifs that we see today, using cables and other Aran configurations, had anything to do with the influx of Aran patterns to the outworkers of the Hebrides that resulted from Kiewe's researches. In the later investigations of Gladys Thompson (*Guernsey and Jersey Patterns*, 1955), we note the culmination of the art; significantly enough, by this time all the examples are knit up by a knitters' cooperative in Dublin. They are now in the archives of the Irish Folklore Department at the University of Dublin.

A visit to the Aran islands today unfortunately reveals little of this heritage. The islands of Inishmore, Inishmaan and Inisheer continue the knitting craft in name only; it is more of a tourist attraction than a continuing tradition. The reason for this is quite simple: in recent years most of the original population has moved away. As in the Shetlands, the contract system continues today on the mainland where many knitters are employed in making up garments for sale in their own shops.

The origin of their distinctive patterns is now lost in history. Two factors are instrumental in this disappearance. The first and most important is that Aran knitting is a much older tradition than that of Shetland and the fisher ganseys of England and Scotland. At its

oldest the gansey tradition is derived from the hosiery knitting of the 17th century; Shetland two-colour knitting, albeit practised since the craft began, has only come into prominence in the last hundred and fifty years. The second factor is that those people with direct access to the tradition have long since left the islands. As we have seen, there have been serious efforts in the past to determine the patterns' origins, most recently by Heinz Kiewe who has spent much time relating the patterns to Irish Celtic heritage, to the religious backdrop of Irish society and to the nature of the islanders' economy. In a well-publicised list of patterns and their meanings, he created a web of symbolism around them. For example, the 'Holy Trinity' stitch (more commonly named the blackberry stitch) is made, he points out, by knitting 'three in one and one from three'; the 'Tree of Life' stitch represents Jacob's dream of the ladder to heaven; 'plait' stitches are symbolic of the plaited holy bread of the Old Testament, and of a devout family bound up with God.

Aran sweater, featuring allover bobbles, diamonds with moss stitch and double cables worked front and back.

Hand knitted Aran sweater.

My own personal view is to find this connection a little too tenuous. The islanders' relationship with the Church, of course, cannot be denied; indeed, there has been a monastery there since AD 530. But too much has been made of it. It is certainly true that the patterns on the pullovers have a design image that can be related to a Celtic tradition 1200 years old. But whether such patterns have been knitted for that long is in dispute because the tradition now has no roots through a direct line; like the Fair Isle and guernsey traditions, their origins and meanings must remain open for further discussion.

The contribution that I have to make is simply to put into perspective the Celtic tradition, and make people aware that when they knit up these patterns they are reproducing images that are literally over a thousand years old.

On page 218 you will find an illustration from a religious manuscript produced in Ireland in the 8th century, the *Book of Kells*. I make no claim that today's Aran patterns come directly from this manuscript or others like it. What can be said is that the imagery is similar; indeed, some of the patterns shown in the manuscript, such as the trellises, whorls and interweaving which were expressions of the monks' knowledge of classical geometry, can be found in Aran patterns. But the relationship is surely a cultural one.

I am particularly interested in the *Book of Kells* because of the history of my own area of Northumberland. At one time its ties with Ireland were indivisible and we owe much of our culture to the influence of the classical teachings of the Irish monks.

When the *Book of Kells* was written, Ireland and Northumbria had an identical religious atmosphere and St Columba had already established many monasteries in both areas. King Oswald of Northumbria turned, not to Canterbury and the Roman Church of St Augustine, but to the Irish Church and to St Aidan who established the monastery of Lindisfarne in AD 635. The whole of Northumberland was thus influenced by the Irish classicists, particularly by Benedict Biscop who founded the monasteries of St Peter at Wearmouth (674) and St Paul at Jarrow (682) which is less than three miles away from where I am writing now. By the beginning of the 8th century Wear-mouth and Jarrow were amongst the most important centres of scholarship in Western Europe. The tradition that permeated Northumberland through their influence was a Celtic one whose design imagery came from the east *via* Persia and Italy, Greece and Rome. This Hellenisation of the West is, in art and cultural terms, expressed as Orientalisation. From the previous geometric and primitive style of decoration, Celtic designs turned to the imagery of the east, the beast and the mask in particular. The most prominent expression of this was the tendril or snake which could be wrought and shaped at will. The *Book of Kells* is, without doubt, an heraldic expression of this tradition. It is possible that the knitting patterns of Aran are the last such expressions of these designs. But there is also some justification for the view that the Aran patterns we know today are a very recent phenomenon. Most of the local wool was woven into Irish tweed, dyed blue for the men's shirts or made into colours for the decoration of their heavy duty belts (*criosanna*) which were elaborately woven.

Most of the patterns decorating the pullovers were like the one shown here made in 1948 (*above, left*). Miss Muriel Gahan, who presented it to the Folklore Museum as part of a series of jerseys, was adamant that it was 'a typical native design'. It comes from Inishmaan and, as you can see, bears a close resemblance to the ganseys of England and Scotland. Made up in white wool spun in Galway, it consists of fine horizontal bands of double moss stitch, each band edged with a row of garter stitch.

Navy blue was the popular colour, dyed from natural plant material, and the man's jersey (*see page 227*) is also typical. Close examination of these two garments reveals that they were knitted in the round in exactly the same way as all our previous patterns, the sleeves being picked up at the shoulder with gussets under the arms. In the other examples illustrated, the pattern on the front is different from that on the back, which may account for their having been knit over two needles only. So it is difficult to decide from the available evidence whether the general practice was to knit over two needles or in the round.

This uncertainty of evidence appeared to me, as though it permeated the whole object of my intent. In this atmosphere of uncertainty I created a process for judging 'something' to be authentic. I used this process to ask what it means to be 'authentic' in the context of knitting traditions for these islands. The process I came up with is as follows:

The criteria for establishing 'the knitting of Aran' as 'Authentic' is to be clear about the conditions that are necessary, in our case, to establish that the craft of knitting practise is a 'tradition'; ie: where customs, beliefs, and skills are passed from generation to generation. Encircling this process it is necessary that every aspect of this tradition displays provenance; ie a pathway from the present back to its earliest known history, and transparency: the pathway is clear, devoid of influence outside its provenance.

Finally, where the tradition's provenance and transparency is established, then can we term the tradition as 'Authentic'. No matter where I looked within the archives I examined, my process could not determine anything as 'Authentic'.

There was no definitive statement describing a knitting community, producing knitwear, like Muriel Gahan described in her submission to the Folklore Museum *(page 225)*. Neither is there material evidence of hand knit sweaters like Mary Thomas described *(page 222)*. The lack of evidence drew me to conclude that whatever knitting was done on these islands, it had nothing to do with the culture that enveloped the life of these islanders.

In my opinion the knitting of Aran was entirely commercial—an act of survival.

So, turning from this disappointment with local tradition—I began to reference near current history and found in local newspapers reference to the work of the Congested District Board; who, with the help of P. A. Siochain (a Galway businessman) arranged for knitters from the Outer Hebrides to go to Aran to teach Galway knitters how to commercialise the sweaters; by restricting the range of pattern sequences, speeding up production and completion to International sizing and standards of finish. Through his company Galway Bay Products he pioneered export of Aran sweaters throughout the world. The Knitting of Aran became so famous a commercial success that Aran Sweaters were even taken on as image creators by The Clancy Brothers (an erstwhile Folk group of the 1950's and 60's) Their mother read news of the terrible ice and snow storms in New York City and sent Aran sweaters for her sons and Tommy Makem to keep them warm. The group wore the Arans on the Ed Sullivan show and the result was an increase in orders. When John F. Kennedy visited Galway the effect on the local community was similar to the Royal Patronage in the Shetlands. The local news ran stories illustrating the President and his children playing together—all wearing Arans. The result was an explosion in orders. This explosion, we are informed, saturated the knitters of Aran and other parts of Eire; and there was difficulty fulfilling these orders. In 1974 when I visited the Aran islands evidence of this boom had long disappeared.

Having at least established that Aran had a venerable history of knitting manufacture, the consistent and burning issue remained. Who created Aran patterns?

Two possibilities emerge. Did an expert knitter, and a group of like-minded friends develop the patterns, or were the patterns imported from overseas from an existing tradition?

It is an uneasy concept to accept that an expert knitter from a local community could influence a country's traditions.

And yet it is easier to understand when she would be described as 'an incredible, expert craftsman, a creative risk taker, who would readily share her transparent and creative decision making with those knitters of equal skill willing to let her take the lead, glad to share her creative adventures'. Knitters such as these were the centre for everything creative in knitting within their communities. Other knitters would gravitate towards these experts, and in consequence the knitting within a community would take on a shared set of characteristics.

In the context of Aran knitting, the development of patterns that would be described as unique to Aran is an enormous jump to take from the previous gansey patterns that were evident in the archives.

I propose that the development of Aran patterns could have been as follows: The knitting traditions which have been the subject of our examination in this book, have within their skill set one common theme that informs the decoration of the knitted fabric of these traditions. This knitting is essentially a mathematical expression of a relationship between stitches and rows. This relationship is usually termed the 'ground'.

In the tradition of Fisher Ganseys—the base ground is always in stocking stitch. Within this stocking stitch ground creativity begins by making a knit stitch into a purl. This purl stitch stands out in contrast against the stocking stitch ground; thus, repetition reveals countless decorative purl knit combinations.

Strangely, and almost poetic in its contrast, we find that the majority of the knitted fabric of Aran is grounded in purl stitch. Here creativity begins where a purl stitch is disturbed by making it a knit stitch. The

Navy blue Aran sweater, made up of decorative welts, trellis and bobble diamonds.

knit stitch is then worked against the purl ground in countless twisting combinations. The revelation of vision by this expert knitter is for her to realise that success is a result of physically manipulating the knit stitch this way and to also realise that this pattern generation is not like the old geometric stocking stitch method. She realises that the process of pattern making becomes organic on a purl background. Thus she is soon able to make her knitting creep and crawl snakelike, creating whorls and tendrils, tassels and teasels over the surface of her fabric unfettered by the geometric restraints of a stocking knit ground.

Imagine then that her group of knitters develops a vocabulary of patterns to create garments decorated with these new creations which, in turn, serves to generate sales to a little shop in Dublin on Stephens' Green called Countryworkers Ltd. opened in 1935 by Dr Muriel Gahan.

Imagine Heinz Edgar Kiewe, in the summer of 1936, after browsing the range of crafts available, purchasing an Aran sweater, not unlike the example on page 223. Imagine that the sweater he purchased was knitted by this same expert, who was also chosen by Dr Gahan as an exhibitor in her submission to the Folklore Museum in 1948.

Imagine that Heinz Edgar Kiewe noticed that this knitwear resonated with his memory of his heritage, his culture and the nature of the knitting he would be familiar with from his childhood in, East Prussia. Imagine the excitement he must have felt thinking how similar the sweater patterns were to those finely crafted patterns he remembered that decorated his climbing socks and how quickly they could be knit with a thick yarn by women of these islands.

I have no knowledge of the extent of Kiewe's knitting manufacture, or whether he had a commercial relationship with Galway Bay Products. I do know of his extraordinary steps to link his knitting to a Celtic heritage some 600 years earlier. I think I am beginning to understand why he has been so tenacious in promoting Celtic connections. Heinz Edgar Kiewe had to create a tradition because none existed. No tradition—no provenance—no sense of connectedness to the past. He provided it all by linking his Bavarian culture to the Irish Celts. It was a masterly move. In the war of survival, pragmatism wins. As they reap the rewards of this deception there will be few Irish to deny the connection.

For a review of the patterns our expert knitter and her group could have created you will find one full pattern and three full half round pattern combinations included at the end of this section, an ideal project for your knitting development with the "Tyrolean" or Bavarian twist stitch.

LIST OF ABBREVIATIONS

K	knit
P	purl
tog.	together
inc.	increase
y.fwd.	yarn forward
dec.	decrease
y.b.	yarn back
tbl	through back of loop
y.r.n.	yarn round needle
P loop inc.	pick up purlwise from the row below between stitches and purl into back of it
K loop inc.	pick up knitwise from the row below between stitches and knit into back of it
M1	make one stitch by putting yarn forward (if working knitwise) or round needle (if working purlwise)
S1	slip one stitch
psso	pass the slipped stitch over
moss 4	work 4 stitches in K1, P1 moss stitch
S1f	slip one stitch forward onto cable needle and drop to front of work
S1b	slip one stitch back onto cable needle and drop to back of work
Kss	knit the slipped stitch
Pss	purl the slipped stitch
K1b	knit one stitch through back of loop
P1b	purl one stitch through back of loop
Kssb	knit slipped stitch through back of loop
Pssb	purl slipped stitch through back of loop
CB	cable back
CF	cable front
C4	cable 4 (slip 2 sts to back, K2, K2 off the pin)
C6	cable 6 (slip 3 sts to back, K3, K3 off the pin)
C8	cable 8 (slip 4 sts to back, K4, K4 off the pin)
R.Tw.	right twist: knit into 2nd stitch on left hand needle, then into 1st stitch; slip both loops off needle together
L.Tw.	left twist: knit into 2nd stitch on left hand needle through back of loop; then into 1st and 2nd stitches together through back of loop; slip both loops off needle together
M.B.	make bobble
M.K.	make knot
F.Cr.P.	front cross purl

CLASSIC ARAN PATTERN No. 1

Aran sweater of the 1950s.

In my notes on knitting technique at the beginning of this book *(pages 12–25)*, I have mentioned that it is crucial to make tension swatches of the different yarns used when making traditional knitwear so that you can accurately assess the number of stitches required to cast on for the size of your choice. The tension swatch is usually done in the form of a 4 inch (10 cm) square worked in stocking stitch. In Aran knitting the complexity of the design precludes this method, since the working of many of the patterns pulls in or extends the garment. There is really no alternative but to work a couple of inches in pattern to establish the number of stitches required and also to make sure that your combination of patterns is pleasing. The best way to be sure of this is to make up two swatches of every pattern you have. Place one in the centre and more of your favourites side by side until you are satisfied. With two samples of each pattern you will get an accurate idea of what the pullover will look like across the whole of the front or back. As you will probably realise, there is some virtue in always using the same brand of wool so that your knitting is constant and you will not have to make new swatches every time you change your wool brand.

To start you off, here is a fully worked out pattern, which you can either knit up as it is, or use for reference when putting together your own patterns. It is a splendid Aran which includes decorative welts, open and closed Marriage Lines, open worked chevrons and cables.

If you feel that there is too much decoration, you might prefer to knit the welt in plain K4 P3 rib. But for future reference, the patterned welt given here also looks marvellous on an otherwise plain pullover.

Size: to fit 41 inch chest (104 cm) ; length 24 inches (61 cm); sleeves 21 inches (53 cm).

Wool: 46 oz (1.3 kg) Regency Bainin pure Aran wool.

Needles: Five No. 10 (3¼ mm) double-pointed pins *or* 1 set circular twin pins.

Tension: 5½ stitches and 7 rows to 1 inch (2.5 cm) over pattern.

Abbreviations: See page 229.

The body

The front and back are identical. For each, cast on 105 sts over two needles. For the welt, work K4, P3 rib, with a single cross travelling stitch on the purl ribs as follows:

1ST ROW (right side):   *K4, K1b, P2, repeat to end.
2ND ROW: *K2, P1b, P4, repeat to end.
3RD ROW: *K4, S1f, P1, K1b, P1, repeat to end.
4TH ROW: *K1, P1b, K1, P4, repeat to end.
5TH ROW: *K4, P1, S1f, P1, Kssb, repeat to end.
6TH ROW: *P1b, K2, P4, repeat to end.
7TH ROW: *K4, P1, S1b, K1b, Pss, repeat to end.
8TH ROW: *K1, P1b, K1, P4, repeat to end.
9TH ROW: *K4, Kssb, K1b, Pss, P1, repeat to end.

Repeat from 2nd row until the welt measures 4 inches (10 cm), ending with a right side row.

NEXT ROW: Knit, to divide welt pattern from the first body pattern.

The body now begins. The pattern above the welt (30 sts repeat) is a horizontal panel made up of open diagonal shapes as follows:

1ST ROW: K1, *M1, S1, K1, psso, K10, K2 tog., M1, K1, M1, S1, K1, psso, K10, K2 tog., M1, K1, repeat from* to end.
2ND AND EVERY ALTERNATE ROW: Purl.
3RD ROW: K2, *M1, S1, K1, psso, K8, K2 tog., M1, K3, repeat from * to last 2 sts. K2.
5TH ROW: K3, *M1, S1, K1, psso, K6, K2 tog., M1, K5, repeat from * to last 3 sts. K3.
7TH ROW: K4, *M1, S1, K1, psso, K4, K2 tog., M1, K7, repeat from * to last 4 sts.K4.
9TH ROW: K5, *M1, S1, K1, psso, K2, K2 tog., M1, K9, repeat from * to last 5 sts. K5.
10TH ROW: Purl.
NEXT ROW: Purl, increasing evenly to 139 stitches. The first pattern is now complete.

The vertical patterns now begin. On the extreme side sections is a Marriage Line configuration (15 sts); next, a double cable (9 sts); then open Marriage Lines with moss stitch (26 sts); a single narrow cable (6 sts); and in the centre a panel of double chevrons (27 sts).

At the same time as working this sequence of patterns, increase one st on each side every 10th row (in stocking stitch), until the height to the armpit is 18 inches (46 cm) or as desired.

Marriage Lines
24 rows and 15 stitches
1ST ROW: P1, K1, P1, K12.
2ND ROW: P11, (K1, P1) twice.
3RD ROW: K2, P1, K1, P1, K10.
4TH ROW: P9, K1, P1, K1, P3.
5TH ROW: K4, P1, K1, P1, K8.
6TH ROW: P7, K1, P1, K1, P5.
7TH ROW: K6, P1, K1, P1, K6.
8TH ROW: P5, K1, P1, K1, P7.
9TH ROW: K8, P1, K1, P1, K4.
10TH ROW: P3, K1, P1, K1, P9.
11TH ROW: K10, P1, K1, P1, K2.
12TH ROW: (P1, K1) twice, P11.
13TH ROW: K12, P1, K1, P1.
14TH ROW: (P1, K1) twice, P11.
15TH ROW: K10, P1, K1, P1, K2.
16TH ROW: P3, K1, P1, K1, P9.
17TH ROW: K8, P1, K1, P1, K4.
18TH ROW: P5, K1, P1, K1, P7.
19TH ROW: K6, P1, K1, P1, K6.
20TH ROW: P7, K1, P1, K1, P5.
21ST ROW: K4, P1, K1, P1, K8.
22ND ROW: P9, K1, P1, K1, P3.
23RD ROW: K2, P1, K1, P1, K10.
24TH ROW: P11, (K1, P1) twice.
Repeat from row 2.

Double cables
14 rows and 11 stitches
1ST ROW: P1, K4, P1, K4, P1.
2ND ROW: K1, P4, K1, P4, K1.
3RD TO 6TH ROWS: Repeat 1st and 2nd rows twice.
7TH ROW: P1,*S2f, K2, K2ss, P1*, repeat from * to *.
8TH ROW: As 2nd.
9TH TO 12TH ROWS: Repeat 1st and 2nd rows twice.
13TH ROW: As 1st.
14TH ROW: K1, *S2f, P2, P2ss, K1*, repeat from * to *.
Repeat from row 1.

Open Marriage Lines with moss stitch
33 rows and 10 stitches
1ST ROW: K1, y.fwd., S1, K1, psso, moss 7.
2ND ROW: moss 7, P3.
3RD ROW: K2, y.fwd., S1, K1, psso, moss 6.
4TH ROW: moss 6, P4.
5TH ROW: K3, y.fwd., S1, K1, psso, moss 5.

6TH ROW: moss 5, P5.
7TH ROW: K4, y.fwd., S1, K1, psso, moss 4.
8TH ROW: moss 4, P6.
9TH ROW: K5, y.fwd., S1, K1, psso, moss 3.
10TH ROW: moss 3, P7.
11TH ROW: K6, y.fwd., S1, K1, psso, moss 2.
12TH ROW: moss 2, P8.
13TH ROW: K7, y.fwd., S1, K1, psso, P1.
14TH ROW: P10.
15TH ROW: K8, y.fwd., S1, K1, psso.
16TH ROW: P10.
17TH ROW: moss 8, K2 tog., y.fwd.
18TH ROW: P2, moss 8.
19TH ROW: moss 7, K2 tog., y.fwd., K1.
20TH ROW: P3, moss 7.
21ST ROW: moss 6, K2 tog., y.fwd., K2.
22ND ROW: P4, moss 6.
23RD ROW: moss 5, K2 tog., y.fwd., K3.
24TH ROW: P5, moss 5.
25TH ROW: moss 4, K2 tog., y.fwd., K4.
26TH ROW: P6, moss 4.
27TH ROW: moss 3, K2 tog., y.fwd., K5.
28TH ROW: P7, moss 3.
29TH ROW: moss 2, K2 tog., y.fwd., K6.
30TH ROW: P8, moss 2.
31ST ROW: P1, K2 tog., y.fwd., K7.
32ND ROW: P10.
33RD ROW: K2 tog., y.fwd., K8.

Single narrow cable
14 rows and 6 stitches
1ST ROW: P1, K1b, P2, K1b, P1.
2ND ROW: K1, P1b, K2, P1b, K1.
3RD TO 10TH ROWS: Repeat 1st and 2nd rows 4 times.
11TH ROW: P1, S1f, P1, Kssb, S1b, K1b, Pss, P1.
12TH ROW: K2, P2b, K2.
13TH ROW: P2, S1f, K1b, Kssb, P2.
14TH ROW: K1, S1f, P1b, Kss, S1b, K1, Pssb, K1.
Repeat from row 1.

Double chevron
8 rows and 27 stitches
1ST ROW: P5, K5, P7, K5, P5.
2ND AND EVERY ALTERNATE ROW: Purl.
3RD ROW: P3, P2 tog., K2, y.fwd., K1, y.fwd., K2, P2, P3 tog., P2, K2, y.fwd., K1, y.fwd., K2, P2 tog., P3.
5TH ROW: P2, P2 tog., K2, y.fwd., K3, y.fwd., K2, P1, P3 tog., P1, K2, y.fwd., K3, y.fwd., K2, P2 tog., P2.
7TH ROW: P1, P2 tog., K2, y.fwd., K5, y.fwd., K2, P3 tog., K2, y.fwd., K5, y.fwd., K2, P2 tog., P1.
8TH ROW: Purl.
Repeat from row 1.

When you have reached armpit height, slip the extra sts you have made at each side onto holders and continue in pattern to your shoulder height.

The shoulders
Work to the last 8 sts, turn. Work back to the last 8 sts, turn. Work to last 16 sts, turn. Work back to last 16 sts, turn. Work to the last 27 sts, turn. Work back to last 27 sts, turn. You will now have 51 sts for each shoulder and 37 sts in the centre (*i.e.* the central pattern panel plus 5 sts either side) for the neck. Put the neck sts and shoulder sts on separate holders. When you have completed the front and the back, graft the shoulders together.

The sleeves
Since you will now have the pattern in your memory, it is suggested that you knit the sleeves in the round. Pick up 100 sts around the armhole, including the underarm sts from the holder. Work in the patterns, placing the central section to the shoulder seams.

Decrease 2 sts at the underarm on every 6th row until you have 56 sts. Work to the desired length then knit the welt to match the body.

The neck
Pick up sts evenly around the neck and work in K1, P1 rib for 5 inches (12 cm). Cast off loosely.

Finishing
Sew the side seams.

Aran Islanders meet the Galway boat *c.*1900.

CLASSIC ARAN PATTERN NO. 2

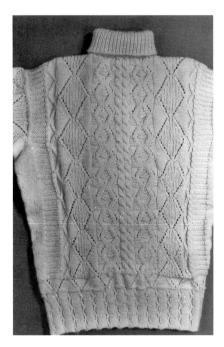

Aran sweater of the 1950s.

Side panel
30 stitches

1ST ROW: K2, P5, K2, P1, K1, P4, M1, S1, K1, psso, (P1, K1) 5 times, P1, K2 tog., M1.

2ND ROW: P2, (K1, P1) 5 times, K1, P2, K4, P1, K1, P2, K5, P2.

3RD ROW: K9, P1, S1f, P1, Kss, P3, K1, M1, S1, K1, psso, (K1, P1) 4 times, K1, K2 tog., M1, K1.

4TH ROW: P4, (K1, P1) 3 times, K1, P4, K3, P1, K2, P9.

5TH ROW: K2, P5, S1f, K1, Kss, P2, S1f, P1, Kss, P2, K2, M1, S1, K1, psso, (P1, K1) 3 times, P1, K2 tog., M1, K2.

6TH ROW: P4, (K1, P1) 3 times, K1, P4, K2, P1, K3, P2, K5, P2.

7TH ROW: K9, P3, S1f, P1, Kss, P1, K3, M1, S1, K1, psso, (K1, P1) twice, K1, K2 tog., M1, K3.

8TH ROW: P6, K1, P1, K1, P6, K1, P1, K4, P9.

9TH ROW: K2, P5, S1f, K1, Kss, P4, S1f, P1, Kss, K4, M1, S1, K1, psso, P1, K1, P1, K2 tog., M1, K4.

10TH ROW: P6, K1, P1, K1, P7, K5, P2, K5, P2.

11TH ROW: K9, P4, S1b, K1, Pss, K5, M1, S1, K1, psso, K1, K2 tog., M1, K5.

12TH ROW: P15, K1, P1, K4, P9.

13TH ROW: K2, P5, S1f, K1, Kss, P3, S1b, K1, Pss, P1, K5, K2 tog., M1, K1, M1, S1, K1, psso, K5.

14TH ROW: P15, K2, P1, K3, P2, K5, P2.

15TH ROW: K9, P2, S1b, K1, Pss, P2, K4, K2, tog., M1, P1, K1, P1, M1, S1, K1, psso, K4.

16TH ROW: P6, K1, P1, K1, P6, K3, P1, K2, P9.

17TH ROW: K2, P5, S1f, K1, Kss, P1, S1b, K1, Pss, P3, K3, K2 tog., M1, (K1, P1) twice, K1, M1, S1, K1, psso, K3.

18TH ROW: P6, K1, P1, K1, P6, K4, P1, K1, P2, K5, P2.

19TH ROW: K9, S1b, K1, Pss, P4, K2, K2 tog., M1, (P1, K1) 3 times, P1, M1, S1, psso, K2.

20TH ROW: P4, (K1, P1) 3 times, K1, P4, K5, P10.

21ST ROW: K2, P5, S1f, K1, Kss, S1f, P1, Kss, P4, K1, K2 tog., M1, (K1, P1) 4 times, K1, M1, S1, K1, psso, K1.

22ND ROW: P4, (K1, P1) 3 times, K1, P4, K4, P1, K1, P2, K5, P2.

23RD ROW: K9, P1, S1f, P1, Kss, P3, K2 tog., M1, (P1, K1) 5 times, P1, M1, S1, K1, psso.

24TH ROW: P2, (K1, P1) 5 times, K1, P2, K3, P1, K2, P9.

25TH ROW: K2, P5, S1f, K1, Kss, P2, S1f, P1, Kss, P2, M1, S1, K1, psso, (P1, K1) 5 times, P1, K2 tog., M1.

26TH ROW: P2, (K1, P1) 5 times, K1, P2, K2, P1, K3, P2, K5, P2.

27TH ROW: K9, P3, S1f, P1, Kss, P1, K1, M1, S1, K1, psso, (K1, P1) 4 times, K1, K2 tog., M1, K1.

28TH ROW: P4, (K1, P1) 3 times, K1, P4, K1, P1, K4, P9.

29TH ROW: K2, P5, S1f, K1, Kss, P4, S1f, P1, Kss, K2, M1, S1, K1, psso, (P1, K1) 3 times, P1, K2 tog., M1, K2.

30TH ROW: P4, (K1, P1) 3 times, K1, P5, (K5, P2) twice.

31ST ROW: K9, P4, S1b, K1, Pss, K3, M1, S1, K1, psso, (K1, P1) twice, K1, K2 tog., M1, K3.

32ND ROW: P6, K1, P1, K1, P6, K1, P1, K4, P9.

33RD ROW: K2, P5, S1f, K1, Kss, P3, S1b, K1, Pss, P1, K4, M1, S1, K1, psso, P1, K1, P1, K2 tog., M1, K4.

34TH ROW: P6, K1, P1, K1, P6, K2, P1, K3, P2, K5, P2.

35TH ROW: K9, P2, S1b, K1, Pss, P2, K5, M1, S1, K1, psso, K1, K2, tog., M1, K5.

36TH ROW: P15, K3, P1, K2, P9.

Repeat diamond pattern from row 13. Repeat the step pattern, small rope and travelling stitch as necessary: they do not repeat evenly with the diamond pattern.

Centre panel

39 stitches

Repeat once from * to * after the 9 central sts on every row except the 10TH and 12TH.

1ST ROW: *P1, K3, P7, K3, P1*, K4, P1, K4.

2ND ROW: *K1, P5, S1, P2 tog., psso, P5, K1*, P4, K1, P4.

3RD ROW: *P1, K1, M1, K2, P5, K2, M1, K1, P1*, K4, P1, K4.

4TH ROW: *K1, P5, S1, P2 tog., psso, P5, K1*, P4, K1, P4.

5TH ROW: *P1, K2, M1, K2, P3, K2, M1, K2, P1*, K4, P1, K4.

6TH ROW: *K1, P5, S1, P2, tog., psso, P5, K1*, P4, K1, P4.

7TH ROW: *P1, K3, M1, K5, M1, K3, P1*, S2f, K2, K2ss, P1, S2f, K2, K2ss.

8TH ROW: *K1, P13, K1*, P4, K1, P4.

9TH ROW: *P5, K2, M1, K1, M1, K2, P5*, K4, P1, K4.

10TH ROW: K1, P15, (K1, P4) twice, K1, P15, K1.

11TH ROW: *P3, P2 tog., K2, M1, K3, M1, K2, P2 tog., P3*, K4, P1, K4.

12TH ROW: K1, P15, (K1, P4) twice, K1, P15, K1.

13TH ROW: *P2, P2 tog., K2, M1, K5, M1, K2, P2 tog., P2*, K4, P1, K4.

14TH ROW: *K1, P15, K1*, S2f, P2, P2ss, K1, S2f, P2, P2ss.

15TH ROW: *P1, P2 tog., K2, P7, K2, P2 tog., P1*, K4, P1, K4.

16TH ROW: *K1, P5, S1, P2 tog., psso, P5, K1*, P4, K1, P4.

17TH ROW: *P1, K1, M1, K2, P5, K2, M1, K1, P1*, K4, P1, K4.

18TH ROW: *K1, P5, S1, P2 tog., psso, P5, K1*, P4, K1, P4.

19TH ROW: *P1, K2, M1, K2, P3, K2, M1, K2, P1*, K4, P1, K4.

20TH ROW: *K1, P5, S1, P2 tog., psso, P5, K1*, P4, K1, P4.

21ST ROW: *P1, K3, M1, K5, M1, K3, P1*, cross cables as in rows 7 and 14.

Repeat from row 8.

CLASSIC ARAN PATTERN NO. 3

Aran sweater with cross-stitch configuration. To make this pattern, start the 42-stitch side panel 11 stitches in, beginning with the diamond.

Side panel

42 stitches

Repeat once from * to * on every row.

1ST ROW: *P2, (K1b, P1) 3 times, K1b, P2, K1b, P1, K1b, P4, K1b, P1, K1b*.

2ND ROW: *P1b, K1, P1b, K4, P1b, K1, P1b, K2, (P1b, K1) 3 times, P1b, K2*.

3RD ROW: *P2, (K1b, P1) 3 times, K1b, P2, K1b, P1, S1f, P1, Kssb, P2, S1b, K1b, Pss, P1, K1b*.

4TH ROW: *(P1b, K2) 4 times, (P1b, K1) 3 times, P1b, K2*.

5TH ROW: *P2, (K1b, P1) 3 times, (K1b, P2) twice, S1f, P1, Kssb, S1b, K1b, Pss, P2, K1b*.

6TH ROW: *P1b, K3, P2b, K3, P1b, K2, (P1b, K1) 3 times, P1b, K2*.

7TH ROW: *P2, (K1b, P1) 3 times, K1b, P2, K1b, P3, S1f, K1b, Kssb, P3, K1b*.

8TH ROW: *P1b, K3, (P1b) twice, K3, P1b, K2, (P1b, K1) 3 times, P1b, K2*.

9TH ROW: *P2, (K1b, P1) 3 times, (K1b, P2) twice, S1b, K1b, Pss, S1f, P1, Kssb, P2, K1b*.

10TH ROW: *(P1b, K2) 4 times, (P1b, K1) 3 times, P1b, K2*.

11TH ROW: *P2, slip 3 stitches onto cable needle to front, knit into back of next purl stitch, purl next knit stitch, knit into back of next purl stitch, purl next stitch, knit into back of first stitch on spare needle, purl next stitch, knit into back of 3rd stitch, P2, K1b, P1, S1b, K1b, Pss, P2, S1f, P1, Kssb, P1, K1b*.

12TH ROW: *P1b, K1, P1b, K4, P1b, K1, P1b, K2, (P1b, K1) 3 times, P1b, K2*.

13TH ROW: *P2, (K1b, P1) 3 times, K1b, P2, K1b, S1b, K1b, Pss, P4, S1f, P1, Kssb, K1b*.

14TH ROW: *(P1b) twice, K6, (P1b) twice, K2, (P1b, K1) 3 times, P1b, K2*.

15TH ROW: *P2, (K1b, P1) 3 times, K1b, P2, K1b, S1f, P1, Kssb, P4, S1b, K1b, Pss, K1b*.

Repeat from row 2.

Centre panel

18 stitches

1ST ROW: K1b, P5, K1b, P1, (K1b) twice, P1, K1b, P5, K1b.

2ND ROW: P1b, K5, P1b, K1, (P1b) twice, K1, P1b, K5, P1b.

3RD ROW: K1b, P4, (S1b, K1b, Pss) twice, (S1f, P1, Kssb) twice, P4, K1b.

4TH ROW: P1b, K4, P1b, K1, P1b, K2, P1b, K1, P1b, K4, P1b.

5TH ROW: K1b, P3, (S1b, K1b, Pss) twice, P2, (S1f, P1, Kssb) twice, P3, K1b.

6TH ROW: P1b, K3, P1b, K1, P1b, K4, P1b, K1, P1b, K3, P1b.

7TH ROW: K1b, P2, S1b, K1b, Pss, S1b, K1b, Kss, P4, S1f, K1b, Kssb, S1f, P1, Pss, P2, K1b.

236

8TH ROW: P1b, K2, P1b, K1, (P1b) twice, K4, (P1b) twice, K1, P1b, K2, P1b.

9TH ROW: K1b, P1, (S1b, K1b, Pss) twice, S1f, P1, Kssb, P2, S1b, K1b, Pss, (S1f, P1, Kssb) twice, P1, K1b.

10TH ROW: (P1b, K1) twice, P1b, (K2, P1b) 3 times, K1, P1b, K1, P1b.

11TH ROW: K1b, (S1b, K1b, Pss) twice, P2, S1f, P1, Kssb, S1b, K1b, Pss, P2, (S1f, P1, Kssb) twice, K1b.

12TH ROW: (P1b) twice, K1, P1b, K4, S1f, P1b, Pssb, K4, P1b, K1, (P1b) twice.

13TH ROW: K1b, (S1f, P1, Kssb) twice, P2, S1b, K1b, Pss, S1f, P1, Kssb, P2, (S1b, K1b, Pss) twice, K1b.

14TH ROW: (P1b, K1) twice, P1b, (K2, P1b) 3 times, (K1, P1b) twice.

15TH ROW: K1b, P1, (S1f, P1, Kssb) twice, S1b, K1b, Pss, P2, S1f, P1, Kssb, (S1b, K1b, Pss) twice, P1, K1b.

16TH ROW: P1b, K2, P1b, K1, (P1b) twice, K4, (P1b) twice, K1, P1b, K2, P1b.

17TH ROW: K1b, P2, S1f, P1, Kssb, S1f, P1, Kssb, P4, (S1b, K1b, Pss) twice, P2, K1b.

18TH ROW: P1b, K3, P1b, K1, P1b, K4, P1b, K1, P1b, K3, P1b.

19TH ROW: K1b, P3, (S1f, P1, K1b) twice, P2, (S1b, K1b, Pss) twice, P3, K1b.

20TH ROW: P1b, K4, P1b, K1, P1b, K2, P1b, K1, P1b, K4, P1b.

21ST ROW: K1b, P4, (S1f, P1, Kssb) twice, (S1b, K1b, Pss) twice, P4, K1b.

22ND ROW: P1b, K5, P1b, K1, S1f, P1b, Pssb, K1, P1b, K5, P1b.

Repeat from row 3.

Pilgrimage to St McDara's Island, 1943.

CLASSIC ARAN PATTERN NO. 4

Aran sweater made up of centre trellis, waved ribbon, leaf patterns and heart cable. Work moss stitch at the sides for the full width.

Leaf pattern

11 stitches

1ST ROW: P1, K1b, P1, K1, P1, K5, P1.
2ND ROW: K1, P5, K1, P1, K1, P1b, K1.
3RD ROW: P1, K1b, P1, K1, M1, P1, S1, K1, psso, K3, P1.
4TH ROW: K1, P4, K1, P2, K1, P1b, K1.
5TH ROW: P1, K1b, P1, K1, M1, K1, P1, S1, K1, psso, K2, P1.
6TH ROW: (K1, P3) twice, K1, P1b, K1.
7TH ROW: P1, K1b, P1, K1, M1, K2, P1, S1, K1, psso, K1, P1.
8TH ROW: K1, P2, K1, P4, K1, P1b, K1.
9TH ROW: P1, K1b, P1, K1, M1, K3, P1, S1, K1, psso, P1.
10TH ROW: K1, P1, K1, P5, K1, P1b, K1.
11TH ROW: P1, K1b, P1, S1, K1, psso, K3, P1, K1, M1, P1.
12TH ROW: K1, P2, K1, P4, K1, P1b, K1.
13TH ROW: P1, K1b, P1, S1, K1, psso, K2, P1, K1, M1, K1, P1.
14TH ROW: (K1, P3) twice, K1, P1b, K1.
15TH ROW: P1, K1b, P1, S1, K1, psso, K1, P1, K1, M1, K2, P1.
16TH ROW: K1, P4, K1, P2, K1, P1b, K1.
17TH ROW: P1, K1b, P1, S1, K1, psso, P1, K1, M1, K3, P1.
18TH ROW: K1, P5, K1, P1, K1, P1b, K1.
Repeat from row 3.

Side panel—Heart cable

20 stitches

1ST ROW: K1b, P7, S2f, K2, K2ss, P7, K1b.
2ND ROW: P1b, K7, P4, P7, P1b.
3RD ROW: K1b, P6, S1b, K2, Pss, S2f, P1, K2ss, P6, K1b.
4TH ROW: P1b, K6, P2, K2, P2, K6, P1b.
5TH ROW: K1b, P5, S1b, K2, Pss, P2, S2f, P1, K2ss, P5, K1b.
6TH ROW: P1b, K5, P2, K4, P2, K5, P1b.
7TH ROW: K1b, P4, S1b, K2, Pss, K4, S2f, P1, K2ss, P4, K1b.
8TH ROW: P1b, K4, P2, K1, P4, K1, P2, K4, P1b.
9TH ROW: K1b, P3, S1b, K2, Pss, S1b, K2, Kss, S2f, K1, K2ss, S2f, P1, K2ss, P3, K1b.
10TH ROW: P1b, K3, P2, K1, P6, K1, P2, K3, P1b.
11TH ROW: K1b, P2, S1b, K2, Pss, S1b, K2, Kss, K2, S2f, K1, K2ss, S2f, P1, K2ss, P2, K1b.
12TH ROW: P1b, K2, P2, K1, P8, K1, P2, K2, P1b.
13TH ROW: K1b, P2, K1, S1f, P1, Kss, S2f, P1, K2ss, K2, S1b, K2, Pss, S1b, K1, Pss, K1, P2, K1b.
14TH ROW: P1b, K2, P1, K1, P1, K1, P6, (K1, P1) twice, K2, P1b.
15TH ROW: K1b, P2, K1, P1, S1f, P1, Kss, S2f, P1, K2ss, S1b, K2, Pss, S1b, K1, Pss, P1, K1, P2, K1b.
16TH ROW: P1b, K2, P1, K2, P1, K1, P4, K1, P1, K2, P1, K2, P1b.
17TH ROW: K1b, P2, S1f, P1, Kss, S1b, K1, Pss, P1, S2f, K2, K2ss, P1, S1f, P1, Kss, S1b, K1, Pss, P2, K1b.
18TH ROW: P1b, K3, S1b, K1, Kss, K2, P4, K2, S1f, K1, Kss, K3, P1b.
Repeat from row 3.

Waved ribbon

8 stitches and 12 rows

1ST ROW: P2, K4, P2.

2ND ROW: K2, P4, K2.

3RD ROW: As 1st.

4TH ROW: As 2nd.

5TH ROW: P2, S2b, K2, K2ss, P2.

6TH ROW: As 2nd.

7TH TO 10TH ROWS: Repeat 1st and 2nd rows twice.

11TH ROW: P2, S2f, K2, K2ss, P2.

12TH ROW: As 2nd.

Repeat from row 1.

Centre trellis

24 stitches

1ST ROW: P1, K1b, P3, K2, (P4, K2) twice, P3, K1b, P1.

2ND ROW: K1, P1b, K3, S1f, P1, Pss, (K4, S1f, P1, Pss) twice, K3, P1b, K1.

3RD ROW: P1, K1b, P2, (S1b, K1, Pss, S1f, P1, Kss, P2) 3 times, K1b, P1.

4TH ROW: K1, P1b, (K2, P1) 6 times, K2, P1b, K1.

5TH ROW: P1, K1b, P1, (S1b, K1, Pss, P2, S1f, P1, Kss) 3 times, P1, K1b, P1.

6TH ROW: K1, P1b, K1, P1, (K4, S1f, P1, Pss) 2 times, K4, P1, K1, P1b, K1.

7TH ROW: P1, K1b, P1, S1f, P1, Kss, (P2, S1b, K1, Pss, S1f, P1, Kss) 2 times, P2, S1b, K1, Pss, P1, K1b, P1.

8TH ROW: K1, P1b, (K2, P1) 6 times, K2, P1b, K1.

9TH ROW: P1, K1b, (P2, S1f, P1, Kss, S1b, K1, Pss) 3 times, P2, K1b, P1.

Repeat from row 2.

Aran family *c.*1900.

239

A Final Word

My enthusiasms revolve around the process and practice of creative endeavour in all its forms, in particular—around knitting. It has been my experience within the traditions, that creativity has depths of subtlety that explores culture with the nuance of circumstance and practice; more than the individual, more than image, more than touch and texture.

This creative depth of traditional knitting has, however, been denied recognition through what I would term—a narrow definition of creativity when looked upon as unique, visual, enthusiastic expressive individuality.

I learned by experience that this denial of equal status given to creative works that do not adhere to these cultural values is to deny the majority of most of the worlds creative endeavour.

These values lie within the processes of creative activity and the circumstances that they are practiced. In the context of this book these processes and practices are about a thorough understanding of knitting skills, an understanding of the people who practice knitting, their circumstance for the knitting, the conditions under which the artifact was made and a deep knowledge of the patterns and conventions the knitters applied. Once achieved we can be witness to adventurous personal creative interpretations, and thus decode the meaning behind the making and in consequence increase our sensitivity and therefore our understanding of their creations.

In my conversations with knitters about their motivation, their wishes, desires and their reflections they invariably expressed such traits in the form of a powerful sense of self. There was no concern more important than respect from and for their fellow knitters. This respect came not from skill; skill was to be expected. Respect came from a deep knowledge of its application, often expressed as subtle stitch relationships that ordinary knitters would miss.

I believe that within these pages the criteria for understanding traditional knitting has been addressed and that with your deepening knowledge of the craft and its traditions, applied with an open mind you will be able to generate bursts of creative endeavour which will have direct relevance to the traditions by serving as an influence for its gradual change.

About the Author

Here is the chronicle of events detailing my involvement with Knitting. For a number of years as a young man, I was involved with producing machine-knitted winter garments for outdoors, camping and climbing. I managed a cell system of production almost identical to the system used before the industrial revolution. I ran twenty cells. There were ten workers in each cell—nine machine knitters working under the guidance of a manager who was responsible for the distribution of material, the production of the work, quality control and maintaining the number of knitters in the cell. Once a week I distributed the designs and raw material and picked up the finished material. I was successful—an early accolade was the right to attach the Woolmark to my garments.

However in 1972, my life was about to change. One winter Sunday I was sitting in my local pub having a pint with the 'lads'—salmon fishermen making the most of their time before catching the tide (2 am this time of the year), oil riggers just back from Aberdeen, their pockets bulging with 5 pound notes tightly rolled up and held together by elastic bands, an electrician, a plumber, a bank clerk—and me. We had just finished a game of soccer on the beach below the pub and now, hot and sweaty, we were up for a pint or two—till closing time, and then home to a well deserved Sunday Lunch after a hard week plying our trades. The language was raw, rough and loud—our woman were at home cooking, with grandma minding the 'bairns.' Granda was in one of the corner bars with his mates, scouring the betting and sports pages of the Sunday paper.

As I continued my pint, Mr Paris Stone, a salmon fisherman came over and sat at the opposite side of the small table where I was sitting sharing my version of a story out of the local newspaper. I didn't know Mr Stone, nor did he know me beyond what we shared of our lives in the pub and on the playing field. We did know, however, each other's work. He was welcome at the table; there was no formality, and he joined immediately in our conversation. I finished my drink and got up from the table as it was my turn to buy the next round.

Paris intervened and said he would 'get them in'. He brought the drinks back and my companions took theirs, thanked him and moved out of earshot. No one buys another's round unless they want attention.

I said, "So what's happening Paris. Is there anything I can do for you?' Paris replied, "Well…aye, there is Mike." He pulled out of his bag a dark navy pullover that had seen better days. He called the pullover a 'gansey', and I noticed that he handled this bedraggled object like I and my machine knitters did the pullovers we produced. Paris carefully explained to me that this bundle of wool was knitted some thirty years previously for his father, who in turn had given it to him. He surveyed the condition of the gansey and said to me, "This gansey is supposed to be passed on to my eldest. The state this is in, it can't be repaired—at least that's what me grannie says. She can't knit because of her hands and my wife can't because she doesn't knit. So I thought since you are in the business you would know."

He smiled and looked at me as though his problem was solved. "I knit on machines Paris. Anyway why don't you just buy another one like it," I replied, thinking I was stating the obvious. Paris was visibly taken aback at my dismissal, "You can't buy this. This is a Cullercoats gansey!!" He thrust the 'gansey' at me and asked me to have a look at the pattern. He said "That is a special pattern—every village has their own" I saw that he appeared quite concerned at my ignorance of what was to him was an important part of the fabric of his life. He asked whether I could find a knitter to reproduce the gansey with exactly the pattern in exactly the same pattern sequence. As he took the gansey he said "My son cannot go to sea without his gansey—it would be bad luck." "Ok", I said quietly under my breath, "You said 'All the fishing villages have patterns'. They are all secret"!

It did not take long for me to visualise the creative and commercial possibilities. In 1974 Paris gave a gansey to his son. We all had one made. I received a modest grant from the Northern Arts Association to pay for many more to be knit, ready for an exhibition that I curated with Tyne & Wear Touring Exhibition Service, who exhibited the fruits of my search for gansey patterns from the Humber to the Northern reaches of Scotland. The exhibition opened in1976 to great acclaim and travelled far and wide, from the Scottish Fisheries Museum in Anstruther, to the most famous bookshop in London, Foyles in Charing Cross Road, London.

During this time, I heard that my interest had sparked others to record the patterns of their own locality. In 1977 Michael Harvey and Rae Compton came out with *Fisherman Knitting*, Shire Album No.31 and Mary Wright published *Cornish Guernseys & Knit Frocks* through Alison Hodge in association with Ethnographica.

Between 1976 and 1981, I formed a publishing company, Esteem Press, and produced two editions: *Traditional Knitting of the British Isles: The Fisher Ganseys of North East England,* and *Traditional Knitting of the British Isles: The Fisher Ganseys of Scotland and the Scottish Fleet.* For craft books, they were well received.

I completed my research by delving into the colour knitting of Fair Isle and Shetland and the Tradition of Aran. This research opened my eyes, curing me of any romantic notion that these traditions were indeed traditions. In 1984 Collins published my research where I hinted at the commercial reality of these 'traditions'.

In 1985 I was invited through the International Wool Secretariat to visit Australia, and through their Wool Corporation, to exhibit my collection of knitting and run a series of workshops all over Australia. There were two major consequences, both of which changed my life completely again: I met my future partner at one of my workshops, and I discovered that I enjoyed the process of teaching so much, that on the day after receiving my Australian citizenship, I kick-started a new life in Australia by returning to University at 45! Over the next five years, I completed masters and postgraduate teaching qualifications which led to 20 years lecturing in design and creative process.

I am retired now and live in Fremantle Western Australia up on the hill by Fother Gill.

Notes

The following British terms have been used in the text and their American equivalents are given below:

gauge—tension
pins—knitting needles
twin pins—circular knitting needles
s.d.—shillings and pence in old British currency

Conversion chart for knitting needles

UK (old size)	UK (metric)	USA
3	6½ mm	10
4	6 mm	9
5	5½ mm	8
6	5 mm	7
7	4½ mm	6
8	4 mm	5
9	3¾ mm	4
10	3¼ mm	3
11	3 mm	2
12	2¾ mm	1
13	2¼ mm	0
14	2 mm	00

Occasionally, knitting needles even smaller than UK size 14 are mentioned in the book. Historically, these very fine needles (*e.g.* UK sizes 16 and 17) were used for fine hand-knitting of woollen garments such as socks, which nowadays would all be machine-knitted.

Measurement Charts

Man's Size	Small		Medium		Large		X-Large		XX-Large	
	in	cm	in	cm	in	cm	in	cm	in	cm
1. Chest	34-36	86-91.5	38-40	96.5-101.5	42-44	106.5-111.5	46-48	116.5-122	50-52	127-132
2. Center Back Neck to Cuff	32-32½	81-82.5	33-33½	83.5-85	34-34½	86.5-87.5	35-35½	89-90	36-36½	91.2-92.5
3. Back Hip Length	25-25½	63.5-64.5	26½-26¾	67.5-68	27-27¾	68.5-69	27½-27¾	69.5-70.5	28-28½	71-72.5
4. Cross Back	15½-16	39.5-40.5	16½-17	42-43	17½-18	44.5-45.5	18-18½	45.5-47	18½-19	47-48
5. Sleeve Length to Underarm	18	45.5	18½	47	19½	49.5	20	50.5	20½	52

Woman's Size	S		M		L		1X		2X	
1. Bust	32-34	81-86	36-38	91.5-96.5	40-42	101.5-106.5	44-46	111.5-117	48-50	122-127
2. Center Back Neck to Cuff	28-28½	71-72.5	29-29½	73.5-75	30-30½	76-77.5	31-31½	78.5-80	31½-32	80-81.5
3. Back Waist Length	17	43	17¼	43.5	17½	44.5	17¾	45	18	45.5
4. Cross Back (Shoulder to Shoulder)	14½-15	37-38	16-16½	40.5-42	17-17½	43-44.5	17½	44.5	18	45.5
5. Sleeve Length to Underarm	17	43	17	43	17½	44.5	17½	44.5	18	45.5

Stitch tension 28sts/10 cm

Inches	34	36	38	40	42	44	46	48	50	52	55
cm	86	91	97	102	107	112	118	122	127	132	140
Actual	238	252	266	280	294	308	322	336	350	364	378
+Standard ease 10%	262	278	294	308	324	340	354	370	385	400	416

Formula for Estimating Yarn

A	Knit 1 ball	
B	Height x width =	?? square cm
C	Garment height x width of front =	?? square cm
	Garment height x width of back =	?? square cm
	Sleeve height x sleeve width =	?? square cm
C/B =	Number of balls needed	?? total square cm
D	Add one ball for safety	

Allowance (ease) cm. The Ease Percent Matrix

Size	tight	close	standard	large	baggy
Bust/chest and hip fit					
66	-3.5	-2	+4	+8	+12
71	-3.	-2	+4	+8.5	+14
76	-4	-2	+4.5	+9	+15
81	-4	-2.5	+5	+10	+16
86	-4.5	-3	+5	+10.5	+17
91	-4.5	-3	+5.5	+11	+18
97	-5	-3	+6	+11.5	+19
102	-5	-3	+6	+12	+20
107	-5.5	-3	+6.5	+13	+21
112	-5.5	-3.5	+6.5	+13.5	+22
117	-6	-3.5	+7	+14	+23

Note: this is an ease percent matrix!

Armhole/Upper arm/wrist/thigh/ankle

	-5	0	+10	+25	+40

Further Reading

Margaret Dixon, *The Wool Book*, Hamlyn, 1980.

* Sarah Don, *Fair Isle Knitting*, Mills and Boon, 1979.

Eve Harlow, *The Art of Knitting*, Collins, 1977.

Marie Hartley, *The Old Hand-Knitters of the Dales*, Dalesman, 1951.

* Shelagh Hollingworth, *The Complete Book of Traditional Aran Knitting*, Batsford, 1982.

* Sheila McGregor, *Complete Book of Fair Isle Knitting*, Batsford, 1981.

* Mary Phillips, *Creative Knitting*, Van Nostrand Reinhold, 1971.

* Gladys Thompson, *Patterns for Guernseys, Jerseys and Arans*, Batsford, 1969.

Maggie Twatt and Mary Smith, *Shetland Knitting Patterns*, Shetland Times, 1979.

Mary Wright, *Cornish Guernseys and Knitfrocks*, Alison Hodge/ Ethnographica,
   1979.

* Reprint edition available from Dover Publications, Inc.

Yarn

It is worth mentioning the type of yarn knitted in the Gansey tradition and the Shetland Heritage, because if you knit up the incorrect yarn your finished product will be a disappointment.

The following explanation is a simplified description by THL Siobhan nic Dhuinnshleibhe, the full article can be referenced at http://kws. atlantia.sca.org/Woolen_vs_Worsted_Explained.pdf

"Woollen", basically means that the individual fibres of varying lengths are going in many different directions, overlapping each other at a variety of angles and leaving air spaces between the individual fibres. "Worsted" means that the individual fibres are roughly the same length and are running parallel to each other and only overlapping at the tips, leaving little to no space between the individual fibres...

Fiber preparation:
(Woollen spun- Shetland Fair Isle) When fibres are carded, be it on hand cards, a drum carder or purchased from a vendor as roving, the fibres are brushed back and forth in order to remove any second cuts or vegetable matter and to break up the separate locks of wool. Shorter fibres and longer fibres are blended together. (For example, a fleece where the undercoat is blended with guard hairs) When drawn out into roving or rolled off a card into a rolag, the individual fibres themselves overlap at a variety of angles and all along the length of the individual fibres, leaving air spaces throughout the roving/rolag and having a very soft, lofty appearance. When these fibres are spun together, they will trap air spaces between the jumbled-up fibres and make a yarn that is very warm with a soft feel. With frequent wear, these fibres or yarns will be prone to felting and/or pilling because they do not have the tight smooth finish of worsted fibres, but they will be infinitely warmer than worsted fibres because of the air spaces and softer finish.

(Worsted spun—Guernsey 5ply Worsted Wool) When fibre is combed with wool combs or the ends of locks are flicked with a flicker, the fibres are arranged parallel to each other and only overlap each other at the tips instead of the widely varying angles that carded fibres do. This was traditionally done with the longer wools, so that any shorter fibres are removed (think separating and undercoat or second cuts from longer fibres), leaving all the remaining fibres roughly the same length. As the fibres are parallel, there is very little air space between the fibres so that when the fibres are spun as is or pulled out into top, the fibres will have a smooth, often dense appearance. When these fibres are spun together there will be little to no air spaces between these fibres and make a yarn that is very strong and smooth with a silky or harder feel than carded yarns. These yarns are not prone to felting and pilling with frequent wear, but they will not feel as soft against the skin nor be as warm as carded yarns.

Suppliers

Here is a list of Guernsey 5 ply wool suppliers that I believe have the relevant expertise to supply appropriate yarns for the patterns in this book.

It is also a good idea to get feedback from Portals such as Ravelry and Pinterest.

Frangipani wool suppliers have a colour range of 26. The yarn is 100% worsted five ply Guernsey wool supplied in 500 g cones. The supplier says this way of supplying the wool keeps prices down and they advise " you will not have joins every 100g."

Recent research (Interweave Knits 2006) has discovered that many Scottish fisher lassies knitted their own versions of ganseys and their choice of colours: pink, raspberry and pale green have been added to their range. To order simply email: jan@guernseywool.co.uk.

Blacker Yarns states that the construction of five ply worsted makes a yarn which locks together, creating a crisp and lean yarn with excellent stitch definition.

They have started a natural range of colours from the following breeds, sourced locally in Devon and Cornwall: Romney, Manx/Hebridean/Romney cross, Max/ Hebridean cross.

They also produce a Jacob yarn from 3 Jacob flocks on the Isles of Scilly, which they advertise as a limited supply each year.

The supplier has available Navy, Oxblood, Slate and Olive. Over-dyed shades are Rich Dark Peak, metallic Bronze, Foamy Cream and Pewter.

Contact: Blacker Yarns,
Kenny Gill way
 Launceston,
Cornwall PL15 7PJ.
www.Blackeryarns.co.uk.

Thomas Ramsden group is the creator of Wendy Poppleton's Guernsey 5 ply, a traditional hard twist worsted spun British wool such as has been used in the knitting of traditional fisherman's jerseys or ganseys (also called Knit Frocks in Cornwall) for generations.

When knitted up it is windproof, water resistant and hard wearing. Guernsey wool is not an oiled wool, but relies on the tightness of the spinning to give it these properties. Garments knitted in 5 ply Guernsey are suitable for all outdoor activities such as sailing, shooting, walking and golf.

The yarn is suitable for both hand and machine knitting and is as traditional as you can get. It is available in Aran cream, Atlantic blue, Crimson red and Navy blue.

www.tbramsden.co.uk
Netherfield Road, Guiseley, Leeds, LS20 9PD.
sales@tbramsden.co.uk (Sales); enquiries@tbramsden.co.uk (Enquiries)

BritishWool.com R.E.Dickie is a long-standing manufacturer of traditional yarns. Their 5 ply production is in 100 g balls in the traditional shades.

R E Dickey,
West End Works,
Parkinson Lane,
Halifax, West Yorkshire.
HX1 3UW.
Email: wool@dicky.co.uk.
Email sales: sales@Dickie.co.uk
www.britishwool.com

Jamieson and Smith have created a selection called Shetland Heritage which recreates the original characteristics of hand spun yarn used in old Fair Isle garments. The yarn is replicated from that found in knitted Fair Isle garments in the collection of Shetland Museum and Archives, and developed from Jamieson & Smith's worsted spun combed tops give a soft feel, and a smooth finish.

Jamieson & Smith (Shetland Wool Brokers LTD)
90 North Road
Lerwick
Shetland
ZE1 0PQ
www.shetlandwoolbrokers.co.uk
sales: sales@shetlandwoolbrokers.co.uk

Acknowledgements

Acknowledgements must first go to all the knitters and their families whom I met while on my travels. All were generous in their hospitality and willingness to share their lifestyles and traditions. It is to them that all credit must go, since they gave their patterns and delved into their family albums and collections of knitwear to provide the majority of imformation and photographs.

I would also like to thank the many people who have helped me compile the book: the Northern Arts Council, whose enthusiasm and research grant began the whole venture; the Tyne & Wear Museum Service for their sponsorship and support of the resulting exhibition of traditional knitwear that toured Britain; and for the expert help of Mary Wright on the ganseys of Cornwall, Shelagh Hollingworth on Aran and Martin Warren on the ganseys of Norfolk. I would like to thank the knitters who checked the patterns, especially Mary Coghill, and thanks must also go to the knitters who have been so helpful in knitting up the very many swatches and samples over the years, especially Mrs Pickering, Mrs Renwick and Mrs Ellis.

I owe acknowledgements to the following for access to material and permission to reproduce archival photographs and artefacts:

England

Bude Historical and Folk Museum, Bude, Cornwall
Canty Museum and Art Gallery, Truro, Cornwall
City Art Gallery, Leeds
Cornwall Museum Service, Truro, Cornwall
Fisher & Sons, Filey, Yorkshire
Frank Meadow Sutcliffe Gallery, Whitby, Yorkshire
Humber Keel and Sloop Preservation Society, Hull, Yorkshire
International Wool Secretariat, London
Norfolk Museum Service, Cromer Museum, Norfolk
Norfolk Museum Service, Great Yarmouth Museum, Norfolk
Poppyland Publishing, Cromer, Norfolk
Scarborough Museum, Yorkshire
Shipley Art Gallery, Gateshead, Tyne & Wear
Tyne & Wear Records Office, Newcastle-on-Tyne, Tyne & Wear
Upper Dales Museum, Hawes, Wensleydale, Yorkshire
Yorkshire Museum Service, Museum Gardens, York

Scotland

Country Life Archives, National Museum, Edinburgh
Johnston Collection, Carnegie Public Library, Wick, Caithness
Library Archives, Peterhead, Aberdeen
Scottish Fisheries Museum, Anstruther, Fife
Shetland Museum, Lerwick, Shetland

Ireland

D.D.C. Pochin Mould
Irish Folklore Museum, Dublin
Irish Tourist Board, Dublin
National Museum of Ireland, Folklife Division, Dublin
The Irish Times, Dublin
Trinity College Library, Dublin

In this expanded version I must first acknowledge Dover for their decision to include my book in their craft catalogue.

More specifically, I acknowledge Mary Carolyn Waldrep for the management and editing of the material. Equally important is the acknowledgement I extend to my partner Patricia Hanson for her help in keeping me on track and to Kim Cannon who I met 25 years ago when I taught her the techniques I illustrate within these pages. Kim's organisational skills at making sense of the material I had stored away 30 years ago in boxes and files in no particular order has been spectacular. I could not have done the book without their help.

Index